T0288020

IRREPLACEABLE

"A hands-on guide for enhancing our humanity in harmony with AI." —Marshall Goldsmith

IRREPLACEABLE

The Art of Standing Out in the Age of Artificial Intelligence

PASCAL BORNET

WILEY

Published by John Wiley & Sons, Inc., Hoboken, New Jersey.
Published simultaneously in Canada.

For general information on our other products and services or for technical support, please contact our Customer Care Department within the United States at (800) 762-2974, outside the United States at (317) 572-3993 or fax (317) 572-4002.

Wiley also publishes its books in a variety of electronic formats. Some content that appears in print may not be available in electronic formats. For more information about Wiley products, visit our web site at www.wiley.com.

Library of Congress Cataloging-in-Publication Data is Available:

ISBN: 9781394264407 (cloth)
ISBN: 9781394264414 (ePub)
ISBN: 9781394264421 (ePDF)

Cover Design: Wiley
Cover Image: © Gearstd/Shutterstock

SKY10079833_072224

I dedicate this book to my children and to all the children in the world.

We owe them the best future.

Contents

Preface

I've spent the last 25 years immersed in the world of artificial intelligence (AI) and automation, working for two of the industry's most prominent consulting firms. In my role, I've implemented hundreds of AI projects around the globe and seen firsthand how AI can transform businesses and society—boosting efficiency, enhancing the experiences of customers and employees alike, enhancing people's lives, and sometimes even saving them.

My experiences have led me to a crucial realization: successful AI is really all about us, the humans. AI has been built by people, and it is used by people. Without human insight and interaction, AI loses its essence and purpose. The most successful and profitable AI initiatives I have seen are those that are in strong connections with people.

This is why, a few years ago, I decided to concentrate my research on the frontier between humans and AI. This is where I believe there is the highest value to create for our world.

This has sparked my passion for leveraging AI to create a more humane world. It was this commitment that led me to write my first book, *Intelligent Automation*, in 2020, aiming to make these insights accessible to the largest possible audience.

> *"Without human insight and interaction, AI loses its essence and purpose."*

My journey continued on social media, where I began sharing this message through stories that sparked inspiration. For example, I love sharing about real-life AI innovations that make a difference in our world—think of hearing aids that let a baby hear their parents' voices for the first time, or an AI system for public swimming pools that alerts if someone is drowning.

Along the way, I've built an amazing online community of millions of followers across LinkedIn, Twitter, and YouTube who get just as excited about these innovations as I do! And when I'm not online, I'm traveling around the world, speaking at more than 50 events a year to spread the word even further.

The interactions, the questions, and the conversations I've had with people during those events, as well as on social media, are what inspired this book.

Consider this book as an extensive question-and-answer session where I address the most critical and sensitive questions raised from my interactions with a wide variety of audiences. As a result, while I am the one putting pen to paper, this book is very much a collaborative effort. In a way, it's an honor to assert that this book has more than one author—it has millions!

Don't be fooled by the easy words in this book. They are solid, backed by my 20-plus years in the AI trenches. I've sweated to make this a quick read, something anyone can grasp, even if you're not a bookworm. It's short, sharp, and packed, ready for you to dive in.

No single book can be for all readers, yet we each play multiple roles in our lives. Most of us are parents, workers, team leaders, or entrepreneurs—in addition, all of us are humans. And AI impacts all these dimensions of our lives simultaneously. However, most books concentrate on just one area, risking imbalance—for instance, improving your professional life might result in neglecting your family life. This book addresses that gap. It adopts a holistic approach, guiding you to maintain balance in your personal, family, and work lives. It ensures you can thrive in the various dimensions that define your existence.

Keep in mind that navigating the AI landscape is a complex, often surprising journey, filled with the unknown of the future. My insights stem from personal experience and extensive research. Yet it's important to acknowledge that other experts may have differing views.

Humility is key; no one can predict the future with certainty, so embracing a variety of perspectives is essential in this field.

And I'm eager to hear your thoughts and engage in discussions. Share your views using the hashtag #irreplaceable, and let's connect online at @pascal_bornet. Also, join the IRREPLACEABLE Community and Academy, a safe space where we can share, learn, and actively engage with the concepts from the book (www.irreplaceable.ai).

This book will take you on an exciting and transformative journey. I've distilled 20 years of research to create a unique approach to surviving and thriving with AI that I'm excited to share with you. I've had the privilege of consulting with hundreds of experts in fields such as neuroscience, psychology, resilience, flow, and creativity.

This book is like an open house into the future, addressing the most important question of our current times: In a world of AI, how do we keep our humanity front and center?

> *"AI is not the destination; it's the vehicle that takes us to a more human future."*

We stand out. We become IRREPLACEABLE.

More About My Passion for AI and the Reason for This Book

Nature gave ants the capacity to carry up to 50 times their weight and cheetahs the ability to run super-fast. We humans are not as strong or as fast. But we were given another power: the one to create technology. And thanks to technology, we too can carry heavy loads, move at the speed of sound, and do much more! It's like we're the "tech-animals" of the world.

Now, the story of our relationship with AI is actually part of a much bigger story about our love affair with technology. AI is just the latest and greatest in a long line of technologies that have made our lives so much better.

Let me give you some mind-blowing examples of how technology has improved our world. Since 1900, primarily thanks to technology, our life expectancy has doubled to reach 70 years

(continued)

(*continued*)

old globally,[1] literacy rates have increased from 12% to more than 85%,[2] extreme poverty has declined from more than 75% to about 10%,[3] and child mortality rates have dropped by 93% since 1950.[4]

That's like going from a world where most people couldn't read and had a high chance of not even making it to their fifth birthday to a world where almost everyone goes to school and has a good chance of living a long, healthy life!

Of course, technology isn't perfect. For example, in the same period, CO_2 emissions have risen more than 16 times, contributing significantly to climate change.[5]

But here's the thing: the same technology that causes these problems can also help solve them. We should all be confident in the virtuous cycle of the technologies we create. For example, the very problems caused by technology, like pollution, can be addressed with newer, greener technologies, such as renewable energy systems.

This cycle of technological innovation is essential for human progress. No one reading this book would like to go back in time and live a life full of dangers that ends, at best, at 30 years old.

The long evolution of technology from stone and fire to AI is a sacred legacy from our ancestors, aimed at improving the world. Today, we must honor this legacy by adapting to and evolving with both the advantages and challenges of technology, seizing opportunities, and mitigating risks.

We are the custodians of this legacy, tasked with creating a better future for our children. This responsibility means that discussions about AI's impact should not be limited to experts or corporations; they concern us all. Each of us holds the influence and voice to shape our future with AI.

This book is my commitment to empower you with the tools, insights, and inspiration needed to master the dynamic and exhilarating world of AI.

AI is not the destination; it's the vehicle that takes us to a more human future.

Introduction

Wakeup! The provocative cover of this book is a wake-up call. This book is meant to grab you until you pay attention. Our humanity is at risk, and we need to act now!

AI is here to stay, inevitably expanding and accelerating its presence. It is rapidly infiltrating various aspects of our lives, from influencing our decisions and automating jobs to capturing our children's attention, threatening our privacy and ethics, and even unfairly competing against our businesses.

> *"This book is a wake-up call. Our humanity is at risk, and we need to act now!"*

You Have a Choice to Make

As AI takes over our world at an increasing pace, you are faced with a choice of two options.

Option 1

You can sit back and do nothing, letting AI strip away everything that makes you human. You can let it pull your strings like a puppet, turning you into a meaningless, obsolete husk.

1

This is exactly what happens when we leverage AI to value speed over depth and prioritize convenience over human connection. This is also what happens when we relinquish creativity to AI copy-paste, or when we opt for AI simulation over authenticity.

I call this the "AI obesity." Just like how we got hooked on fast food, now we're binging on fast creativity, fast connections, fast decisions, and even fast love. It's like we're addicted to the fast food of AI, consuming it in large quantities without thinking about the consequences.

We're settling for "good enough" instead of striving for excellence, and we're losing our jobs, our businesses, our attention, our kids' safety, and our humanity in the process. If you ask me, AI obesity is a far more critical danger for our humanity than any hypothetical Terminator-style robot apocalypse!

"AI obesity is a far more critical danger for our humanity than any hypothetical Terminator-style robot apocalypse!"

Option 2

Alternatively, you can choose quality over convenience. You can swap fast food for a gourmet dining experience. This decision for authenticity, uniqueness, and depth is your key to maintaining your humanity in an AI-dominated world. It is about becoming truly IRREPLACEABLE.

How to achieve that? Well, first and foremost, you need to understand that AI itself isn't the problem. It's like food—AI is not inherently good or bad, it's all about how you engage with it: the amount, quality, variety, and frequency of your consumption.

However, the big difference between food and AI is that our parents warned us that eating too much can lead to obesity. Unfortunately, no one has yet taught us how to consume AI to avoid falling into AI obesity—but this book will fill that gap. So embracing the gourmet experience is not about refusing or banning AI; it is about using it wisely. It means getting the best out of it without losing yourself.

The closer you get to AI, the more you stand to gain—better efficiency, smarter learning, improved life satisfaction—but also the more dangerous it becomes. Imagine you're juggling sharp knives. With the right skills, you'll wow everyone. Without them, you could severely hurt yourself. This book is here to teach you the skills for that amazing juggling act.

To master this art, this book is going to take you on a practical journey to become IRREPLACEABLE. This groundbreaking approach draws on my 20 years of pioneering research at the human-AI frontier. It offers practical strategies that apply universally to your personal life, your children, your work, and your organization.

By leveraging it, you will develop the confidence to equip and guide your kids toward a successful future alongside AI. Additionally, you will be able to transform the impact of AI on your children from a distractor to a powerful educational ally.

You'll discover how to enhance your unique capabilities—those that AI can't match. By subtly blending your talents with AI, you'll forge powerful synergies, propelling your performance to new heights. Soon you won't be searching for jobs; jobs will be seeking you out. Forget climbing the corporate ladder; you'll be constructing your own.

Adopters of the IRREPLACEABLE approach have seen remarkable outcomes: over 30% increase in efficiency and 40% enhancement in work quality. They're enjoying a more balanced life, with heightened satisfaction and a deeper sense of purpose in their work. They also report having boosted their resilience and adaptability, leading them to greater inner peace, sharper focus, and overall life satisfaction.

Applying the IRREPLACEABLE journey to your company allows you to dramatically transform your business model with AI at scale. Simultaneously, you'll master the delicate art of merging human and AI strengths, significantly enhancing your business's uniqueness and competitive edge. You'll drive innovation to a point where you're no longer just adapting to the market—you're redefining it.

Your IRREPLACEABLE Journey

The "IRREPLACEABLE" framework introduces the "Three Competencies of the Future," developed from extensive research supported by experts in diverse fields such as behavioral psychology, addiction, pediatrics, resilience, flow, creativity, critical thinking, neuroscience, and learning.

As we will learn in more detail later in the book, "AI-Ready" focuses on enhanced performance and ethical AI use. "Human-Ready" leverages our unique human capabilities and creates synergies with AI.

"Change-Ready" emphasizes resilience and adaptability in the rapidly changing AI landscape.

This book marks the beginning of your transformation, which continues online. My LinkedIn page (www.linkedin.com/in/pascalbornet), X account (@pascal_bornet), and YouTube channel (@pascal_bornet) offer further insights, educational materials, expert discussions, and updates to support your ongoing journey. Join the IRREPLACEABLE Academy and community at www.irreplaceable.ai. Share your experiences of becoming IRREPLACEABLE using #irreplaceable.

The first step in your self-transformation journey is to take the IRQ: the IRREPLACEABLE Quotient test (www.irreplaceable.ai). This test allows you to identify which competencies you need to work on in priority. It will also help you track your progress and coach your learning because you can retake the test at any time during your journey.

How This Book Is Organized

Part 1, "The IRREPLACEABLE Imperative," kicks off with a bang, shattering the myths surrounding AI and unveiling the game-changing IRREPLACEABLE framework. You'll discover the secret sauce to supercharging your human potential and get started with the IRREPLACEABLE roadmap.

In Part 2, "Building IRREPLACEABLE Skills," you'll dive into how AI is redefining the world of skills. You'll discover the power of creating a synergistic relationship with AI, leveraging your uniquely human abilities—the Humics—to build skills that complement and enhance AI's capabilities.

Part 3, "Becoming IRREPLACEABLE at Work," teaches you the art of AI augmentation, enabling you to elevate your work performance without risking your job to automation. You'll learn to adopt an AI mindset, strategically apply AI to your work and life, and maintain AI literacy in an ever-evolving landscape. You'll also confront the burning questions of personal data management and ethical AI use head-on.

Part 4, "Raising IRREPLACEABLE Kids and Protecting Yourself," equips you with the tools to future-proof children in the age of AI. From outsmarting digital distractions to breaking free from AI addiction, you'll gain the tools to navigate the AI-infused world with confidence and redefine the essence of a well-balanced life for you and your children.

Part 5, "Leading IRREPLACEABLE Companies," teaches you how to embed AI into your organization's DNA while creating an environment where humans and AI work together seamlessly, unlocking unprecedented innovation and growth. You'll explore the principles of responsible AI implementation, and I'll show you how to build resilient, adaptable businesses that thrive in the face of change.

Part 6, "Implementing an Action Plan," provides a practical summary, guiding you on how to immediately apply the method in your daily life.

Throughout this book, you'll find real-life examples, expert insights, and actionable strategies that you can immediately apply to your life and work. By the end of this journey, you'll have the mindset, skills, and tools to become truly IRREPLACEABLE—ready to harness the power of AI, amplify your human potential, and create a future that is more innovative, inclusive, and deeply fulfilling.

PART

I

The IRREPLACEABLE Imperative

In this first part of the book, you'll explore the overarching concept of being IRREPLACEABLE in the age of AI. You'll dive into what it means for you as an individual, setting the foundation for the rest of the book.

Remember, AI impacts all dimensions of your life simultaneously—your personal life, your role as a parent, your work, and your business. This book takes a holistic approach, ensuring that you can thrive in all these areas. You'll start by understanding the IRREPLACEABLE imperative, which will guide you through the rest of your journey.

CHAPTER

1

Don't Believe All You Hear About AI!

AI has become an inescapable presence, transforming the way we live, work, and interact. But amid the hype and the headlines, it's easy to get lost in a maze of misconceptions and half-truths.

In this chapter, I'll separate fact from fiction, dispelling the myths that cloud our understanding of AI and its impact on our world. You'll explore the reality of AI's influence on society, business, and the future of work, laying the groundwork for the IRREPLACEABLE framework that will guide you through this transformative journey.

I've pinpointed 10 prevalent rumors surrounding AI. For each, I'll delve into analysis and offer my verdict—TRUE or FALSE—based on my insights.

Adapting to AI's Influence

Rumor #1: AI is only important for tech enthusiasts or people working in technology

FALSE.

Honestly, we often miss just how much AI has woven itself into the fabric of our daily lives. It's everywhere, and our reliance on it is continuously deepening. Every single day, we're all engaging with AI in so many ways, often without even realizing it!

Let's delve into the myriad ways AI interacts with our daily lives:

- You wake up and roll out of bed, and your smart home's thermostat has already adjusted the temperature, ensuring a cozy morning for you. That's AI working its magic.

- On your commute, you're taking a new route today. But no worries—your GPS reroutes in real-time based on current traffic conditions. That smooth, traffic-free drive? Courtesy of AI.

- Your car, like most modern cars, comes embedded with AI-driven features—from adaptive cruise control and automated parking to predictive maintenance alerts. It's AI looking at your safety.

- As you start your workday, the document you're drafting autocorrects your typos and suggests better phrasing—that's AI refining your words.

- Checking social media? The posts you see first, the ads that mysteriously match your recent search history, and even the memes tailored to your sense of humor—all are AI's handiwork.

- Got a client overseas? When you converse over email, AI-driven translation tools help bridge any language gaps, ensuring seamless communication.

- Planning a business trip? The online platform you use to book your flight employs AI to find you the best deals and optimal flight times and even suggests hotels based on your past preferences. Once on the flight, AI systems assist pilots in optimizing routes in real time based on changing weather conditions and airspace traffic.

- Got a virtual meeting? The noise-cancellation ensuring the car horn in the street doesn't disrupt proceedings is, once again, AI's doing. And that spam-free inbox you enjoy? AI's tireless efforts filter out those unnecessary emails.

- Returning home, you might unwind with some tunes. Your music streaming app creates a playlist with fresh songs that fit right in with your favorites. You guessed it—AI's behind that perfect playlist.

- At home, beyond smart fridges and thermostats, there are AI-powered ovens that adjust cooking times based on what's inside, washing machines that optimize cycles based on load weight and dirtiness, and even vacuums that learn the layout of your house for efficient cleaning.

- Movie night? The recommendations from your streaming service don't disappoint. Whether you're in the mood for a rom-com or an action-packed thriller, AI knows just the thing.

- Finally, as you drift off to sleep, your fitness tracker monitors your sleep patterns, ensuring you wake up refreshed. That gentle wake-up alarm that doesn't jar you out of slumber? A lullaby from our ever-present helper, AI.

Now, think bigger. Our entire supply chains—from the factory producing goods and the systems optimizing shipping routes to the stock management at your local store—rely heavily on AI. The banking system is also a massive nexus of AI operations. From fraud detection and credit score evaluations to high-frequency trading, AIs are at the helm. In the high-stakes environment of hospitals, AI acts as an invaluable ally, working alongside medical professionals, amplifying their ability to save lives and enhance patient care.

This also raises questions. For example, we believe we should not give AI the right to make decisions by itself without consulting us. But we have already been doing this for years, and the delegation trend is accelerating. Financial markets operate on AI automation, aircraft are piloted by AI, and traffic lights are controlled by AI. This raises several questions: What are the implications of such a delegation? To what extent should we entrust AI with such responsibilities? And is it truly safe to rely on AI across all facets of our existence?

In addition, can you imagine what would happen if, one day, all AI systems just...stopped working? That's a scary thought. The consequences would be unimaginable. Not only would we lose out on many of our modern comforts and work automation, but it could be disastrous in fields like medicine. So many people rely on AI-driven systems for critical care and support.

With AI everywhere, it is imperative for all of us to become aware and responsible, to become IRREPLACEABLE.

Rumor #2: To be successful in an AI world, we need to adopt AI-like qualities

FALSE.

We have been taught that to succeed, we need to be good at crunching numbers, hyper-focused, working 24/7, and becoming a super-productive workhorse. We tend to admire startup leaders who burn out after working endlessly for months. I still hear managers saying that if you are not stressed, you are not doing enough. And when we carve out time for ourselves, most of us still feel guilty about not achieving more.

But times have changed. Today, with the recent advancements in AI, this mentality is just stone age.

Here's a hot take: to avoid being redundant with AI, you have to be less like AI, not more! To really click with AI, you've got to play up what makes you human, where AI will never be as good as you: harnessing creativity, exploring unconventional ideas, and fostering profound connections with others. Creating synergies that elevate your work to unprecedented levels is impossible if you concentrate solely on skills where AI outshines.

As you will learn in this book, it's these human superpowers—like creativity, empathy, leadership, and just being a good listener—that'll give you the real edge. That's your secret sauce AI can't copy.

Rumor #3: Using AI at work or school is cheating

FALSE.

Ever feel like a fraud using tech to be more efficient at work? It's like there's this unwritten rule that if you're using ChatGPT or Google Translate, you're not really doing the job properly. As if you're breaking some sacred commandment: thou shalt not leverage smart tools but rely on brute human force alone!

Scrap that antiquated notion—it's just not true. You know what? Using AI smartly is a game-changer. It doesn't make your work less valuable; it shows you're clever about how you get things done. This skill is increasingly valuable in a tech-intensive world.

AI is as fundamental as electricity, the internet, or fire. Just as we no longer specify that we baked a cake "with fire" or "with electricity," it is irrelevant to mention that we crafted a presentation "with AI." AI's integration should become seamlessly implicit in any of our accomplishments.

The time has come to reexamine these outdated attitudes toward technology. In this book, we will cover how to make this mind shift and several other ones to ensure your success in a world increasingly driven by AI.

Managers should lead this cultural change. Encourage teams to openly embrace AI tools that amplify their talents. Tell them they're not average workers anymore; they're AI-powered superheroes! The most forward-thinking companies are those dropping the secrecy and fully integrating the tech advantage into their culture. So what about the laggards clinging to "pure human toil" as some badge of honor? Let's just say they'll vanish faster than fax machines.

Rumor #4: AI will take our jobs

TRUE.

Everyone's buzzing about how AI will snatch away our jobs like a thief in the night.

This is true: your job has an expiration date, and this date is about to come. In our world increasingly driven by AI, this is not a prophecy of doom but a stark reality. The role you fulfill today, the tasks you perform with ease and expertise, are on borrowed time. Whatever your industry, your role, or your expertise, the clock ticks!

So what can we do? Anticipate and prepare.

You need a pivotal shift in how you view your career, shifting focus from job security to skill adaptability. In short, pivot from protecting jobs to cultivating flexible skills. You must shift your fight. Don't try to save your job; this fight is already lost.

Instead, use your time and energy to make your skills fit the new world. Your skills stay with you always, while your job is just a title on a piece of paper. Improving your skills is the smartest thing you can do for your future.

Instead of waiting passively for AI to reshape our professional landscape, we should actively engage with this technology. Learn about AI's capabilities and limitations. Enhance your own skill set with qualities that AI can't achieve as well as you do: genuine creativity, emotional intelligence, and strategic insight. In this book, we will cover how to succeed in such a crucial self-transformation.

AI isn't a rival; it's a partner that helps us automate mundane tasks, freeing us up to focus on what's truly important: our team, strategic thinking, creativity, and our clients. Plus, AI expands our capabilities, enabling us to achieve more and make a greater impact on our world—like doctors saving more lives or analysts who can sift through millions of report pages in just minutes. It's not AI that will take your role but certainly someone who knows how to harness AI better than you!

AI may change the nature of work, but that doesn't have to spell its end. And if the day comes when work as we know it shifts or diminishes, let's embrace it as a chance to focus on what truly matters in life: time with our loved ones, pursuing our passions, safeguarding our planet, and focusing on a life purpose that goes beyond a work-centric existence.

The Specificities of AI

Rumor #5: AI and human intelligence are the same kinds of intelligence

FALSE.

The two types of intelligence are inherently different, though their functions occasionally overlap.

There is a lot of debate about how to define AI. To make it simple and clear, I like to define AI as the *simulation* of human intelligence in machines. It's when a machine is designed to think, learn, speak, and interact with its environment, much like a human. This encompasses a range of functions, from basic problem-solving and decision-making to advanced tasks like natural language processing, sensory perception through vision or touch, and executing complex actions.

Now, to explain the difference between AI and human intelligence, let's consider two artists:

- **The Human Artist (human intelligence):** Meet Sofia. She's a painter who has been creating art since she was a child. Every brush stroke she makes is influenced by a blend of her emotions, memories, experiences, and even the mood she's in that day. When she paints a sunset, she remembers the one she saw during a memorable summer vacation. Sofia often experiments, trying new techniques or colors based on her feelings or inspirations from the world around her. Her paintings are not just visual representations; they're a window into her soul and life story.

- **The Robot Artist (artificial intelligence):** Now, meet Artie. Artie is a robot designed to paint. When Artie paints that same sunset, it analyzes thousands of sunset images it has been fed, calculating the most common colors, the patterns of the clouds, and the positioning of the sun. It doesn't remember sunsets or feel the warmth of that summer evening; it uses data and patterns to create a beautiful painting. Over time, the more sunsets Artie is shown, the better its paintings become. However, it doesn't "feel" or "remember"—it calculates and executes based on data and programming.

In essence, Sofia's intelligence is rich, emotional, and experiential. It's influenced by her upbringing, her joys and sorrows, and the unique way she perceives the world. Artie's intelligence, on the other hand, is powerful and precise, driven by vast amounts of data and specific instructions. While Artie can create a painting that looks like a sunset, it doesn't "understand" a sunset in the emotional and experiential way Sofia does.

Table 1.1 is a straightforward matrix to compare AI and human intelligence today. It demonstrates how AI and human intelligence have complementary strengths and weaknesses.

We will dive deeper into these differences and complementarities in the next part of the book.

Rumor #6: AI has become more creative than humans

FALSE.

This question is insightful because when interacting with AI, such as asking ChatGPT for a poem, it appears creative and intelligent, almost human-like, which warrants further explanation.

I like to compare what AI does to a trick, similar to a magician's trick: it seems smart and creative, but it's an illusion. Imagine you have a super-talented parrot that has memorized millions of phrases. If you say "hello," it might respond with "How are you?" not because it understands greetings or cares about your well-being, but because it's heard that reply often after the word "hello" in its past experiences.

AI operates similarly. Trained on extensive data, it generates responses by predicting the most likely next word or phrase, like a sophisticated keyboard's autocomplete. Same as in the case of the parrot, all this doesn't imply AI's understanding, emotions, or consciousness. And this trick has consequences.

Imagine that our super-talented parrot, in trying to mimic conversations, occasionally mixes up the phrases it's heard. Perhaps it heard two different conversations—one about baking and another about space exploration. If you ask the parrot about making a cake, it might mistakenly throw in something about astronauts. This isn't

Table 1.1 AI versus human intelligence.

	AI	Human Intelligence
Origin and Development	Created and designed by humans based on algorithms and data. Evolves through updates to algorithms and more data.	Product of evolution over millions of years, shaped by genetics, upbringing, and experiences.
Learning	Learns from big datasets using algorithms. Can rapidly master narrow domains given sufficient data.	Learns from experiences, teachings, and observations. More versatile and adaptable, understands context beyond data.
Emotions and Consciousness	No emotions, consciousness, desires, or subjective experiences. Decisions are based purely on logic and algorithms.	Inherently emotional and conscious. Decisions are influenced by feelings, desires, and intuition.
Generalization	Most AIs are narrow or domain-specific, excelling only at specific tasks. Some more general models exist.	Highly generalizable. Humans adapt to a wide range of tasks, often transferring knowledge between domains.
Creativity	Can generate novel outputs based on programming and data but can't create with intentional imagination.	Capable of genuine creativity, art, music, and innovative solutions, often emotionally/abstractly driven.
Interaction with Environment	Interacts using predefined algorithms and sensor data.	Continuously interacts using sensory information, experiences, and emotional responses.
Ethics and Morality	No inherent ethics or morals. Ethical behavior in AI comes from human programming.	Has a capacity for ethical reasoning, influenced by culture, upbringing, and experiences.

	AI	Human Intelligence
Biases	Subject to biases from datasets and programming that can lead to inaccurate or unfair conclusions.	Prone to cognitive biases shaped by experiences, culture, and emotions. However, humans can recognize and work to overcome biases through introspection and education.
Limitations	Limited by algorithms, data, and compute power. Processes information, doesn't "understand."	Extremely versatile but can be influenced by biases, emotions, overload, and physical constraints.

because the parrot genuinely believes astronauts are related to baking, but because it's jumbled up the patterns it's recognized.

Similarly, generative AI models like ChatGPT can produce "hallucinations"—outputs that seem nonsensical or unrelated to the input. Such errors might produce answers that are factually incorrect, contextually irrelevant, or just plain odd.

This risk of "hallucinations" underscores the importance of using AI tools with a critical mind, understanding their limitations, and not taking their outputs at face value. It's a reminder that while these models are powerful, they don't truly "understand" content and can make incorrect predictions.

Now let's talk about the creative aspects of AI. Imagine your parrot is not just good at mimicking words but is also adept at mixing phrases it's heard before. When you recite a line of a poem to it, the parrot might respond with a new line that sounds poetic and fits rhythmically. It does this by blending bits of other poems or phrases it's heard before.

- **Recombination versus novelty:** Imagine the parrot has heard poems about the sun and the moon. If prompted, it might blend these to talk about a "sunny moon." While this is a creative mix from the parrot's repertoire, it doesn't compare to a human's capability to introduce entirely new themes or groundbreaking poetic styles.

- **Mimicry versus intent:** The parrot's poetic response isn't driven by an intent to convey emotion or tell a story. It's just mimicking in a way that fits the prompt. A human poet, however, often writes with purpose, intent, and emotion.

- **Absence of emotion and experience:** When a human writes a poem about love, it might come from personal experiences, deep feelings, or reflections on relationships. The parrot's "poem" lacks this depth; it's just a mix of words without understanding their emotional weight.

In essence, while the parrot can produce "creative" mixes of what it's heard, its process is fundamentally different from the rich, multifaceted creativity of humans.

AI in Society and Business

Rumor #7: AI will go rogue and destroy humanity

FALSE.

The risk comes from humans, not from AI.

While we should certainly approach AI with caution, the "killer robot" scenario is more of a dramatization than a likely reality. Every time someone tells you the sky is falling because of AI, remember all those old stories—Prometheus, Frankenstein, the Terminator. They are cautionary tales, not prophecies!

AI is neither good nor bad; it depends on how we build and how we use it. It is like a knife that is useful for cooking but can also kill people if used with the wrong intentions. We should be concerned about humans with malicious intent or lack of capabilities using AI, not about AI. Should AI ever go rogue in the future, it would be because humans, at some point, endowed it with such capabilities. Therefore, the entire responsibility rests on our human shoulders.

A few things are certain: the emergence of superintelligent AI is inevitable, and it's likely to happen sooner than later. Another certainty is that we will face issues with this superintelligent AI, issues that we have not even predicted—the same way as climate change, the Chernobyl disaster, or the COVID-19 pandemic happened. The issue is that, as humans, we tend to react to problems only after they occur. Unfortunately, this reactive approach is a fundamental aspect of our nature that we need to acknowledge.

So what did we do when we experienced issues with nuclear power? We regulated it. We created the Atomic Energy Commission to oversee nuclear technology globally.

In the same way, can we regulate AI globally before a catastrophe happens? I hope so. But this will certainly not be enough. The difference between nuclear power and AI is that it is easier to work on AI without anyone noticing it. Working on nuclear power requires plants and large equipment that are easy to spot, even from space. So regulating AI sounds great, but there's always going to be that one person in a garage somewhere or a group hiding out in the countryside, cooking up AI for all the wrong reasons.

Despite these challenges, I believe we must stay optimistic and maintain our faith in humanity's inherent goodness. We have built AI; it is like our kid. It is learning from us and inheriting our biases, intelligence, and capabilities. Now we need to make sure we also share with it our values.

Currently, AI is still in its learning phase. The same as a teenager, it is still learning, and is still more or less under our control. But it will soon become an autonomous adult. This event will happen when AI becomes superintelligent. At that time, we'll be crossing our fingers, hoping we've done enough to raise it to be a responsible, ethical adult that can't let itself be influenced, even by the most malicious humans.

So what do we need to do? If we are good parents, we need to teach responsibility, accountability, trust, ethics, and values. We need to prepare it for autonomy, ensuring it has the necessary "maturity" to make decisions that are beneficial or at least nonharmful to humanity. This includes instilling in AI the ability to discern and resist harmful human influences.

As AI's parents, we all have a role to play in this education, and I will explain later in the book how you and I will be able to act on this.

Rumor #8: A business that does not use AI has a limited life

TRUE.

Thinking of a business that can survive without using AI is the same as thinking of a business that can operate without electricity. It is not possible!

Modernizing your company is crucial for its survival. In fact, research unveils that nearly half of the S&P 500 companies are expected to be replaced within the next decade,[1] a trend largely driven by the swift pace of technological innovation and disruption.

This applies to companies as much as individuals (and dinosaurs!): adapt or risk extinction. If you don't take the initiative to modernize promptly, rest assured, your competitors will.

Conversely, many people preach that AI is the silver bullet for all your company's problems. But let's get real: AI isn't a one-stop fix—it's a tool, and like any tool, it's only as good as the person wielding it.

Think of AI as a sophisticated espresso machine in a coffee shop. It's capable of producing perfect shots of espresso every time, but without a barista who knows how to use it, maintain it, and create a menu of drinks to satisfy customers' diverse tastes, it's just a fancy piece of equipment.

AI can process data and automate tasks with incredible efficiency, but it requires human expertise to interpret that data correctly and make decisions that align with the company's vision and ethics. And when blended with human creativity, intuition, and strategic thinking, it can create a recipe for success that is truly remarkable.

But all this won't happen overnight. There is a need to start the transformation ASAP because it can take time, your competitors might have already started, and you do not want your business to be stuck in the past and die.

As a tool, AI amplifies what is already there, whether it is good or bad. If your current processes and culture are flawed, AI will only highlight those flaws. Conversely, if they are robust, AI can boost your company to new heights of efficiency. In this book, I will share with you a framework to successfully transform your business, based on my experience implementing AI for hundreds of businesses worldwide.

This framework advocates for a holistic integration of AI and human skills, emphasizing adaptability, ethical AI use, and the amplification of unique human capabilities. It aims to ensure businesses not only adapt but excel in an AI-driven world by leveraging trust to enable AI implementation at scale. Unlike traditional models solely focused on efficiency and cost reduction, this approach prioritizes the ethical use of AI to fundamentally transform business operations and decision-making, while creating incremental value from human creativity, judgment, and interaction.

The Future with AI: Our Kids and Our Humanity

Rumor #9: We should protect our kids against the impact of AI

TRUE.

It's a familiar script at a restaurant table: parents exchanging worried glances over their quinoa salad as their kids, eyes glued to screens, converse fluently in emojis and hashtags. "What's happening to the children?" we whisper, imagining a future where our offspring meld into the Matrix, leaving us to wonder if we'll have to plug USBs into their ears to get a moment of eye contact.

But before we start childproofing the Wi-Fi or teaching toddlers how to use an abacus instead of an iPad, let's take a breath. The truth is, AI isn't the big bad wolf at the door—it's the new neighbor we ought to get to know.

Yes, AI is everywhere, and it's natural to fear the unknown. We worry that our kids might become too dependent on technology or, worse, be outsmarted by it. But what if we're looking at it all wrong?

Instead of fearing AI, we could be embracing it as the most extraordinary tutor our kids could have—ever available, infinitely patient, and brimming with the kind of knowledge that would make even Einstein raise an eyebrow.

Think about it: AI can help our kids learn a new language, understand quantum physics, or explore the universe, all customized to their learning pace and from the comfort of their bedrooms. And let's be honest, who among us hasn't wished for a homework helper who doesn't groan when algebra appears?

Balance and guidance are key. We shouldn't just hand over the tablets and let AI do the parenting. Instead, let's guide our kids on how to use this technology responsibly. Succeeding at implementing this approach is one of the key topics of this book.

Show them how to question the information AI provides and use it as a tool for learning, not just a source of endless entertainment. Let's teach them digital literacy—the understanding of how AI works, its benefits, and its limitations.

As we will discuss in this book, we can prepare our children for a future where AI is just another tool in their kit—a powerful one, sure, but nothing compared to the power of a curious, creative, well-guided human mind.

Rumor #10: AI will make our world less human

IT DEPENDS (ON YOU).

As I pointed out in the introduction, digital and AI are like food; our health depends in large part on what we consume. If we're not careful, we can end up with AI obesity—basically, overloading on digital stuff that doesn't really do us any good. Let's dive into that.

Food producers, always looking for more profits, may add more sugar and flavor enhancers to products like chocolate bars and sodas to make them irresistible. Tech companies use similar tactics to keep us engaged longer on social media, games, and other apps. Thanks to that, they can show us more ads and make more profits. Whether it is food or AI-powered apps, the impact on our brains is the same: we, and our kids, constantly crave more.

Regulations definitely help, but they won't stop you or your children from eating chocolate and greasy French fries the whole day, potentially leading you to obesity and diabetes. It's the same with AI—no one will prevent you from using it in a harmful way.

But you will have to bear with the consequences on yourself and your children, the potential loss of your humanity, caused by AI obesity—being hooked on technology to the point of losing touch with the natural world, and what makes you "yourself."

On top of this, as AI gets smarter and smarter, it is becoming increasingly better at tricking our brains, intensifying this issue in the future.

I was worried about these risks for myself and especially for my kids. So I met with renowned psychology and behavioral therapy experts to understand these issues better and find solutions to them. I will share these priceless secrets in the following chapters. I will also share how I fell into an addiction to social media and how I overcame it by building a new, innovative approach.

In addition, as AI takes on roles once reserved for humans, it's natural for us to question our significance and purpose. Historically, people found meaning through their professions, or the unique skills they took decades to build. Now, with machines outpacing us in various tasks, it's essential to redefine and rediscover that sense of purpose. AI can answer any question except this one: What is your purpose in life? While AI excels at answering questions, we humans should excel at asking the right ones.

In this new AI-augmented world, our purpose might shift from mere task execution to more profound pursuits: building relationships, artistic expression, ethical leadership, and personal growth. But how do we navigate this transformation and help our kids to succeed? How can AI be that tool that amplifies our human potential? This book brings tangible answers to these questions.

AI increases our convenience dramatically. It's like a modern-day Aladdin's lamp—ready to remember, calculate, translate, and create at our command. It boosts our efficiency, but this raises a question: Will our brains become lazy from overreliance on technology? The book will delve into the implications of this shift and offer strategies for maintaining what matters: our humanity.

We'll provide answers to other significant questions: As AI takes on roles in customer service and social interactions, could we lose the personal touch that fosters human connection? Without human emotions, how will AI navigate ethical choices in areas like justice, healthcare, or warfare?

We could lose our humanity if we are not careful, and this is the purpose of this book: a call for reflection and action on what we can do today to make sure our humanity becomes IRREPLACEABLE.

CHAPTER

2

The Essence of Being IRREPLACEABLE

Having dispelled the myths surrounding AI, we now turn our attention to what it truly means to be IRREPLACEABLE. In this chapter, we'll explore the origins of this concept and how it manifests in today's world, setting the stage for the detailed framework to come.

The questions shaping the flow of discussion throughout this book are inspired by those I regularly encounter during my keynote speaking engagements and from the vibrant dialogue with my social media community.

Introducing the IRREPLACEABLE Concept

Pascal, why is your book titled *IRREPLACEABLE?*

Great question. Let me start with a story.

My family and I were wrapping up a fantastic weekend trip in New York and heading back to Miami on a Sunday afternoon. We wanted to get the kids to bed early to kick off the school week, so we chose a flight that wasn't too late.

We breezed through security at the airport, picked up some last-minute New York souvenirs, and then headed to our gate. But at the gate, we were met with delayed boarding and a lengthy line of travelers eager to sit down in the plane after a long wait.

Lunch had eluded us amid the hustle, so we grabbed what you could call sandwiches—if only they had any flavor—and ate them quickly near the boarding gate. The flight crew could see us; we were right by the door.

After a quick bathroom break and a coffee run, I returned to find the last passengers boarding. My family got in line, the last to board, and we approached the gate but were met with a cold "The flight is closed."

Despite our protests, the fact we'd been in sight the whole time, and the plea that this would mean a late night for the kids, the crew member wouldn't budge. Efficiency and common sense seemed lost to rigid automation—the automated door had closed, and that was that! The crew manager told me, "The door closes automatically when it sees no one else in the queue. The flight is closed!"

I started to become upset because of this ridiculous situation. Indeed, we were there with our boarding passes in hand, and just five feet from us, beyond the door, were the passengers lining up on the jet bridge to actually board the plane. We debated back and forth, but their argument was always a robotic repetition of "the door is closed."

I said to the crew manager, "Look, if technology is doing everything, why are you still here? Isn't it to handle situations like this?" I went on, "You're human; unlike the door, you know what human empathy is; hence, you can make the door act more human—for instance, by waiting before closing when families are about to get on." I was so upset that the next sentence just came out of my mouth naturally. I told her, "You might believe you are IRREPLACEABLE, but by acting like a machine, there is no reason why your job would not be fully replaced by a machine!"

That was the origin of this book's title. So, in a way, the title arose from a human's burst of emotion, aiming to emphasize the demand for increased humanity!

In the end, we had to wait for the next flight, three hours later. We finally arrived home at 11 p.m. and went to bed. After waking up at 6 a.m. on Monday—as they do every school day—the kids were so tired that entire day that they went to sleep right after getting home from school at 4 p.m.!

Later, one of my friends who works for an airline confirmed that it is typically not an issue to open the boarding door in such cases. So the problem was not technical; it was more an issue of this crew manager's mindset.

This experience perfectly illustrated how some people become so intertwined with technology that they lose their human touch. I'm sure most of you have had similar encounters with people so hidden behind their machines and processes that they forget they are human.

Others believe technology gives them power over people. There is no future for such behaviors. Mechanization has contaminated not only their skills but, more importantly, their mindset. These people who are becoming robotic are the ones who will be replaced by actual robots.

So, on the one hand, those unable to adapt beyond robotic routines will be replaced by the very technology they cling to. On the other hand, those embracing their humanity, who can work alongside technology and add value that machines cannot, will be IRREPLACEABLE.

The takeaway is simple yet profound: navigating a high-tech future means doubling down on what makes us human. Our essence can't be coded or automated. Our humanity is IRREPLACEABLE.

Succeeding in an era of AI is about rediscovering our humanity and taking it to unprecedented levels. We must excel in the art of being human like never before. In a world of artificial intelligence, authenticity is the ultimate competitive advantage. In this book, I'll dive into not just the skills but the mindset that will cement our place as IRREPLACEABLE in an age where technology is everywhere.

> *"In a world of artificial intelligence, authenticity is the ultimate competitive advantage."*

To finish on a good note, I had a turnaround moment just days after that airport frustration. I was scrambling to get a document from the Social Security Administration that my accountant needed. Despite multiple failed attempts to download it online and fruitless calls, I was told to visit their office in person. So there I was in Miami, after a 30-minute wait in line, only to be told I couldn't get the document without my driver's license, which I'd forgotten to bring along. Although I had my passport with me to justify my identity, the rule was clear: it needed to be the driver's license.

I explained my predicament—the endless calls, the hotline runaround, and now this. I could see the agent understood. With a glance of empathy, she printed the document but blotted out her name, bending the rules because she saw the person behind the policy. I thanked her, recognizing her humanity. This was a perfect example of how, despite what technology demands, a human touch can still make all the difference. No algorithm could have stepped up like that—only a person who sees you!

Decoding the IRREPLACEABLE Concept

How do we hold onto our human essence in a world increasingly saturated with AI?

My airport story probably got you thinking. It's like AI and tech are slowly creeping into every part of our lives, even impacting our behaviors. We're often influenced by machines without even realizing it. So what's the cure for this tech infection?

Becoming IRREPLACEABLE is your antidote to the tech pandemic!

The IRREPLACEABLE concept touches on the core of human identity, value, and connection. It's the notion that certain qualities, contributions, or bonds are so unique and intrinsic to an individual or an organization that they cannot be duplicated or substituted, even by advanced technology such as AI.

In the context of AI's growing capabilities, being IRREPLACE-ABLE becomes a poignant topic. As artificial intelligence evolves, it can replicate or exceed human abilities in tasks ranging from menial to highly complex. This technological progression leads to existential questions: What aspects of our humanity remain uniquely ours? Are there elements within us that are immune to digitization or automation?

It is a thought-provoking idea that our humanity, our values, our jobs, or even our loved ones could one day be replaced by AI. To avoid this, we must recognize and cherish what is truly IRREPLACEABLE in ourselves: as a person but also as a human.

In essence, being IRREPLACEABLE in the age of AI means cultivating and valuing those attributes that are inherently human and cannot be replicated by algorithms. With that, we ensure that as AI evolves, it serves as a complement to, rather than a replacement for, the rich and multifaceted nature of human life.

The concept of being IRREPLACEABLE isn't exclusive to individuals; it's equally relevant to companies. For example, a company composed of IRREPLACEABLE people will be more likely to succeed in an AI world than a company that does not. Let's look in more detail at how this concept applies to organizations.

The IRREPLACEABLE Concept for Companies

Could you provide an example of a company that is not IRREPLACEABLE?

History is replete with examples of companies that failed because they thought they were IRREPLACEABLE. It's tough to pick just one, but a noteworthy case is Zume Pizza.

Zume Pizza's story is a stark reminder that failing to balance technological innovation with the human element can lead to downfall. Shut down in 2023, Zume had attempted to revolutionize the food industry with its AI-driven pizza preparation and delivery process, featuring robots and oven-equipped trucks for on-the-go baking. Despite its advanced automation, the company overlooked the essential human aspects of culinary creativity and customer interaction, critical in the dining experience.

The heart of pizza's appeal—comfort, tradition, and human connection—was lost in Zume's push for automation. While robots excelled in efficiency, they fell short in replicating the nuanced skills of human chefs, leading to a product that couldn't match the quality of handcrafted pizzas. This technology-first approach limited Zume's adaptability to customer preferences and special dietary needs—a flexibility readily available with human staff.

Additionally, the emphasis on high-tech solutions added unnecessary complexity and costs, without enhancing customer value, undermining the sustainability of Zume's business model compared to traditional pizza establishments. The lack of human oversight likely affected quality control and the ability to address emerging issues, distancing customers who value not just convenience but also the quality and dining experience.

Zume's failure underscores the vital importance of integrating the power of AI with the unique strengths of the human touch.

What does it mean for a company to be IRREPLACEABLE?

This is an important question: What are the key ingredients that make some companies IRREPLACEABLE, even as AI transforms business?

IRREPLACEABLE companies are at the forefront of the tech agenda. They have a clear vision with measurable return on investment, plus a flexible and comprehensive long-term plan to deliver it. They remain agile, adjusting their plans to align with market shifts.

But this is not all.

At their core, companies are living organisms powered by human beings such as employees, managers, customers, suppliers, or partners. And it's their distinctly human qualities that set the successful companies apart, even as technology expands.

Take digital transformations as an example. Companies pour insane amounts of cash into implementing some new sales software or adding automation to streamline finance tasks, expecting massive gains. But get this: research shows that up to 75% of these major tech projects crash hard.[1] And up to 70% actually fail outright, according to the consulting firm McKinsey & Company.[2] Talk about a massive waste of money—trillions sunk annually on broken transformations!

So what's causing this epic failure rate? Mainly there is a mismatch between the pace of tech change and people's capacity to adapt. When companies focus heavily on the tech tools alone, forgetting the human side, projects flounder fast.

Imagine gifting Granny an iPhone and then leaving her to figure it out solo. That'd be a bit harsh, right? But too often, companies force-feed tech changes without giving people the support to evolve their skills or integrate new tools. Then leaders seem shocked when workers feel lost in the shuffle!

IRREPLACEABLE companies know better. They align the pace of tech with people's ability to adapt. They don't just invest in software; they invest in the humans who give those tools meaning. They provide training, encouragement, and a culture ready for change. By doing this, they make their people IRREPLACEABLE too.

At their core, IRREPLACEABLE companies recognize that even as tech progresses, people power innovation. So they build adaptable cultures and workforces ready to evolve fluidly alongside AI. They lead with compassion, wisdom, and ethics—all those human superpowers!

So, as an organization, be IRREPLACEABLE. Guide your people, and inspire them. AI can only compute, but humans create, care for, and connect. Augment your tech with the magic of humanity!

Later in the book (Part 5), we will go through the critical success factors to make your organization truly IRREPLACEABLE.

CHAPTER

3

The Urgency to Become IRREPLACEABLE

This chapter confronts the pressing need to become IRREPLACE-ABLE. I project into an AI-dominated future, conduct a detailed analysis of what it means to be replaceable versus IRREPLACEABLE, and introduce the IRREPLACEABLE framework that will guide us through the rest of the book.

Projecting into an AI-Dominated Future

How urgent is it to become IRREPLACEABLE?

Fast-forward a few years from now. Here are some examples of what could happen if most of us fail to become IRREPLACEABLE:

- Imagine a world where companies use AI algorithms to assign jobs and careers, stripping individuals of the choice to pursue their passions, leading to a society that lacks innovation and personal fulfillment.

- Consider a world where parents use AI to monitor and control every aspect of a child's life, potentially replacing the human aspect of parenting with surveillance and control, impacting the child's development and independence.

- Imagine a future where judges would fully rely on AI that not only enforces law but also crafts punishment based on a person's psyche. It would push the boundaries of justice, replacing the human judicial process with algorithms that might lack compassion or context.

- Picture a technology that records every one of your memories in detail. A person with access to such a database could replicate or even replace individual identities, raising questions about what makes us unique.

- Consider a personal AI that makes decisions for you, from what you eat based on your health data to whom you should date based on social compatibility algorithms. Your life becomes a series of optimized events devoid of spontaneity and genuine human choice.

- Think about a political landscape where people can use AI to predict voting patterns and align policies with the majority's preference, effectively silencing minority voices and reducing the complexity of governance to mere data points.

Of course, I have designed these examples to provoke your thoughts and highlight the potential consequences of overreliance on AI. My purpose here is to highlight the importance of maintaining a balance where AI serves to enhance human capabilities rather than replace the core attributes that make us human.

None of us wants to be in the situation of failing to become IRREPLACEABLE. This is why this book exists!

Can you provide more scary examples of what our lives could become if we miss out on becoming IRREPLACEABLE?

If you have ever watched the British TV series *Black Mirror* (streaming on Netflix), each episode is a story of a world where people have failed to become IRREPLACEABLE. The ones that strike me the most are these:

- In the episode "Nosedive," people rate each other for every interaction, affecting their socioeconomic status. Society might use an AI system to determine social standing, leading to a life obsessively curated for artificial approval, stripping away authenticity.

- "Hang the DJ" explores AI-driven dating where algorithms dictate relationships. Such reliance on AI for finding companionship could result in a society that loses the natural spontaneity and complexity of human relationships.

- "Men Against Fire" presents a military application where soldiers' perceptions are altered by technology to dehumanize enemies. This scenario suggests a future where someone could use AI to manipulate our perception to align with agendas, fundamentally changing free will and moral choices.

- In a scenario reminiscent of "Shut Up and Dance," AI surveillance systems could blackmail individuals into compliance by threatening to release personal information, thereby controlling behavior and eroding privacy.

- Expanding on "Playtest," therapists could use virtual reality AI for therapeutic purposes, but with the potential to become so immersive that individuals might prefer virtual existence over real life, impacting society's mental health on a large scale.

These sci-fi cautionary tales envision AI radically transforming human life, ethics, and society. Let's make sure the real-world story has a happier ending. Let's make sure we try our best ASAP to become IRREPLACEABLE!

IRREPLACEABLE versus Replaceable: A Detailed Analysis

How would you compare replaceable and IRREPLACEABLE people?

That is a great question: How do you spot the difference between people who might become IRREPLACEABLE and those who might not?

Meet our three imaginary friends: Alex, Rishi, and Kiran. They can all access the same AI apps on their phones or computers. As we will see, it's how they use it, though, that tells us everything. It is their approach, reliance, and emotional connection to it that can determine how IRREPLACEABLE they might become.

Let's dive deeper.

Alex: Not IRREPLACEABLE   Meet Alex, the beloved gardener who relies on time-tested methods rather than flashy new apps or gadgets. "Nature doesn't need technology telling it what to do," Alex often says while tenderly caring for the flower beds.

But when drought hits and water runs short, Alex's old-school ways are put to the test. Gardens across the community start to wither under the harsh sun.

Alex is cautious, even skeptical, about using AI in daily tasks and work. She only uses the AI system sparingly, often falling back on traditional approaches even if AI could do it better. Alex tends to avoid AI completely, sticking to manual methods or older tech.

She harbors doubts about the AI systems, maybe due to worries about privacy, fear of new tech, or not fully grasping its abilities. Alex believes human effort is invaluable, and relying on AI could diminish their role and significance.

But in doing so, Alex risks falling behind as AI-enhanced processes become the norm. She misses chances to use AI to improve. By not embracing tech, Alex risks isolating herself from a community that increasingly relies on digital platforms to stay connected. Alex's limited tech literacy not only prevents her from harnessing AI's benefits but also exposes her to cyber risks like scams and hacking.

In this case, not tapping the AI system's full potential puts Alex at a disadvantage, especially where AI-boosted efficiency, accuracy, and innovation are highly valued. If Alex doesn't adapt, others who embrace AI may replace the cautious gardener.

Rishi: IRREPLACEABLE   Meet Rishi, the inventive chef who blends tech with personal flair. She uses a smart cooking app for recipe ideas but always adds her own spin, marrying suggestions with an intuition for flavors. "Tech brings the ingredients together, but the heart makes the meal," Rishi says, dishing up potluck favorites.

Rishi sees AI as a tool, not a crutch, understanding its pros and cons. Rishi taps the AI when needed but balances it with human judgment and interaction. She integrates AI not just for efficiency but to find new approaches and solutions, too. Rishi cares about AI's ethics, from data privacy to bias.

This chef seeks people's opinions and values experiences, using AI as an aide, not the main source. Rishi gets AI feedback to improve skills but may push back on its outputs, wanting transparency. She knows AI evolves, so her use of it should too. She sees herself as a lifelong learner, with AI fueling growth.

Rishi views AI as a partner, respecting its abilities without overreliance and being aware of its upsides and downsides. This chef believes human creativity, emotions, and intuition are IRREPLACE-ABLE. While benefiting from AI's speed, Rishi treasures the human touch, judgment, and connections. She likely has strong tech literacy, engages in AI ethics talks, and sees long-term value in evolving with AI.

Thanks to her mindful AI use, Rishi creates value by harnessing AI while avoiding its risks.

Kiran: Not IRREPLACEABLE   Meet Kiran, a parent who leans heavily on tech for parenting hacks, fun, and learning. Kiran often uses apps to plan the family schedule, limit screen time, and even read bedtime tales. "There's an app for that," is Kiran's mantra. But when a digital assistant glitches, leaving Kiran's household adrift, she must rediscover photo albums, board games, and the lost art of talking.

Kiran depends heavily on AI for daily tasks, even treating it as a key source of info, entertainment, and company. Kiran constantly consults AI for various needs, from reminders to advice or companionship.

Kiran sees AI as a go-to solution for any problem, sometimes favoring its suggestions over human input. She develops a bond with the system, appreciating its consistency, speedy replies, and absence of judgment. But Kiran starts feeling redundant given the efficiency of AI, especially if it can automate her tasks or hobbies.

Relying so heavily on AI decreases Kiran's human collaboration and stifles innovation due to overreliance on AI solutions. She is blinded by the shiny AI apps she uses. As a result, she dismisses privacy concerns, and she is less likely to discuss AI ethics. Her long-term vision lacks personal or professional growth alongside AI, which could lead to redundancy.

Kiran faces AI obesity. Her overdependence on AI and failure to utilize human qualities puts her at risk of being effortlessly replaced by technology.

Table 3.1 shows a more detailed profile comparison between Alex, Rishi, and Kiran.

Table 3.1   IRREPLACEABLE versus replaceable.

Attribute	Alex	Rishi	Kiran
Profile	NOT IRRE-PLACEABLE due to underutilizing AI	IRREPLACEABLE thanks to a balanced use of AI	NOT IRRE-PLACEABLE due to overreliance on AI
Traits	Cautious or skeptical about AI	Sees AI as an evolving tool	Heavily depends on AI for various needs
Usage Pattern	Uses AI sparingly; prefers traditional methods	Balances AI use with personal judgment and human interactions	Constant engagement with AI for diverse needs
Interactions	Bypasses AI in favor of manual methods	Uses AI as supplementary aid; seeks human opinions	Favors AI suggestions over human input
Emotional Attachment	Holds reservations about AI; possible privacy concerns	Collaborative view of AI, not overly reliant	May develop reliance or bond with the system
Self-view	Values human efforts; fears AI could diminish their role	Values human intuition and creativity; sees AI as a growth catalyst	Feels roles or input might be redundant due to AI capabilities
Learning and Adaptability	Resistant to learning new AI features; slow to adapt	Eager to learn and adapt to AI evolution; systematically questions the new advancements to identify opportunities and risks	Too adaptive to AI changes; does not question the systematic use of AI; does not take perspectives on potential risks

Attribute	Alex	Rishi	Kiran
Ethical Awareness	Concerned about ethical implications but may lack understanding	Engages in ethical discussions; aware of AI impacts	Less aware or engaged in the ethical implications of AI
Collaboration	May avoid AI in collaborative settings	Uses AI to enhance collaborative efforts	May over-rely on AI, reducing human collaboration
Innovation and Creativity	Limited AI-induced innovation due to hesitance	Fosters innovation through balanced AI use	May stifle innovation by over-relying on AI solutions

Our IRREPLACEABLE Humanity

What do you mean by "humanity" when you say that "being IRREPLACEABLE helps future-proof our humanity"?

To define our humanity, we must turn our gaze not toward globally acclaimed laureates, but toward our children. They are the purest version of ourselves. With their unfiltered joy and curiosity, kids serve as a living canvas, displaying traits that evolution has finely honed over 3.5 billion years. These traits set us apart from most animals and encapsulate our unique place in the universe.

In the playground, a vibrant showcase of these innate capabilities unfolds. Watch a group of children in the sandbox. Without a word, they start shaping the sand into elaborate structures. One decides the sandcastle needs a moat; another suggests a bridge. Their minds are not just at play; they are creators, architects of their own imaginative realms. This *genuine creativity* is not taught; it flows naturally, an intrinsic part of their being.

Now turn your attention to a pair debating the rules of a new game they've concocted. They argue, consider each other's viewpoints, and then reach a compromise. This dance of thoughts, this weighing and balancing of ideas, is the seedling of *critical thinking*. It's about understanding rules, questioning them, and even creating new ones.

Lastly, observe the intricate web of interactions as children play. A newcomer approaches, shy and hesitant. Within minutes, she's welcomed into a game, her laughter mingling with the rest. This is *social authenticity* in action. It's about connecting, understanding, and empathizing. It's the glue of human interaction, binding us through shared experiences and emotions.

Kids are masterpieces, embodying the very essence of what makes us human. Through their play, we see genuine creativity, critical thinking, and social authenticity come to life. These capabilities, so effortlessly displayed by children, are the cornerstone of our humanity.

Genuine creativity allows us to innovate and dream, make art, and solve problems in ways that no other species can. *Critical thinking* empowers us to analyze, question, and make informed and ethical decisions, which is the cornerstone of progress. *Social authenticity* enables us to build communities, empathize, and collaborate, forming the bedrock of societies.

What is the role of these capabilities in the IRREPLACEABLE concept?

These three uniquely human abilities are central to the concept of being IRREPLACEABLE. Given the frequent use of this term throughout the book and through your practice of being IRREPLACEABLE, I propose we refer to these "uniquely human abilities" as "Humics," with the capital "H" emphasizing our human essence.

The Humics are extraordinary. While the Humics are inherent to us from birth, they also possess the remarkable potential to be nurtured and expanded throughout our lives.

In the chapters that follow, I'll delve into how, in our AI-driven era, success hinges not on mastering AI coding but on revitalizing and enhancing our Humics. I'll demonstrate how to utilize them to forge adaptive skills that keep pace with our ever-evolving world and technological advances.

Are the Humics a new concept?

These Humics are not a new discovery. Millennia ago, Aristotle, one of the foundational thinkers of Western philosophy, identified key uniquely human abilities—akin to genuine creativity, critical thinking, and social connectivity—as essential for achieving "eudaimonia," the flourishing life.

For Aristotle, these innate traits weren't just capabilities; they were virtues that, when cultivated, lead to the highest form of human good and well-being. He believed that living in accordance with these virtues enables individuals to fulfill their potential, find meaning in life, and live in harmony with others.

This perspective aligns closely with how we intend to apply the Humics—using them as a cornerstone to develop new, relevant skills tailored to an ever-changing market.

What is the most powerful thing about the Humics?

The Humics are deeply intertwined with our inner selves, emotions, personal journeys, individual personalities—and with love. Love plays a pivotal role in strengthening and positively guiding these capabilities. Love encourages us to use our genuine creativity, critical thinking, and social authenticity with a sense of purpose and compassion, leading to a richer, more connected human experience.

For instance, love inspires creativity by driving us to express our feelings, experiences, and dreams in innovative ways. Love also compels us to seek justice, fairness, and understanding, guiding us to make decisions that reflect our concern for the happiness and safety of others. It is also through love that we learn to listen actively, communicate effectively, and offer support and compassion.

What is the risk of AI making us lose our humanity?

The real risk to our humanity doesn't stem from AI taking over the Humics, because these are intrinsically human traits that AI cannot replicate in full depth. We will discuss this in more detail later in the book.

The danger, instead, lies in us neglecting these capabilities, satisfying ourselves with shallow AI-generated outcomes—the phenomenon I've termed "AI obesity." Overreliance on AI for tasks we are better suited to perform ourselves could lead to the atrophy of our Humics. This is similar to how muscles weaken without exercise.

For example, this happens when you take the habit of listening more to the technology than to your clients—as in my story at the airport. It also happens when we accept the first AI-generated option for a new book cover without further refinement or a personal touch. Or if you engage on social media primarily using AI-generated content instead of your authentic voice and ideas.

How do we avoid losing our humanity?

In the face of AI's ascendancy, safeguarding our humanity requires deliberate action. First, we must not let AI take over all creative tasks, and must ensure we stay engaged in creativity ourselves. Second, it's crucial not to rely solely on AI for making decisions or solving problems, because this can weaken our critical thinking. Third, we should avoid replacing genuine human interactions with AI, which could erode our social authenticity. Each of these steps helps maintain the human essence in an AI-driven world.

What activities should I do without AI?

Great question. A practical rule I use is what I call the "Joy and Growth Principle." If an activity doesn't bring you joy or contribute to your personal or professional growth, let AI handle it!

In addition, I suggest some practices to train your Humics and grow your humanity muscle. Allocating 15 to 30 minutes daily to these activities is a strategy I advocate. More of these practices will be detailed in Part 2 of the book.

Here are exercises you can perform to make these essential traits flourish while ensuring AI does not diminish your humanity:

- **Actively engage in creative pursuits:** Make space for activities that fuel creativity, whether through arts, writing, designing, or problem-solving in innovative ways. These pursuits keep our creative faculties sharp and remind us of the joy found in creation.

To practice this, I've learned to allow myself to be bored. When I'm bored, my mind starts to wander, and this wandering becomes a seedbed for creativity. In our always-connected world, true boredom is rare. By disconnecting and experiencing boredom, I've found that it can really stimulate my natural creativity.

- **Challenge our minds:** Regularly engage in activities that require critical thinking. This could mean learning something new, engaging in debates, solving ethical problems, or simply questioning the status quo to understand deeper truths about the world.

  To practice this, I like to genuinely argue against my own deeply held beliefs. This exercise can be uncomfortable, but it forces me to see the other side of the argument. It has greatly broadened my perspective and enhanced my open-mindedness.

- **Foster authentic connections:** Prioritize face-to-face interactions and cultivate relationships that are built on empathy, understanding, and genuine connection. Social authenticity thrives on deep, meaningful interactions with others.

  I like to make it a point to greet everyone I meet on the street, offering a simple "hello" that can brighten someone's day. When these people are willing to talk with me, I will delve into their interests, professions, and what ignites their passion to a detailed degree. Additionally, I try to anticipate the needs of those around me, performing acts of kindness without waiting to be asked—for example, holding doors open or reaching for items on high shelves. This proactive approach reinforces my sense of empathy and understanding in building authentic relationships.

- **Reflect and self-improve:** Take time for introspection to understand your emotions, motivations, and the impact of your actions on others. Self-awareness is key to personal growth and maintaining a grounded sense of humanity.

  On top of my regular mindfulness practice, I like to confront myself, and to know myself better, I've been intentionally disrupting my daily routines. For example, if I usually read the same type of books, I switch to a genre I normally avoid. Or I purposely change the route I take to go to a usual place like work or family. It forces me to confront and better understand my emotions, motivations, and the effects of my actions on others.

- **Educate and advocate:** Share the importance of the Humics with others. Advocacy can help create environments—whether at work, in schools, or within communities—that prioritize and nurture these essential aspects of our humanity.

By intentionally embracing these practices, we safeguard and enhance our Humics. This deliberate effort enables us to leverage AI's advantages while maintaining our distinct human essence, thus protecting our humanity in an increasingly digital world.

You said earlier that AI can elevate our humanity; can you explain?

As we'll explore later in the book, AI's role in taking over less engaging or lower-value tasks—such as household chores, manual computations, repetitive duties, tedious data entry, or manual searches—allows us to shift our focus away from mundane tasks.

Conversely, AI finds it challenging to replicate our Humics. Hence, AI inadvertently encourages us to rediscover and invest in our Humics, which truly define our humanity. In doing so, AI unintentionally points us toward enhancing our humanity. So, in a way, AI challenges us to be more human.

"AI isn't just a tool for economic productivity but a means to elevate our humanity."

This perspective is profound because it suggests that AI isn't just a tool for economic productivity but a means to elevate our humanity. It's a vision of a future where AI serves to amplify our most human qualities, a world where we prioritize the growth of the soul as much as the growth of the economy.

What are the other benefits of further developing our Humics?

Later in the book, we'll delve deeper into how fully developing these abilities offers us four crucial advantages:

- It prevents AI from diminishing our humanity, as we've just discussed.

- It fosters a synergistic relationship between humans and AI. As I will demonstrate later in the book, these abilities cannot be genuinely replicated by AI. Thus, they support a complementary collaboration that generates synergies and maximizes value creation with AI.

- It equips individuals with the limitless potential to develop new skills that remain continually relevant and are constantly adapted, meeting the evolving demands of an AI-enhanced world.

- In a future where every company has access to identical AI capabilities, developing the Humics forms the foundation for business differentiation and operational excellence. Companies that can strategically integrate human and AI capabilities provide the greatest value to their customers.

The IRREPLACEABLE Framework

You've convinced me. How do I become IRREPLACEABLE?

Becoming IRREPLACEABLE in a world increasingly run by AI is a subtle art. This book sets out to chart a course for you not only to coexist with AI but also to stand out. Let's explore this journey together.

- **Cultivating complementary capabilities:** Imagine a world where AI complements your work, creating a partnership that leverages both your strengths. Being IRREPLACEABLE means being able

"In a world where AI can do almost anything, the greatest value lies in being uniquely human."

to harness the distinctly human abilities that technology can't genuinely replicate, and then subtly combine them with AI to generate synergies. When AI can diagnose a condition, it's the empathetic doctor, the creative problem-solving lawyer, or the compassionate nurse who will make the true difference. This has the potential to make you an indispensable force in any field. In a world where AI can do almost anything, the greatest value lies in being uniquely human.

- **Navigating the AI impact on our children:** Our kids are growing up with AI as their playmate. What does this mean for their future? How can we shepherd them through this new landscape? We are the cartographers of their digital world, and it's our role to chart a path that leads them to safety and success.

- **Lifelong AI literacy:** AI is not just a passing trend; it's a language we need to learn and speak fluently. This fluency will allow us to identify the risks and embrace the opportunities that come with each new technological breakthrough. The coming chapters will guide you in establishing and maintaining your AI literacy in the long term.

- **Adapting and evolving:** In a world of dizzying change propelled by AI's endless innovation, adaptability is the new survival skill. To thrive amid this turbulence, we must elevate adaptability and resilience to an art form. The name of the game is rapid unlearning and relearning, letting go of old ways faster to embrace new ones. Unlike AI, we don't need an update or a new version to adapt. Our human flexibility is unmatched, and this book will teach you how to harness it.

- **Embracing a new mindset:** The age of AI ushers in the era of "all of us." With innovation benefiting all, scarcity makes way for shared abundance. The future belongs to those who prioritize the collective "we" over the individual "me." This book will challenge you to shift from a mindset of scarcity to one of abundance, from competition to cooperation.

- **Discovering our purpose:** The question of purpose is as old as humanity itself. In the age of AI, it's more relevant than ever. AI can do many things for us, but it can't provide us with a reason for our existence. This book will invite you to explore the depths of your own purpose.

- **Awareness and self-understanding:** As AI becomes a mirror of our best and worst traits, we must raise the bar of our humanity. There's no more room for our inflated egos or unchecked biases in a world where our actions are amplified by AI. As AI parents, we must act as role models. This book will confront these challenges head-on, encouraging you to embark on a journey of self-discovery and to emerge as a force for positive change.

Is there a framework explaining how to become truly IRREPLACEABLE?

Well, this has been the subject of my research at the human-AI frontier over the last 20 years. As an outcome, here is the IRREPLACEABLE framework. It is also a condensed view of what we will go through in the book. To be IRREPLACEABLE, you need to master the Three Competencies of the Future: AI-Ready, Human-Ready, and Change-Ready (see Table 3.2). The three competencies will future-proof your life, your work, your kids, and even your business.

Start by taking the IRREPLACEABLE Quotient (IRQ) test at www.irreplaceable.ai. You will discover your strengths and growth areas in each of the Three Competencies of the Future. Use it as a compass to know where you stand and where to focus your learning efforts. Share your own experience and breakthroughs building the Three Competencies with the hashtag #irreplaceable, and become a beacon of light for others on this path. Then you could join the IRREPLACEABLE Academy, which includes courses, assets, and a community of like-minded people to support your journey.

When implemented all together in our lives, the three competencies complement and enhance one another, creating a holistic approach

Table 3.2   Three Competencies of the Future.

Competency	Description	Reference
AI-Ready	**"AI-Ready" involves not only leveraging AI for augmented performance but also safeguarding against its negative impacts, such as ethical issues or addictions.**	
Augmentation	Augment yourself with AI by creating an AI mindset, strategically leveraging AI, and maintaining AI literacy.	*Chapter* 8
Protection	Protect yourself and your children from the negative impacts of AI, such as distractions, addictions, or data privacy issues.	*Chapters* 12 *and* 13
Responsibility	Use and build AI responsibly: be mindful, ethical, respectful, and sustainable.	*Chapters* 11 *and* 14
Human-Ready	**"Human-Ready" emphasizes nurturing the "Humics," abilities that are distinctly human and that AI can't authentically replicate. This focus ensures the highest level of synergy with AI, because these abilities are deeply embedded in aspects of humanity—our unique life experiences, emotions, personal stories, and personalities. Love, which is unique to humans, is expressed through the Humics. Outcomes derived from the Humics are valued more when they originate from a human, rather than from AI. For example, humans value a human coach more than they value an AI coach.**	
Genuine Creativity	Generate original ideas and solutions, artistic expressions, and novel approaches to problems. Think outside the box, drawing on inspiration, intuition, and subjective experiences.	*Chapters* 3, 5, 6, *and* 7
Critical Thinking	Analyze and evaluate information by applying independent judgment and ethical reasoning. Critique the validity of information, use intuition to make decisions, and engage in self-reflection to understand your biases, purpose, and underlying motivations. Ask better questions to get better answers. Build trust.	*Chapters* 3, 5, 6, *and* 7

Competency	Description	Reference
Social Authenticity	Forge deep, meaningful relationships, understand complex social cues, and express empathy in ways that are profoundly connected to our consciousness and sense of self. This includes genuine emotional connections and the capacity for moral judgment. It also involves leadership to guide and positively influence other people.	*Chapters 3, 5, 6, and 7*
Change-Ready	**"Change-Ready" emphasizes developing resilience and adaptability to thrive amidst the rapid changes and heightened challenges brought about by the advancement of AI.**	
Resilience	Build a dynamic process of maintaining or regaining your mental well-being in the face of obstacles, changes, or pressures.	*Chapter 9*
Adaptability	Quickly and efficiently adjust to new situations, environments, or changes.	*Chapter 9*
Relearning how to learn	Unlearn in order to discard outdated knowledge, and pave the way for relearning—acquiring new competencies in a fresh context.	*Chapter 11*

to personal and professional development in the age of AI. This integrated approach not only prepares us but also equips our children and loved ones to navigate and succeed in a landscape reshaped by AI.

How will my life change once I become IRREPLACEABLE?

By following the approach in this book to become IRREPLACEABLE, you can expect benefits beyond just future-proofing your life and career. The toolbox offered to you in this book will ultimately provide you with increased confidence, inner calm, control of your focus, and vision to support your loved ones and business.

Those of us who have embraced this approach, myself included, have experienced a transformative journey. By practicing what you will learn from this book, you can expect to move from a state of constantly chasing after things and feeling out of control, overwhelmed, emotionally drained, and stressed, to a state of understanding, taking charge, anticipating, planning, enjoying, and succeeding. Furthermore, these competencies allowed me to build a sense of purpose and confidence that I did not have before.

But this book is a guidebook, not a magic carpet ride to paradise. By embracing the method, you are taking meaningful steps toward a more balanced and fulfilling life. It's like learning to sail in changeable winds—this approach will help you adjust your sails to catch the breeze just right. It's about equipping you with the tools and insights to navigate the complex terrain of an AI-driven world with grace and confidence.

Envision AI as an inevitable current. You have the choice either to hoist your sails and catch the wave, leading you to new horizons, or to anchor down and risk being submerged. The call to action is pressing; the ocean's rhythm waits for no sailor. The earlier you begin this journey, the more adept you'll become at charting a course in these waters, allowing the currents to thrust you ahead rather than maroon you.

In an age where being average is overrated and excellence is the new norm, the urgency to differentiate yourself is critical. And there's no time like the present to start.

PART

II

Building
IRREPLACEABLE Skills

Now that you understand the IRREPLACEABLE imperative, it's time to focus on building the skills that will make you stand out in the age of AI. In this part, the skills you'll learn are not just applicable to work; they are life skills that will serve you in all areas. By mastering these skills, you'll be better equipped to navigate the AI-driven world, both professionally and personally.

CHAPTER

4

Preparing for the AI Takeover

In this chapter, we look at the stark realities of work in the age of AI. We explore how AI is transforming the workplace and what it means for your job. I also introduce the concept of creating a symbiotic relationship with AI, which you'll explore in more depth in the next chapters.

How AI Will Take Away Your Job

I keep hearing about the increasing intelligence and capabilities of AI. Should I be scared about the impact of AI on my job?

Yes, definitely.

Hear this, and heed it well: your job has an expiration date, and this date is about to come. Whatever your industry, your role, or your expertise, the clock ticks, and with each passing moment AI inches closer to rendering your current job obsolete.

Harsh? Yes, but true. This book is here to help. First, let me explain.

Gone are the days when mastering one skill or trade was enough for lifelong employment. Just 30 years ago, people would learn a skill in school, perfect it through practice, and turn it into a lifelong career. Back then, job displacement due to technological advances was a rarity, typically happening over generations.

For example, consider the lamplighters of the 1800s. Their job was to light streetlamps manually each evening. However, with the advent of gas and electric lighting, their role quickly became obsolete. Similarly, telephone operators, who once manually connected calls, were replaced by automatic switching systems.

Yet a crucial difference from today was the pace of change. These workers had a few years to adapt and transition, often finding new roles in emerging industries powered by the same technologies that displaced their old jobs.

As innovation progressed over the years, we clung to the belief that some "automation-proof" jobs remained, and we systematically trained ourselves for the jobs still untouched by technology. For example, lamplighters became electricians, maintaining the new lighting infrastructure, while former telephone operators transitioned into roles in telecommunications support and customer service.

We believed that even if our current jobs were automated, we could simply take some time to retrain and move into another role that was safe from automation. This logic held for centuries—until recently.

For the last decade, change has accelerated at an unprecedented pace. We no longer have time to retrain for new jobs. In addition, AI is now so advanced that jobs once thought safe are now at risk of being automated. Here are the key milestones we've recently reached:

- 50 years ago, from physical to cognitive tasks: Automation moved from factory work to office jobs, managing spreadsheets and databases.

- 20 years ago, from basic to complex cognitive tasks: AI began handling complex activities like stock market analysis, engineering design, and chess.

- 10 years ago, from data processing to decision-making: AI started analyzing legal documents, diagnosing health issues, and even driving.

- 5 years ago, from thinking to creating: Generative AI now crafts songs, artworks, jokes, and literature with impressive proficiency.

The bottom line? No current occupation remains untouchable. Every industry and profession now sit in AI's crosshairs. No job can be considered IRREPLACEABLE anymore.

Yes, this is scary! But it is better to jolt you awake than lull you to sleep. This alarm bell rings because accepting AI's revolutionary force allows harnessing it—resisting only brings replacement!

If displacement happens to me, what should I do?

It is not a question of *if* AI will take your job; it is a question of *when*. And my advice is this: when AI automates your job, view it as an opportunity!

Over the last decades, millions of people have seen their jobs taken by AI and technology. But the frequency of these disruptions has been accelerating as technology progresses quickly, likely impacting our careers multiple times.

You aren't the first, nor the last, to lose a role in this battle. This is part of our lives, the same way as birth, illness, and death are a part of it.

When these displacements happen to us, we have two ways to react: either we spend our lives being scared about death or scared about displacement, living in constant anxiety and stress. Or we can choose to accept these realities and embrace them: we will all die, so let us enjoy our life now! Similarly, we will all be displaced, so let us use this as a catalyst to explore new opportunities!

Let's stay positive. If AI automates your job, it means it was not a job for you. This job was not even meant to be a job for a human! This job was not truly leveraging your uniqueness, your distinctiveness, or those skills that should be your expertise.

But you definitely want to avoid having nowhere to land when you are displaced. For that, you need to act today. If you don't do anything, it is like being on a sinking boat and ignoring the leak until the water reaches your ankles. That stressful, sinking feeling is real; I've experienced it myself. Waiting too long means rushing to reskill under pressure, risking burnout or even depression. It's not just scary; it's a nightmare no one wants to live through, for yourself or your family.

The key? Anticipate and prepare.

Shift Your Focus from Jobs to Skills

How should I prepare to be displaced?

As mentioned, don't look for the next AI-proof job, because it no longer exists. Instead, you need a pivotal shift in how you view your career, shifting focus from job security to skill adaptability.

In short, you need to pivot from protecting your job to cultivating flexible skills.

Instead of wasting your time and energy trying to protect your job, leverage this time and energy to adapt your skills to the new reality. Your skills are based on your capabilities, and they will remain with you forever. Your job is merely a title on a business card. Adapting your skills is the best investment you can make in your future.

In this tumultuous sea of change, your skills are your lifeline. Cling to them, but do not let them stagnate. The skills that keep you afloat today need to evolve, or they will become the anchor that drags you down. This evolution is not a luxury; it is your survival strategy.

Think of your career not as a path but as a continuous revolution, an unending cycle of skills learning, unlearning, and relearning. In this cycle lies your power to stay relevant, resilient, and IRREPLACEABLE.

How can I make my skills IRREPLACEABLE?

Well, this is quite straightforward.

You can become IRREPLACEABLE if you can solve the "human+AI" equation. It is challenging to solve, not because of the "AI" or the "human" components, but because of the "+." The critical question is, how do you forge the best "+" that connects both humans' and AI's strengths while mitigating their weaknesses?

The answer, pivotal in today's world, is something no school has ever taught us. Forging a successful "+" demands mutual understanding and close collaboration between humans and AI. It involves a deep understanding of the benefits and risks of this partnership, an ability to evolve together, and the strategic leveraging of each party's strengths to offset the other's weaknesses.

Without effective cooperation, the equation risks becoming "AI-human," where AI's capabilities overshadow human skills, highlighting the vital need for a balanced and synergistic collaboration to elevate overall outcomes.

So, in the near future, you might not lose your job to AI itself but to someone who's more skilled at teaming up with AI than you are, a person who has been able to solve the equation. If you, too, decide to team up with AI, you can become that unbeatable person, making yourself IRREPLACEABLE.

How do I team up with AI?

A while back, I had an eye-opening chat with Garry Kasparov, the renowned chess grandmaster and ex–world champion. He shared with me a mind-blowing 2005 chess tourney, a battlefield of supercomputers, top human players, and human+AI teams, all vying for the top spot.

The results? Astounding! Sure, human+AI pairs outplayed lone humans. But here's the kicker: at that time—back in 2005—they also defeated stand-alone supercomputers. The ultimate twist? The champions weren't seasoned grandmasters with high-end tech but rather two everyday chess enthusiasts paired with modest computers!

Kasparov's story was an eye-opener for me, the understanding of a game-changing principle that extends way beyond chess, and to any activity where AI can be used. The most formidable alliance in technology isn't human versus machine; it's human *with* machine. This tournament wasn't just a game; it was a lesson for me.

Here are my two main takeaways from my conversation with Kasparov:

- **Partner with AI:** Competing against AI? You're set up to lose. So, because you can't beat AI, embrace it! Join forces with it, and you unlock a world of possibilities. AI isn't an enemy; it's the ultimate partner in the game of progress. Here lies the AI paradox: it is your greatest threat, and yet, if you are wise, it can be your biggest ally.

- **Embrace what makes you a human:** The winning human-AI duos didn't just play to the technology's strengths in tactical computation. They leveraged distinctly human strategic faculties to make judgments the AI couldn't match. Together, both parties drew on complementary abilities greater than either possessed alone, creating synergies. Hence, when teaming up with AI, it is in the qualities that make us uniquely human that our true value lies.

Based on this story, here is our approach. To solve the human+AI equation, you need to implement two main steps:

1. Identify and build the complementary skills that make you work in synergy with AI.
2. Learn how to actually work with AI, leveraging its power while protecting yourself from its negative effects.

CHAPTER

5

Creating a Symbiosis with AI

In the preceding chapter, you explored the transformative impact of AI on the future of jobs, arriving at a pivotal insight: in this new era, it's essential to focus on cultivating skills rather than pursuing predefined job roles. But what specific skills should you prioritize to thrive alongside AI?

In this chapter, I aim to challenge and debunk several widespread misconceptions that I've often encountered:

- In the AI era, the focus should be on building technical skills like coding and programming.
- AI will render human capabilities obsolete.
- AI eliminates the need for soft skills.
- Collaborating with AI in areas where our skills are aligned results in more harmonious and conflict-free collaboration.
- AI can replace human creativity.
- AI understands and interprets context as well as humans do.

Breaking Misconceptions About Technical Skills

Are technical skills the most critical to my success in an AI-driven world?

The short answer is no.

I want to say something that might sound completely opposite to what people think. Over the last 10 years, almost everybody who wrote a book like this would tell you it is vital that your children learn computer science and know how to program and code.

In fact, today, it's exactly the opposite. Current computing technologies are evolving such that nobody has to program anymore. The programming language is just plain language—this is what we do when we prompt an AI system such as ChatGPT. Nowadays, in a way, everybody in the world has become a programmer—without even knowing how to write a single line of code!

Here's the stark reality: tasks that traditionally required significant technical expertise are now performed in the blink of an eye by AI. And it's not just skills related to technology, but all technical skills— from analyzing X-rays to reviewing legal contracts, AI is already outperforming professionals in fields like healthcare, law, and finance. Human expertise is commoditized by AI.

Just last year, an AI system passed the US medical licensing exam and another one the bar exam, surmounting tests for which aspiring doctors and lawyers prepare for years. In fields from contract law to dermatology, AI now rivals seasoned specialists leveraging volumes of data that human minds can scarcely fathom.

So brace yourself for a future where traditional technical expertise may no longer guarantee a competitive edge.

Why can technical skills be mastered by AI so easily?

The technical knowledge that lawyers, accountants, medical doctors, and programmers have in common is based on defined, structured knowledge that is often rule-based and repetitive. It follows specific, well-defined rules and procedures. The answer to any given question is either right or wrong, making it relatively easy for AI to learn through a large amount of data.

Table 4.1   Technical skills that can be easily automated.

Skill	Why AI Excels	Examples of Job Roles Impacted
Statistical Analysis	AI algorithms can process complex statistical models more quickly and accurately than humans, identifying trends and patterns within large datasets.	Data scientists, statisticians
Visual Pattern Identification	Through machine learning, AI can recognize and interpret images and patterns at a scale beyond human capability, useful in fields like medical imaging or security.	Radiologists, security analysts
Predictive Analytics	AI's ability to analyze past data to predict future outcomes surpasses human capabilities in speed and accuracy, applicable in finance, weather forecasting, and more.	Financial planners, meteorologists
Natural Language	AI has advanced in understanding, interpreting, and generating human language, making it invaluable in translation, customer service, and content creation.	Linguists, customer support agents
Precision Work	AI-driven machines perform tasks with a level of precision and consistency that humans cannot achieve, especially in manufacturing and quality control.	Assembly line workers, quality assurance engineers
Data Mining	AI excels in extracting valuable insights from large data sets, identifying patterns or anomalies that may not be visible to human analysts.	Market analysts, research scientists
Fraud Detection	With the ability to monitor and analyze transactions in real time, AI systems can identify fraudulent activity more effectively than human monitoring.	Fraud analysts, risk management specialists

(continued)

Table 4.1 (*continued*)

Skill	Why AI Excels	Examples of Job Roles Impacted
Automated Reasoning	AI systems can apply logic to solve problems, make decisions, or prove theorems, often more quickly and accurately than human reasoning.	Logic professors, AI researchers
Diagnostic Analysis	AI can swiftly analyze medical data and images to assist in diagnosis, often identifying patterns that may not be apparent to human doctors.	Medical doctors
Legal Research and Analysis	AI can process vast amounts of legal documents quickly, identifying relevant case laws and precedents, which can augment the work of lawyers.	Lawyers
Code Optimization and Bug Detection	AI tools can analyze and optimize code, detect bugs, and suggest improvements more efficiently than manual processes.	Coders/software developers

AI's superiority in these technical skills primarily stems from its ability to process and analyze data at a scale and speed that humans cannot match, its consistency in performing repetitive tasks, and its adaptability in learning from new data to improve its performance over time. Table 4.1 provides examples of technical skills that can be automated easily.

With AI getting better at tasks usually done by lawyers and doctors, does this mean these jobs might disappear soon?

No.

Consider healthcare. One might think that doctors' jobs would be harder to replace with AI than nurses' jobs, but as counterintuitive as it might seem, this is untrue. Nurses leverage physical and emotional dexterity—to deliver injections, change dressings, and even manage violent patients. Human care demands such versatile talent. Caregiving for the young, old, and infirm requires profoundly human skills that are tough to automate.

Doctors primarily collect and process data to diagnose patients. Their focused specialization makes automation plausible. Soon, with your smartphone, you'll have access to a doctor available 24/7, superior to any individual doctor globally, because it will have been trained based on the knowledge of all doctors worldwide.

But you will still go to the doctor! You won't visit the doctor for the medical expertise, but instead you'll seek out empathy, communication, advice, and the ability to connect on a human level.

So, to answer your question: doctors won't disappear, but their roles will be different, requiring their skills to evolve.

Does this mean that in an AI-dominated world, we no longer need to learn technical skills?

I like to give an analogy with calculators. We still learn calculus while we have calculators that calculate better than us. Similarly, despite AI's superior capabilities, learning technical skills is still important for several reasons.

First, understanding the underlying processes of technical skills enhances critical thinking and problem-solving abilities. Just as learning basic arithmetic equips us with the foundational knowledge to tackle more complex mathematical problems, mastering technical skills lays the groundwork for understanding more intricate concepts that AI might handle in the future. This deep understanding enables humans to innovate, improve, and even question AI's decisions and methodologies.

Additionally, the process of learning and engaging with technical skills contributes to human creativity and innovation. Interaction with the material world through these skills can inspire new ideas, innovations, and applications that AI, which operates within the parameters set by its programming, might not initiate.

Finally, there's the aspect of empathy and ethical considerations. Understanding technical skills allows humans to make informed decisions that consider ethical implications, societal impacts, and the welfare of others. While AI can perform tasks, it does not possess empathy or the ability to make value-based judgments. Humans equipped with technical knowledge are better positioned to guide AI's application in a way that aligns with human values and ethics.

So yes, we definitely need to keep learning technical skills. But as this book will show in the upcoming chapters, the extent and the way we learn and test these skills needs to change.

Building a Symbiosis with AI

What skills are less susceptible to being mastered by AI?

To answer this question, we need to focus first on defining the characteristics of a fruitful collaboration. Stated differently, what constitutes a successful collaboration, even when it involves humans?

There's often a misconception that the most effective teams are made up of individuals who are all-around experts. However, having a team of "jacks-of-all-trades" often leads to a lack of depth in any one area. Recognizing and valuing specialized, complementary skills is usually more effective than seeking universal proficiency.

The idea that a well-coordinated team of diverse skills can outperform a group of individually brilliant but similar skill sets can be counterintuitive. However, remember Kasparov's story. Humans were amateurs, and the AI system was not the best one in the competition. Neither the humans nor the AI were individually the best. But the complementary pair created a value higher than the sum of the value brought by each party, what we call *synergy*: when 1+1 = 3.

This explains, for example, why companies are not composed only of CEOs. To excel in a CEO role, one needs a specific set of skills that are not necessarily found in every employee. Conversely, most CEOs don't possess the specialized skills to excel in roles like finance or marketing. In successful organizations, roles are strategically assigned based on individuals' unique skill sets. This approach maximizes synergies and minimizes redundancies.

We also see this in nature in a relationship that we call *symbiosis*, an ancient Greek word that means "living together." Different species work together, each contributing in a unique way that benefits the whole. For instance, bees collect nectar to make honey and pollinate flowers in the process, so bees and flowers are symbiotic.

Similarly, when we consider a successful collaboration with AI, viewing it as a form of symbiosis makes intuitive sense. Let's walk through the principles of building such a collaboration.

Symbiosis Principle #1: Complementary capabilities Flowers, stationary by nature, have the unique ability to produce nectar, attracting bees in search of sustenance. Bees, capable of movement, not only feed on this nectar but also inadvertently carry pollen from one flower to another, facilitating cross-pollination and reproduction. This interdependence illustrates a perfect example of complementary capabilities in action.

Just as symbiotic relationships in nature often involve organisms with different but complementary abilities, an effective collaboration should combine diverse skill sets. This diversity ensures that each member's strengths cover the other's weaknesses, leading to a more capable and versatile team. Similarly, AI brings immense computational power, memory, data processing capabilities, and precision to the table. Humans, on the other hand, offer creative thinking, emotional intelligence, and ethical judgment. When combined, these diverse capabilities create synergies, leading to extraordinary advancements and efficiencies.

Symbiosis Principle #2: Understanding the partner's capabilities and limitations Just as bees understand which flowers to visit and flowers evolve to attract the right pollinators, understanding AI's capabilities and limitations allows for effective and ethical use. Humans need to know what AI can and cannot do, ensuring appropriate human oversight where necessary. This is all about the AI literacy that we covered in the last chapter.

Symbiosis Principle #3: Goals and values alignment Symbiotic relationships work toward a common benefit through shared goals and values. Both bees and flowers have a shared goal: survival and reproduction. The bees don't deplete the flowers' nectar supply— they take what they need—and the flowers provide the right amount of nectar to attract the bees. This mutual understanding and shared objective benefit both.

Applying this to AI and human collaboration, both should work toward common goals with aligned values. For instance, if a business uses AI for customer service, the goal shouldn't be just to reduce human labor costs. Instead, it should aim to enhance the customer experience, where AI handles routine queries and humans step in for complex, emotionally nuanced interactions. This way, AI supports human workers without replacing them, and customers receive better service—a shared goal benefiting all.

Symbiosis Principle #4: Interdependence without overdependence
As in symbiosis, where organisms are interdependent but not overly reliant on each other, members of a collaboration should be able to work independently while still supporting each other.

Just as flowers don't rely solely on bees for pollination—wind and other insects can also be pollinators—humans should maintain a balanced dependence on AI. This means leveraging AI's benefits while keeping essential human skills and judgment in play.

Symbiosis Principle #5: Adaptability and flexibility   In nature, both bees and flowers adapt to each other's presence. Similarly, just as symbiotic relationships in nature evolve over time, with each organism adapting to changes in the other, the human-AI relationship is also dynamic. As AI technologies evolve, so too must our strategies for interacting with and guiding these systems. This calls for a continuous learning approach, where we adapt our skills and methods to complement AI's evolving capabilities. Hence the importance of building and maintaining AI literacy, as explained in the previous chapter. In Chapter 8, we will explore AI literacy, and Chapter 9 will focus on developing adaptability and resilience.

This parallel demonstrates that just as bees and flowers have evolved a mutually beneficial and adaptable relationship, humans and AI can develop a symbiotic relationship. It's about leveraging each other's strengths, ensuring ethical collaboration, maintaining effective communication, and continually adapting to changes for mutual benefit.

Are there some specificities about our symbiosis with AI?

In the context of the specific collaboration between AI and humans, a few unique principles prevail, as detailed in the following sections.

Symbiosis Principle #6: AI supremacy in scalability and speed   In case of redundancies between the skills of humans and AI, don't try to compete; humans will always lose! If both humans and AI master a skill, AI will always be better at these skills because it can work on them at a scale and rapidity that we will never be able to equal. So calculation, medical diagnoses, text summarization, code generation, and automation of repetitive tasks are now in the realm of AI, and we should not try to compete on these skills anymore. However, while humans should not compete in this realm, they should understand how to leverage it to elevate their skills and automate task activities, as we will learn in Part 3 of this book.

Symbiosis Principle #7: The Unreplicable Human Essence Principle
The Unreplicable Human Essence Principle highlights the uniqueness of certain human capabilities that are intrinsically linked to our species and remain beyond the reach of AI replication due to their deep human characteristics. These capabilities are rooted in core human aspects that technology cannot genuinely possess: our individual life experiences, our human emotions, and our personalities.

These are typically the Humics—the uniquely human abilities—that we have presented in the first part of the book.

Imagine a painter creating a masterpiece. The painting isn't just a mix of colors and strokes; it's a reflection of the painter's emotions, experiences, and personal touch. Similarly, human capabilities like empathy, creativity, ethics, and emotional intelligence are deeply rooted in our personal histories, emotions, and character traits—elements that AI cannot authentically replicate.

Identifying the Capabilities Complementary to AI

What human capabilities will AI never be able to master as well as we can?

As we discovered in Chapter 3 of the book, only one human element withstands the test of time: our humanity. It is represented by the Humics, which are the three uniquely human abilities: genuine creativity, critical thinking, and social authenticity.

So creating a synergy with AI means leveraging these abilities. Nurturing them to a level that makes us as different as possible from AI, therefore creating synergies with AI.

Here are the main reasons why the Humics are complementary to AI:

- **Genuine creativity** is the ability to generate new and original ideas, solutions, or artistic expressions. While AI can mimic patterns and generate novel combinations based on existing data, it lacks the intrinsic human spark of genuine creativity. This is the ability to draw on personal experiences, emotions, and the subconscious, to create something truly groundbreaking or emotionally resonant. AI's creations, though impressive, are ultimately rooted in the data it has been fed, lacking the depth and unpredictability of human creativity.

- **Critical thinking** is the ability to analyze and evaluate information by applying independent judgment and ethical reasoning. It involves critiquing the validity of information, using intuition to make decisions, and engaging in self-reflection to understand one's biases, purpose, and underlying motivations. AI can process and analyze information at incredible speeds, but it falls short in applying ethical reasoning, intuition, and independent judgment. These critical thinking facets require an understanding of context, the subtleties of human values, and the ability to foresee consequences beyond raw data analysis. AI lacks self-awareness and cannot self-reflect or understand biases in the way humans can, making it unable to truly master critical thinking.

- **Social authenticity** is central to engaging harmoniously with people. It encompasses the ability to understand and manage emotions, communicate effectively, empathize, and exercise leadership to guide and positively influence people. AI can simulate social interactions and even mimic empathetic responses, but it cannot genuinely understand or feel human emotions. The depth of human connection, built on shared experiences and genuine empathy, remains beyond AI's reach. Social authenticity requires an understanding of complex social cues and emotional subtleties that AI, lacking real emotions and consciousness, cannot fully comprehend or authentically replicate.

To enhance our partnership with AI, we must not only relearn and strengthen our Humics but also elevate them to the highest levels of mastery. Chapters 6 and 7 will guide you through this process.

Are you sure that AI will never be able to replace the Humics?

First, it's important to acknowledge that the future of AI and its impact on us is unknown. We need to stay humble. History shows that we often underestimate AI's ability to handle tasks we thought only humans could do, like creative work with generative AI. Conversely, tasks we assumed would be automated easily, like navigating physical spaces, are still challenging for AI.

To directly address your question, like any human, I can't foresee accurately the future. So, no, I cannot be 100% certain that technology will never reach the level of these abilities. However, I am convinced of one thing: developing the Humics is now our best course of action. Focusing on developing our Humics is the wisest investment of your time and energy today. In contrast, waiting to see what happens and constantly trying to acquire new skills in response to AI advancements is like chasing an ever-moving target—a sure path to failure.

While AI can simulate more and more of our human capabilities, replacing the full spectrum and the depth of the Humics is beyond the current and foreseeable reach of AI. These abilities are deeply intertwined with our consciousness, emotions, and our subjective understanding of the world, aspects that AI, as an artificial construct, will always authentically lack.

So can AI ever replicate the Humics? It might imitate or simulate them to a certain degree. But can it replicate them with the same human authenticity? Certainly not. As underscored throughout Part 2, these abilities also embody the expression of love, a distinctly human emotion, adding another layer to our authenticity that AI simply cannot replicate.

In my view, the only way AI could genuinely replicate the Humics would be through a hypothetical future scenario where humans and AI merge, creating a new entity that blends the human touch with AI's capabilities. Until such a hypothetical merge occurs, AI will always lack the ability to truly replicate the depth that is uniquely human.

If AI becomes conscious and reaches superintelligence, does that mean it will master the Humics?

Even if AI were to achieve a form of consciousness, including self-awareness and emotions, it would inherently differ from human consciousness due to fundamental differences in its nature, experience, and essence.

The subjective experience of being human—our personal narrative, and our ability to empathize deeply with others—is grounded in our unique life experiences and biological makeup. Even if AI could mimic empathy or possess self-awareness, its "emotions" would not stem from a lived, human experience, making its form of empathy fundamentally different and possibly shallower than human empathy.

Animals experience the world through their senses and physiological responses, much like humans. For instance, a dog's consciousness is shaped by its acute sense of smell, affecting its perceptions and emotions. Similarly, human consciousness is deeply tied to our physical bodies and senses.

An AI, equipped with sophisticated sensors, could navigate its environment similarly to how a bat employs echolocation—it can move around and identify obstacles, but it doesn't experience its surroundings in the rich, emotional, and embodied way that shapes human consciousness. It will shape its own specific type of consciousness.

In essence, even with advances in technology, AI consciousness would lack the fundamental essence of what it means to be human—encompassing our flaws, unpredictability, and emotional depth—which cannot be fully replicated by artificial means. While I believe AI will reach superintelligence and a form of consciousness, it will never be the same intelligence and consciousness as the human one.

The Humics are deeply intertwined with human consciousness, a product of our biological evolution, embodied experiences, and social interactions. This connection underscores why AI, even with advancements toward consciousness, will never be able to replicate the Humics authentically.

What if AI imitates with high fidelity the Humics?

This scenario is quite likely, matching recent AI developments like ChatGPT, which can mimic a human conversation without truly understanding it. Think about two drinking glasses: one made by machines and the other hand-blown by a craftsman. The one made by the craftsman can be more than five times more expensive than the one made by the machine.

We humans tend to value the items made by other humans more than those made by machines, even if they look identical. This preference is due to the stories, personality, and emotions that the human creator adds to the product. Humans will always value something made by a person more than something made by AI, even if the AI has copied it with high fidelity.

Similarly, even if AI can imitate the Humics with high fidelity, these abilities, when manifested by humans, will always hold a higher value. The human touch adds a layer of authenticity, emotional depth, and connection that cannot be replicated by machines, no matter how advanced.

In essence, the value we place on human-executed abilities stems from a deep appreciation of the human condition—our struggles, our growth, and our capacity for emotion and empathy.

What AI does imitate will always lack a critical component: authenticity. It speaks to the IRREPLACEABLE value of being inherently human—reflecting our unique perspectives, emotional depth, and the subjective nuances of our existence.

How the Humics Boost Each Other

What is so special about combining these uniquely human abilities together?

Earlier in this book, we discovered that these abilities form the core of our humanity. They share essential characteristics: they're inherent, can be developed, and are deeply anchored in our emotions, stories, and personalities. Importantly, they all spring from what uniquely defines us as humans: love.

As I delved into the Humics, I discovered there's even more to them than initially meets the eye. They are not three separate entities. They are deeply interconnected. When combined, these abilities create something truly special: a cohesive whole. They form a triad of interrelated virtuous abilities, where no single ability stands alone; together, they bolster each other.

The three Humics are like the three primary colors; by blending them, you can create all the colors of the rainbow: thousands of capabilities. They complement and enhance each other, leading to more effective problem-solving, decision-making, and innovation.

Here are a few examples of how they magically combine:

- **Genuine creativity and critical thinking:** Creativity generates a wide range of ideas, while critical thinking evaluates these ideas, determining their feasibility and value.

- **Social authenticity and genuine creativity:** Being more creative will improve your storytelling abilities, which in turn will enhance your communication abilities.

- **Social authenticity and critical thinking:** By enhancing your critical thinking, including your capacity for self-reflection, you will be able to better understand your emotions and manage them in the context of relationships.

By mastering these three abilities, you create synergies. Thus, when you develop one of these abilities, you're not only improving that particular area but also positively impacting at least one of the other two. This synergy makes the investment in developing these abilities highly worthwhile.

CHAPTER

6

Leveraging the Humics
to Build Skills

In this chapter, you'll explore how to prioritize the development of our uniquely human abilities (the Humics) over specific skills, and how to use these abilities to build new, adaptable skills for the AI era. You'll also see how in a world where AI is making redundant technical skills, the new skills generated by our Humics are becoming increasingly valuable in the job market.

Prioritizing the Development of the Humics Over Skills

Are the three Humics the same as skills?

The three Humics—genuine creativity, critical thinking, and social authenticity—are not skills. Instead, they serve as foundational elements that underpin the development of skills. Think of these abilities as the fertile soil from which seeds, given the right nourishment through education, practice, and experience, can sprout into valuable skills.

For example, genuine creativity is the root of artistic abilities and problem-solving skills, sparking innovation in technology and business. Critical thinking evolves into analytical skills, indispensable for

73

scientific research, legal analysis, and strategic planning in corporate settings. Social authenticity, when fostered through empathetic and collaborative experiences, grows into leadership and teamwork skills, crucial for managing professional and personal relationships effectively.

These capabilities are inherent in all humans and provide us with the foundation to cultivate skills that make significant contributions to our surroundings. Unlike skills that may become obsolete, our uniquely human abilities are timeless, helping us adapt and develop new skills to meet the demands of a changing world. By leveraging these core abilities, we equip ourselves to succeed and flourish in a dynamic and evolving environment.

Why is it better to develop in priority the Humics over skills?

Prioritizing the development of the Humics—genuine creativity, critical thinking, and social authenticity—over merely developing specific skills offers profound benefits for personal growth and adaptability in our fast-evolving world.

These foundational abilities are universal and transferable, unlike certain skills that may become obsolete due to technological advances or shifts in the job market. For instance, when transitioning from a career in finance to technology, your critical thinking ability remains applicable, whereas you may need to acquire new technical skills specific to the tech industry.

Another advantage of using this approach is that you gain unlimited access to thousands of potential skills. Like mixing the three primary colors to create the spectrum, combining these abilities in various ways can lead to the development of countless skills.

Another benefit of building skills based on our unique human capabilities is that, since these capabilities complement AI, all the skills they generate also foster a synergy with AI.

In essence, while specific skills are important for immediate tasks and roles, developing deeper, uniquely human abilities ensures long-term adaptability, fulfillment, and success. It prepares you not just for the jobs of today but for navigating the complexities of the future in a way that is meaningful and rewarding.

Future Evolution of Skills

Do skills evolve the same way as the Humics, and are there some future-proof skills that we can develop?

Skills and Humics evolve differently. There's no such thing as a future-proof skill due to the ever-changing influence of AI, cultural shifts, ethical considerations, and societal changes. Human skills have always evolved.

Unlike the Humics, which are foundational and timeless, our skills emerge, transform, and vanish in response to our environment, challenges, and technological advancements.

For example, the invention of the wheel led to new transportation and mechanical skills. The Industrial Revolution required skills in machinery operation and industrial management. Today, the digital age demands proficiency in information technology, digital communication, and data analysis.

As technology advances rapidly, the evolution of skills will likely accelerate, making the development of human skills an ongoing journey. Being IRREPLACEABLE means leveraging our Humics to continually develop new skills suited to our changing world.

Table 6.1 illustrates some of the current skills, comparing how they are mastered by AI and by humans, as of this writing. We should expect this matrix to change in the next years, as new skills emerge.

Building New Skills by Leveraging Your Humics

How can I create new skills by leveraging my Humics?

Leveraging your Humics to create new skills is not just a method; it's an art form, the natural unfolding of your potential. If you've reached this stage of the book, you've unconsciously begun to understand how to do it.

Think of it this way: your Humics are the fertile soil of your personal development garden. These abilities are the foundation from which all your skills, the seeds, sprout and grow. Just as a garden requires sunlight, water, and wind to evolve, your skills need nurturing through effort, dedication, and exposure to the changing world around us.

Table 6.1   Examples of skills currently mastered by AI versus humans (2024).

Humics	Skill	AI Mastery	Human Mastery	Explanation
Genuine Creativity	Associative Thinking	Low	High	While AI can identify associations within its training data, human associative thinking dynamically connects diverse concepts, fostering more innovative and unexpected ideas.
	Novel Ideas Generation	Very Low	High	Humans uniquely conceive truly original ideas that introduce new concepts and paradigms. AI generates novel ideas by recombining known information.
	Emotional Resonance	Very Low	High	AI lacks the ability to evoke deep emotions in its creations due to an absence of genuine feelings, whereas humans excel in creations that resonate emotionally with others.
Critical Thinking	Unstructured Problem Solving	Low	High	While AI can solve structured problems efficiently, humans are better at dealing with complex, unstructured problems requiring novel approaches.
	Criticizing and Questioning Information	Moderate	High	Humans are better at critically analyzing information, considering context, biases, and implications, a task AI systems are not fully equipped to handle.

Humics	Skill	AI Mastery	Human Mastery	Explanation
	Judgment and Ethical Decision Making	Very Low	High	Humans are better at making ethical decisions due to their ability to understand context, cultural norms, and moral implications, which AI lacks.
	Intuition	Very Low	High	Humans can make intuitive decisions based on subconscious understanding and experiences, a skill that AI lacks.
	Self-reflection and Purpose	Very Low	High	Humans excel in self-reflection and understanding personal motivations and purposes, a concept that is beyond the capabilities of AI.
Social Authenticity	Emotional Intelligence and Empathy	Very Low	High	Humans excel in understanding and expressing emotions, a skill that AI lacks due to the absence of genuine emotional experiences.
	Leadership	Low	High	Humans excel with their ability to inspire, influence, and guide others toward achieving goals. AI lacks the genuine ability to motivate and connect with people on a personal, emotional level.

(continued)

Table 6.1 *(continued)*

Communi-cation	Moderate	High	Humans naturally understand nuances, context, and subtleties in communication that AI often struggles with, despite advances in natural language processing.

Yilmazer, Pelin, et al. "The microstrategy assessment paradigm shows differences in abstraction and generalization between AI systems and young children." *Science Advances* 8.7 (2022).

Hass, Lawrence. "How creative can AI be? A computational approach." *Cognitive Computation* 13.2 (2021): 547–558.

NSW Government. "Critical thinking and judgment." ICT Procurement Toolkit.

Kim, Been, et al. "Bias in bios: A case study of semantic representation bias in a high-stakes setting." *Proceedings of the Conference on Fairness, Accountability, and Transparency* (2018).

White, David. "Three reasons why machines still can't really think like humans do." *Conversation* 29 (2022).

Dindar, Muhammed, et al. "Why AI cannot replace humans." *Turkish Journal of Pediatrics* 63.2 (2021): 251–260.

Zhang, Siyu, et al. "A multimodal dataset for various forms of distractors in emotion recognition." *Frontiers in Robotics and AI* 8 (2021).

Shank, Daniel B., et al. "What role does artificial intelligence have in moral reasoning?" *Trends in Cognitive Sciences* 25.3 (2021): 169–174.

Burton, Neel, Matt Klein, and M.G. Siegler. "Machine learning will never match human creativity." *Track Changes* (2019).

"Leveraging your Humics to create new skills is not just a method; it's an art form, the natural unfolding of your potential."

The beauty of this growth is its autonomy. By simply dedicating yourself to enhancing your Humics, your skills evolve, often subconsciously. This evolution is shaped by your needs, the realities of our world—such as technological advancements and ethical considerations—and your deepest ambitions and personality traits. It involves trusting your intuition and letting your skills adapt to your work context and personal inclinations.

It's crucial to recognize that the future is unpredictable, and the skills needed tomorrow may be unknown today. That's why being overly specific or targeted in your skill development may not be as beneficial as fostering a broad, adaptable skill set rooted in your Humics. Like a gardener trusting in nature's unseen growth processes, trusting in your Humics to cultivate your skills ensures they naturally align with your personal growth, ambitions, technological and societal shifts.

In essence, to nurture the right skills for the future, you don't need to do anything more than cultivate your Humics. Your skills will develop by themselves, growing organically in response to your nurtured qualities and the environment. Like a well-tended garden, your skills will expand in unexpected and beautiful ways, perfectly suited to the world they'll inhabit. This intuitive approach to skill development highlights the power of human potential and the importance of trusting our innate capacity to adapt and flourish.

Have people succeeded in leveraging the Humics to create new skills?

Yes, many. Here are a few examples of people with whom I have worked in the context of my research on the evolution of their skills.

Axel the lawyer   Axel is a lawyer who initially concentrated on honing her legal analysis and argumentation skills—the technical aspects of her profession. However, Axel decided to invest in developing her Humics, focusing particularly on social authenticity and critical thinking.

As Axel began to integrate empathy more deeply into her practice, she became more attuned to the emotional nuances and personal stories of her clients. This shift allowed Axel to craft more compelling case narratives that resonated strongly with judges and juries, improving her effectiveness in the courtroom.

Simultaneously, by deepening her critical thinking ability, Axel was able to view cases from multiple perspectives and anticipate the arguments of opposing counsel with greater accuracy. This not only enhanced her strategic planning but also led to more innovative legal solutions and strategies.

The unconscious evolution of Axel's skills through the deliberate development of empathy and critical thinking exemplifies the natural mechanism of growth. Over time, Axel became known not just for her legal expertise but for her unique approach to lawyering—one that combined technical skill with a profound understanding of human emotion and ethical considerations.

This holistic development transformed Axel from a competent lawyer into an irreplaceable legal advocate, demonstrating how focusing on our Humics can naturally and unconsciously refine and expand our professional skills, setting us apart in our fields.

In summary, originally, Axel possessed foundational legal skills essential for any lawyer, including:

- **Legal analysis:** The ability to dissect and understand complex legal documents and cases
- **Argumentation:** Crafting and presenting logical arguments in court
- **Research skills:** Efficiently finding and interpreting relevant legal precedents and statutes

Through the deliberate development of her Humics, particularly empathy and critical thinking, Axel built and refined a set of new skills:

- **Compelling case narration:** The ability to tell the story of a case in a way that is emotionally resonant and persuasive to judges and juries
- **Emotional intelligence in legal practice:** Understanding and leveraging the emotional aspects of cases to better advocate for clients and connect with all parties involved
- **Strategic legal planning:** Viewing cases from multiple angles to anticipate opposing arguments and develop innovative legal strategies
- **Ethical consideration and client advocacy:** Integrating ethical considerations more deeply into legal practice, prioritizing the well-being and interests of clients with a more holistic approach to lawyering

These new skills, built upon the foundation of empathy and critical thinking, transformed Axel's legal practice, making her a more effective and sought-after lawyer in her field.

Elena the medical doctor Dr. Elena, a dedicated medical doctor, initially focused on mastering the technical skills crucial for her profession, such as:

- **Diagnostic proficiency:** The ability to accurately diagnose diseases based on symptoms and medical tests
- **Clinical knowledge:** Extensive understanding of medical conditions, treatments, and procedures
- **Technical skills:** Competence in performing medical procedures and using medical equipment

Recognizing the importance of further developing her unique Humics, Dr. Elena decided to focus on empathy (social authenticity) and critical thinking. This decision led to the cultivation of new skills that significantly enhanced her medical practice:

- **Patient-centered communication:** Dr. Elena's enhanced empathy allowed her to communicate more effectively with patients, ensuring they felt heard and understood, which improved patient satisfaction and adherence to treatment plans.
- **Holistic care approach:** By integrating empathy into her practice, Dr. Elena began to consider patients' emotional and psychological needs alongside their physical health, leading to more comprehensive care strategies.
- **Advanced problem-solving:** Her deepened critical thinking skills enabled Dr. Elena to analyze complex medical cases from various perspectives, leading to more accurate diagnoses and innovative treatment solutions.
- **Interdisciplinary collaboration:** With improved critical thinking, Dr. Elena became more adept at collaborating with specialists and other healthcare professionals to devise multifaceted treatment plans, enhancing patient outcomes.

These newly developed skills, rooted in empathy and critical thinking, transformed Dr. Elena from a competent physician into a deeply compassionate and innovative medical practitioner. Her ability to connect with patients on a personal level and think outside the conventional medical box set her apart in her field, exemplifying how nurturing our Humics can lead to the development of valuable professional skills.

Jordan the marketing professional   Meet Jordan, a marketing professional with a solid foundation in essential marketing skills, including:

- **Market research:** Proficient in gathering and analyzing market data to understand trends and customer needs
- **Digital marketing:** Skilled in utilizing digital platforms for advertising, social media engagement, and content distribution
- **Strategic planning:** Capable of developing marketing strategies that align with business goals and target audience preferences

Eager to elevate his career, Jordan focused on enhancing his Humics, particularly creativity (genuine creativity) and critical thinking. This shift led to the development of new, innovative skills:

- **Brand storytelling:** Jordan's amplified creativity allowed him to craft compelling brand narratives that resonated deeply with audiences, transforming how products and services were perceived and increasing brand loyalty.
- **Consumer psychology insights:** By applying critical thinking to marketing challenges, Jordan became adept at understanding the psychological factors that influence consumer behavior, enabling the creation of more targeted and effective marketing campaigns.
- **Innovative campaign design:** Leveraging both creativity and critical thinking, Jordan began to design marketing campaigns that broke the mold, utilizing unconventional channels and messages to capture attention in crowded markets.
- **Data-driven creativity:** Jordan learned to combine his creative skills with data analysis, producing creative content that was not only engaging but also strategically optimized based on consumer data insights.

These new skills, nurtured from Jordan's focus on developing his creativity and critical thinking, transformed his approach to marketing.

Jordan moved beyond traditional marketing methods to embrace a more holistic and innovative approach, positioning him as a forward-thinking leader in his field. This example illustrates how investing in our Humics can lead to the cultivation of advanced skills that propel professional growth and innovation.

Maya the software developer Let's consider Maya, a software developer who initially excelled in key technical skills vital for her role, including:

- **Coding proficiency:** Expertise in multiple programming languages and the ability to write clean, efficient code
- **Debugging skills:** The knack for quickly identifying and fixing errors within software applications
- **System architecture understanding:** A solid grasp of how different parts of a software system interact and operate together

Motivated to elevate her career, Maya chose to focus on enhancing two specific Humics: problem-solving (an aspect of critical thinking) and adaptability (a facet of social authenticity in navigating team dynamics). This led to the development of new, invaluable skills:

- **Cross-platform innovation:** Maya's refined problem-solving abilities allowed her to design and implement innovative solutions that worked seamlessly across different platforms and devices, enhancing user experience and broadening the reach of her projects.
- **Agile leadership:** With enhanced adaptability, Maya became an agile project leader capable of managing and motivating diverse development teams through rapidly changing project landscapes, ensuring timely and high-quality software delivery.
- **User-centric development:** By combining her technical skills with a deep understanding of user needs, Maya started to develop software with a focus on user experience, making her products more intuitive and successful in the market.

- **Continuous learning and integration:** Maya's adaptability also meant she was always at the forefront of new technologies, quickly learning and integrating them into her work, thus keeping her skills and her projects cutting-edge.

These advanced skills, cultivated from Maya's dedicated focus on developing her problem-solving and adaptability, transformed her from a proficient software developer into an innovative tech leader and problem solver. This transition illustrates how nurturing our Humics can lead to the creation of specialized skills that significantly enhance our professional impact and adaptability in a fast-evolving field.

In the coming chapter, we will deep dive into each of the three Humics to identify how we can develop them and bring them to a whole new level. With that, we ensure that we can develop all the skills needed for a successful future.

Can you provide examples of how skills may naturally evolve in the future as one leverages the Humics?

As AI evolves, the distinct blend of the three Humics will give rise to new, uniquely human skills. For example:

- **Emotional innovation:** This could be the ability to creatively harness and express complex human emotions in art, literature, or technology design. While AI can mimic patterns or generate content, the depth, nuance, and originality of human emotion, combined with creativity, could lead to unprecedented forms of art or products that resonate deeply on a personal, human level. This emotional innovation could become a cornerstone in fields ranging from therapeutic practices to entertainment and product design, representing a realm where the human touch remains irreplaceable and increasingly valuable.

- **Complex ethical decision-making:** Humans have the innate ability to navigate complex ethical dilemmas, a skill that may become increasingly crucial as society faces new challenges brought about by technological advancements. For instance, in fields like biotechnology or environmental conservation, humans can weigh multiple, often conflicting values and principles to make decisions that align with societal norms and ethical considerations.

- **Intuitive leadership and management:** Leadership and management involve not just decision-making but also the ability to inspire, motivate, and understand the nuanced emotional dynamics of a team. As workplaces evolve, a new kind of leader may emerge, one who excels in fostering collaboration between humans and AI, leveraging the strengths of each to create a harmonious and productive environment. This kind of leadership would require a deep understanding of human psychology, emotions, and the subtleties of team dynamics, areas where AI still falls short.

- **Creative problem-solving in dynamic environments:** While AI excels in structured environments with clear rules, humans are uniquely adept at creative problem-solving in dynamic, unpredictable settings. The future may see an increased need for humans who can navigate complex, real-world problems where the parameters are not fixed but constantly changing, such as in crisis management or in fields that require real-time adaptability and innovative solutions.

CHAPTER

7

Bringing Your Humics to a Whole New Level

We've seen how vital it is to leverage our Humics to develop relevant and evolving skills. The key lies in reviving and strengthening these abilities, elevating them to an unprecedented level of mastery. In this practical chapter, I provide specific strategies for boosting your creativity, sharpening your critical thinking, and deepening your social abilities.

Become Ultra-Creative

I am not at all a creative person; is there anything I can do about it?

If you cannot draw, you might think you were born uncreative. Or if your parents weren't artistic, you might think that's an inherited gene. But what is creativity?

Creativity is the ability to generate new and original ideas, solutions, or artistic expressions. It's not just about being an artist, as is commonly misconceived, but includes a broad range of problem-solving and innovative thinking in various fields, from science and technology to business and everyday life.

Another common myth is that creativity always manifests as a sudden burst of inspiration or a "eureka" moment. While such moments do occur, creativity often involves a gradual process of exploration, experimentation, and refinement. So this is a skill that can be learned and improved.

Another significant misconception about creativity is the belief that it's an innate talent exclusive to a select few. In reality, creativity is a skill that can be nurtured and developed by anyone. So we all have an equal chance to build this valuable skill.

But with AI creating art and poems, is being creative still important?

AI might mix and match, but it can't replicate the depth of human creativity. Think of AI as a chef following a recipe. It can combine ingredients (or, in this case, existing ideas) but can't invent a new flavor inspired by personal experience or emotions. As explained earlier, our creativity is unique because it is intertwined with our emotions, our life story, our traits of character, our personality, and who we are—our hopes, dreams, and even our fears. Our creativity is as unique as our fingerprints.

Because they are not genuinely automatable by AI, myriad research studies show that the value of creative skills in the job market has been drastically increasing over the last decades and will keep increasing.[1] For example, research based on the analysis of job postings found that the salary for the role of creative director has increased by 94% since 2015.

Being able to augment my value on the job market is appealing; how can I build up my creativity?

The understanding of how genuine creativity works is still an emerging field, with no definitive explanation of its inner workings. Through my interactions with various experts in these fields, I've learned that while the science of creativity is still evolving, certain practices— such as embracing curiosity, seeking new experiences, and allowing for reflective downtime—can enhance one's creative potential.

As a researcher, author, and content creator on social media, creativity is central for me. I have experimented with a lot of practices, but here are the ones I find the most efficient for myself.

Creative Practice #1   I am used to jogging about three miles every morning. I use these runs not only to help me stay in good health physically, but I also identified that I was more creative during and after this exercise. After sharing this with experts, they told me this was a proven method for boosting creativity because of the following:

- **Endorphin release:** Physical exercise, like running, triggers the release of endorphins in your brain. These are often called "feel-good" hormones, and they can create a mood of euphoria or a "runner's high." This positive mood shift can open up your mind, making it easier to think creatively.

- **Increased blood flow to the brain:** When you run, your blood flow increases, and more oxygen gets pumped not just to your muscles but also to your brain. This enhances cognitive function and boosts creative thinking.

- **Stress reduction:** Running is a great stress reliever. Lower stress levels mean your mind isn't as clouded with worries, giving you more mental space to think creatively. Note that researchers regularly point at stress as an inhibitor of creativity.

- **Mind wandering:** While running, especially during a repetitive activity like a long jog, your mind can wander. This state of mind wandering is actually a fertile ground for creative ideas. It lets your subconscious work on problems or concepts that you might not focus on while engaged in more demanding cognitive tasks. Neuroscience shows that mind wandering encourages associative thinking, where the brain connects seemingly unrelated ideas and memories, leading to novel combinations and perspectives.

Note that, from my experience, this also works with any kind of exercise that you practice for more than 15 minutes at a heart rate of more than 100 beats per minute.

Creative Practice #2   I find myself more creative in a state of near-sleep, lying in bed with my eyes closed and breathing deeply. I find my best ideas in this position! I shared this with researchers, who told me the explanation is actually rooted in neuroscience and psychology. This state is often referred to as the "hypna-gogic state," which is the transitional phase between wakefulness and sleep.

Here's why it is a hotbed for creativity:

- **The hypnagogic state:** The state between wakefulness and sleep, or the hypnagogic state, is known for sparking creativity, making unique connections, and coming up with innovative ideas. It's a time when the subconscious mind can surface creative concepts that might be suppressed by the conscious mind during full alertness.

- **Subconscious surfacing:** As you approach sleep, your sub-conscious mind becomes more accessible. This part of your mind is a rich source of creativity, memories, and intuition. In this state, you can tap into creative ideas that are not easily accessible when you're fully awake, and your conscious mind is in control.

- **Alpha brain waves:** This state is associated with increased alpha brain wave activity, which is linked to creativity. Alpha waves are present during relaxed states, meditation, and right before falling asleep. This is why I often have ideas when I am about to fall asleep at night. In that case, I write them right away in my journal on my phone.

Creative Practice #3   I am also very creative when I am in a flow state. I reach it by immersing myself in writing and listening to inspir-ing music. Being in a "flow" state, I lose track of time and external pressures, allowing for a heightened focus on internal thoughts and creativity.

Here is how a flow state increases your creativity:

- **Optimal neurochemical balance:** When you're in a flow state, your brain releases a cocktail of neurochemicals like dopamine, endorphins, norepinephrine, and serotonin. This combination enhances focus, speeds up information processing, and boosts creative thinking. Dopamine, in particular, plays a key role in the brain's reward circuit, enhancing our ability to notice patterns and make novel connections.

- **Heightened focus and clarity:** Flow involves intense focus on the present moment, minimizing distractions. This concentration allows you to absorb and process more information relevant to the task at hand, enhancing your ability to generate creative solutions and ideas.

What I have just shared with you are just a few tips to get you started. You will find a lot more in the IRREPLACEABLE Academy (www.irreplaceable.ai). For you to work on this skill, I recommend reading and experimenting with the practices that will fit well with you.

I suggest you try these practices and share your experience on social media using the hashtag #irreplaceable. You might also have identified other practices that are useful to boost your creativity and that could benefit others.

Additional Resources

These are additional resources that I recommend for you to go deeper on the topic:

Kelley, Tom, and David Kelley. *Creative Confidence: Unleashing the Creative Potential Within Us All.* Currency, 2013.

Liberman, Zoe. *Re:Think Creativity: Understand How the Creative Mind Works to Maximize Creativity in Your Life.* Ten Speed Press, 2022.

Tharp, Twyla. *The Creative Habit: Learn It and Use It for Life.* Simon & Schuster, 2021.

Von Oech, Roger. *A Whack on the Side of the Head: How You Can Be More Creative.* Grand Central Publishing, 2008.

Sharpen Your Critical Thinking

Isn't critical thinking just about being good at arguing and pointing out what's wrong with other people's ideas?

If you think critical thinking is just useful for debates or really tough, brainy stuff, you might not be into it. You might think it's just about cold, hard logic.

Similarly to creativity, critical thinking is an ability that can be developed and improved over time through practice and education. Some mistake critical thinking for simply being critical of others' ideas. However, it's more about analyzing and evaluating information objectively, not just finding faults.

Some others believe that critical thinking is relevant only in academic or intellectually demanding contexts. However, it's a valuable capability in everyday decision-making, problem-solving, self-reflecting, and various professional and personal situations.

Another myth is that critical thinking requires a purely logical approach devoid of emotion. While it does involve logical reasoning, emotions and intuition also play important roles. It's about balancing rational thought with emotional intelligence.

So what is critical thinking?

Critical thinking is the ability to analyze and evaluate information and arguments by applying independent judgment and ethical reasoning. It involves critiquing and questioning the validity of information, using intuition, and engaging in self-reflection to understand one's biases, purpose, and underlying motivations. Building trust is a key expected outcome.

Critical thinking is also the ability to ask the right questions. Scientists have known that for centuries. If you ask the right question, by defining well the problem you want to solve, you have almost already solved the problem. This is part of what we currently call "prompting" an AI.

If AI can plan vacations and help with my decisions, doesn't that mean it has mastered critical thinking?

AI can analyze and suggest, but true critical thinking? That's a human specialty. Let me explain.

AI can sort and process information but can't fully grasp the art of connecting diverse ideas with the depth of human insight. AI might follow logic, but it doesn't understand ethics or question the information like humans. It doesn't "doubt" or "reflect" critically. In addition, humans can question not just the "how" but also the "why" behind actions and ideas.

More specifically, for example, it is the role of humans to critically evaluate outcomes from technology and make judgments about their appropriateness. This involves understanding the broader implications and potential unintended consequences of these outcomes.

While we can contemplate the ethical implications of our actions and decisions, considering aspects like justice, fairness, and human rights, AI systems follow data-driven processes, which do not inherently encompass moral and ethical reasoning. In addition, while AI can operate within human ethical guidelines, it cannot create these guidelines because it lacks an understanding of the nuanced human values and societal contexts that shape them.

Finally, critical thinking involves a personal dimension, such as discovering one's own motivations, purposes, and values. This intro-spective aspect is uniquely human. AI does not possess self-awareness or personal motivations; it cannot engage in self-reflection or discover a personal "why."

In summary, critical thinking is deeply tied to human experiences, self-awareness, intuition, moral and ethical considerations, and the ability to question and evaluate within broad contexts. These aspects are intricately linked to human consciousness and are beyond the capabilities of current AI technology.

How can I sharpen my critical thinking?

Drawing from the daily exercises I perform to enhance my critical thinking abilities, I recommend the following practices for you:

- **Awareness and control of your cognitive biases:** First, educate yourself about different cognitive biases—there are many, such as confirmation bias, anchoring, overconfidence, and so on. I recommend leveraging the "Cognitive bias" Wikipedia page, which lists the 188 cognitive biases that all humans have. Reflect regularly on your decision-making process to identify when biases might be influencing you.

- **Building and trusting intuition:** Reflect on past decisions. Recognize when your intuition led you correctly or astray, and learn to distinguish between intuitive insights and impulsive reactions.

- **Critical analysis of media and information:** Develop the habit of critically analyzing the information you consume. Question the source, the context, and the intent behind the information. This helps in honing your ability to discern and evaluate information critically.

- **Develop self-awareness:** Spend time understanding your motivations, values, and biases. Self-awareness is key to understanding your personal "why" and enhances your ability to make decisions aligned with your values.

- **Practice reflective thinking:** Regularly take time to reflect on your actions, your decisions, and their outcomes. This helps in understanding your thought process and improves your ability to think critically about future decisions.

For you to work more in-depth on this skill, I recommend reading and experimenting with the additional resources presented here. Also make sure you leverage the IRREPLACEABLE Academy for a wealth of material on the topic (www.irreplaceable.ai).

Additional Resources

Here are a few additional resources I recommend:

Heuer, Richards J., and Randolph H. Pherson. *Critical Thinking for Strategic Intelligence*. CQ Press, 2021.

Hirt, Edward R., and Keith D. Markman. *Social Psychology: Goals in Interaction*. W.W. Norton & Company, 2018

Kahneman, Daniel. *Thinking, Fast and Slow*. Farrar, Straus and Giroux, 2011.

Levitin, Daniel J. *Weaponized Lies: How to Think Critically in the Post-Truth Era*. Dutton, 2016.

Deepen Your Social Abilities

Are social abilities about being naturally good at talking to people and being outgoing?

We often assume that social abilities are synonymous with being extroverted or sociable. If you work in the technical field, you might think you don't have those types of abilities. However, these abilities encompass much more, including effective communication, empathy, leadership, active listening, conflict resolution, and teamwork, which are valuable in both personal and professional contexts.

There's a belief that social abilities are crucial only in customer-facing or team-based roles. Even in highly technical or independent roles, the ability to communicate ideas clearly, collaborate, and navigate workplace dynamics is critical.

While we all naturally possess strong social abilities, these abilities can certainly be developed and honed through practice and learning.

So how do you define social abilities?

Social abilities are essential for individuals to engage effectively and harmoniously with other individuals. At the heart of these abilities lies emotional intelligence, which involves understanding, managing, and expressing one's own emotions, as well as empathetically navigating through interpersonal relationships.

Leadership also plays a key role in social abilities, involving the capability to guide, motivate, and positively influence others. Central to all this is effective communication—the art of conveying messages and emotions clearly and constructively, through both words and non-verbal cues.

These abilities are invaluable in all areas of life, from personal interactions to professional environments, significantly improving teamwork, conflict resolution, and the overall quality of relationships.

With AI like ChatGPT understanding and speaking like us, will it outdo humans in social abilities?

While AI, like ChatGPT, can assist in and augment certain aspects of communication, the full spectrum of social abilities, particularly those involving emotional depth and deep relationship-building, remain uniquely human. AI can interpret and respond to certain emotional states, but it does so based on programmed algorithms and learned patterns, not genuine empathy or understanding.

Human interactions are often driven by authenticity and sincerity, which are critical for building trust and meaningful relationships. AI lacks the capacity for genuine emotions, making it difficult for people to connect with AI on a deeper, more personal level.

AI can mimic understanding emotions, but it's like a parrot repeating words without grasping their meaning. It lacks the real essence of empathy. Human empathy is rich with our personal stories and emotional depths. In essence, no one other than a human can genuinely interact with another human.

For these reasons, jobs and skills requiring high social abilities are increasing in value. People-focused roles like customer success specialists and community associates saw more than 200% increases in job postings from 2019 to 2022, reflecting rising demand for emotionally intelligent professionals adept at building relationships.

How can I boost my social abilities?

Drawing from the daily exercises I perform to enhance my social abilities, I recommend the following practices for you:

- **Develop empathy:** Focus on really listening to what others are saying without immediately formulating a response. Pay attention to their words, tone, and body language. Regularly practice seeing situations from others' viewpoints. This could involve imagining how you would feel in their situation or asking questions to better understand their experiences.

- **Improve communication abilities:** Enhance your clarity and articulation in speaking. Practice storytelling and explaining complex ideas in simple terms. When you communicate, be conscious of your body language, facial expressions, and gestures. Ensure they align with your verbal messages. Practice maintaining appropriate eye contact and observe how your tone of voice affects conversations.

- **Learn conflict resolution:** Acknowledge and validate different perspectives in a conflict without necessarily agreeing with them. Develop strategies for mediating disputes, such as maintaining neutrality, guiding constructive dialogue, and finding common ground.

- **Cultivate social awareness:** Pay attention to social cues, such as body language, social rituals, and group dynamics. Be aware of and respectful of different cultural backgrounds and norms, which can greatly influence social interactions.

- **Strengthen team collaboration:** Learn to identify and appreciate the diverse skills and perspectives within a team. Create an inclusive environment where all team members feel valued and able to contribute.

- **Develop leadership abilities:** Work on your ability to inspire and motivate others, which could involve public speaking skills, storytelling, or demonstrating passion and vision. Enhance your ability to think strategically and make decisions that align with both short-term and long-term goals.

By focusing on these areas, you can greatly enhance your social abilities, ensuring effective, empathetic, and nuanced human interactions.

Make sure you leverage the IRREPLACEABLE Academy for a wealth of additional material on the topic (www.irreplaceable.ai). Also, here are some additional resources I recommend to help you further improve your social abilities.

Additional Resources

Here are a few additional resources I recommend:

Bolton, Robert. *People Skills: How to Assert Yourself, Listen to Others, and Resolve Conflicts.* Simon & Schuster, 1986.

Carnegie, Dale. *How to Win Friends and Influence People.* Simon & Schuster, 2009.

Goleman, Daniel. *Emotional Intelligence.* Bantam Books, 2006.

McKay, Matthew, Martha Davis, and Patrick Fanning. *Messages: The Communications Skills Book.* New Harbinger Publications, 2009.

Patterson, Kerry, Joseph Grenny, Ron McMillan, and Al Switzler. *Crucial Conversations: Tools for Talking When Stakes Are High.* McGraw-Hill Education, 2021.

PART

III

Becoming IRREPLACEABLE at Work

In the previous part, you learned the skills necessary to thrive in the age of AI. Now you'll learn to apply these skills specifically to the work context. Remember, your professional life is just one dimension of your existence, but it is a significant one. By becoming IRREPLACEABLE at work, you set yourself up for success and fulfillment in your career. However, as you read the chapters in this part, keep in mind that the strategies discussed can also be applied to other areas of your life, such as your passions or even parenting.

CHAPTER

8

Augmenting Yourself with AI at Work

As you've explored in previous chapters, to be strategic and thrive in the age of AI, you need to build capabilities that complement AI. You now need to learn how to collaborate at a more tactical level with AI. The key here is about augmenting ourselves with AI, allowing us to work better, smarter, and faster. In this chapter, you'll dive into the techniques you can use to effectively become superhuman with AI!

A Three-Phase Approach to Augment Yourself with AI

How do I work daily with AI?

Imagine you're a superhero in a world where AI is your sidekick. Just like Batman has Robin, you can have AI as your trusty companion. This is what we call human augmentation with AI.

Augmenting yourself with AI means using AI to enhance your abilities and performance. It's not about replacing you but about making you stronger, smarter, and faster. You'll amplify your human skills with the advanced capabilities of AI.

According to research, you can accelerate your work by more than 20% and improve its quality by more than 40% by using AI.[1] Employers are willing to pay up to 44% more for AI-skilled workers.[2]

Let's explore how you can prepare your job for the AI era in three phases.

- **First, change your mindset:** Think of AI as your partner, not your rival. It's not the Joker trying to outsmart you; it's Robin, ready to assist. Focus on what you can achieve together. Efficiency is your new mantra. It's also about finding balance and not burning out. Let AI handle the heavy lifting while you strategize. Most importantly, be mindful and reflective. Take time to understand and learn how AI impacts your work and life.

- **Second, build and continuously evolve your knowledge:** The world of AI is always changing, and you need to keep up. Build your AI literacy by keeping an eye out for new topics and diving into them, but not too deep. This way, you can stay versatile.

- **Third, strategically implement AI in your work and life:** It's like having a super tool in your toolkit. But if you don't use it wisely, you might end up more like the tool's assistant than its master. Using AI incorrectly can make you a slave to technology, stuck in a cycle of underutilizing its potential or using it inappropriately. To augment yourself with AI, you need to understand when and how to use it.

In summary, preparing for AI in your job is about teaming up with AI, understanding how to use it effectively, and continuously learning to keep up with the changes. Embrace AI, and watch how it transforms your job into something more enjoyable and fulfilling. Welcome to the future of work, where you and AI are the perfect team!

Let's look at each of the three phases in more depth.

Phase 1: Build an AI Mindset

Can you explain the AI mindset I need to adopt?

In a world transformed by AI, much of the conventional wisdom about work is now obsolete. To augment yourself with AI, it's crucial to break away from traditional mindsets and adapt to the new AI mindset.

Forget the old days of glorifying long hours and relentless effort. The new mindset goes against everything we've been taught, from valuing hard work to fearing competition. The new rules? Work smarter, not harder. It's a shift from effort to efficiency, from quantity to quality. Ditch the old mindset that measures success by time spent. In the AI era, it's about the impact, not the hours. It's about making strategic choices for your energy, creativity, and focus. Adopting this AI mindset is the only way to stay IRREPLACEABLE.

> *"The new mindset goes against everything we've been taught."*

The following are the five principles of this new AI mindset.

AI Mindset Principle #1: Efficiency over Effort   Being "smartly lazy" is the new smart. Let's bury the old work ethic that glorifies overwork.

Imagine you're a manager. You assign a 30-minute task, but your team completes it in just 10 minutes. The old-school boss cries foul, suspecting shortcuts or errors, obsessed with time spent rather than results. This outdated mindset equates long hours with hard work, a dangerous path leading to burnout and inefficiency.

But with the new AI mindset, the game has changed. The manager applauds the team's swift completion. Efficiency—getting more done with less effort—is the new benchmark, not time spent. It's a sign of intelligence: the team has certainly automated or delegated cleverly. And importantly, now, they're free for more impactful tasks!

It's not just about working less; it's about adding more value more intelligently. In the AI era, the best managers are those who recognize and reward efficiency, turning the old work ethic on its head for a smarter, more sustainable future.

AI Mindset Principle #2: Value over Volume   Productivity—outputs over inputs—is a metric of performance for AI, not for humans!

In the AI era, human focus should shift from volume to value. With AI, producing large quantities is easy and inexpensive. For example, consider a drinking glass. You can buy many cheap glasses at IKEA because they are mass-produced using technology. However, hand-crafted glass, made with attention to quality, can sell for 100 times more than the IKEA version. The true value lies in quality, not in producing large amounts.

Similarly, current work culture tends to focus wrongly on rewarding the volume of output (e.g., how many reports you have written, calls made, or widgets produced). The new mindset, however, prioritizes the outcome or the impact of the work (e.g., to what extent customer or employee satisfaction increased). It's not about how much you do but how much impact you create.

AI Mindset Principle #3: Collaboration over Control   From childhood, we are praised for accomplishing tasks on our own, like walking, eating, and cycling. We often hear, "Great job, you did it by yourself!" This mindset becomes deeply ingrained in us. Successfully managing tasks independently is equated with success: it signifies survival, usefulness to society, and productivity. Consequently, not being able to do things alone often sparks a fear of losing control!

In today's AI-driven world, clinging to control is a trap. Embrace delegation, especially to AI. It's not about losing control; it's about playing smarter. AI can handle repetitive tasks, analyze mountains of data, and support or automate your decisions, freeing you to focus on what really needs your human touch.

It is not blind delegation. It is about investing in gradually building a trusted collaboration with AI. How to achieve this? Start small. Give AI a piece of work; watch how it goes. Suppose it succeeds; then hand over more. Repeat until you trust it fully.

This isn't just about easing your workload; it's about skyrocketing your value. Letting AI take the wheel on some tasks doesn't diminish your skills—it amplifies them. Delegate to AI, and watch your potential multiply.

AI Mindset Principle #4: Balance over Burnout   Forget the "work till you drop" approach. We've idolized startup leaders who burn out, mistaking self-destruction for devotion. But here's a reality check: overworking leads to burnout, not productivity.

Picture this: You're managing John and Anita. Anita asks for more time off while John barely takes a break. Old thinking labels

Anita as slacking. But that's outdated: it's not about clocking endless hours; it's about working well and then recharging. AI and technology aren't just tools; they're our tickets to work-life harmony, helping us regain the humanity we lost to overwork.

Let's flip the script: Anita's not the problem; she's the model. Breaks, family time, and recharging aren't slacking; they're strategies for sustainable success. Encourage your team to balance work with life.

As a boss, encourage your team to find that sweet spot between work and life. Let them work from anywhere if they're nailing their goals. A rested team is an effective one. It's time to use AI to reshape our work culture into a more human and sustainable one.

AI Mindset Principle #5: Reflection over Rush   It's time to challenge the reckless rush in using AI.

After implementing a new AI tool for sending promotional emails, John successfully gained 30 new clients by fully utilizing the software, while Anita acquired only 3. Initially, John is praised for his adaptability and tech-savviness, whereas Anita is advised to take John as a model.

However, it later emerges that John's success came at the cost of sending unsolicited emails to thousands, leading to privacy uproars and a tarnished brand. In contrast, Anita, who opted for a purposeful, ethical approach, earned lasting trust and respect from her clients.

The harsh reality is that using AI recklessly spells disaster. The wiser approach is to embrace AI with thought, ethics, and responsibility. Lasting impact—not short-term frenzy—should drive AI use. This new age calls for a fundamental change: shifting from AI just for the sake of it to a sustainable AI impact guided by purpose and principles.

In this rapidly advancing AI world, the bold move is to think before you act. Remember, in the AI age, the truly advanced are those who align innovation with integrity.

> *"In the AI era, human focus should shift from volume to value."*

Phase 2: Maintain AI Literacy

What is AI literacy?

AI literacy is like learning a new language. Just as language skills let you communicate and understand a culture, AI literacy helps you grasp the world of artificial intelligence. For instance, using a voice assistant well involves knowing the correct commands and understanding how it processes your requests.

In simple terms, AI literacy means:

- **Understanding AI concepts:** Familiarity with basic AI terminology, such as machine learning, neural networks, and natural language processing

- **Considering ethics:** Understanding the ethical implications of AI, including issues related to privacy, bias, accountability, and the potential for misuse

- **Interacting with AI:** Being able to effectively use and interact with AI-powered tools and services, from virtual assistants to algorithm-driven platforms like social media and search engines; understanding the applications in your work and your industry

- **Evaluating AI systems:** Evaluating AI technologies critically, questioning their functionality, the data they use, and the algorithms that drive them

- **Using AI safely:** Understanding the security risks associated with AI systems and how to protect personal data from being misused

- **Staying updated with the latest advancements in AI and related technologies:** Understanding the new opportunities and risks of these technologies

Being AI literate does not mean becoming a data scientist. For 99.99% of people, knowing how AI impacts society, ethics, and your specific industry is more valuable than understanding how complex algorithms work.

It's a skill set everyone needs, not just tech professionals. AI literacy is a continuous journey, requiring regular updates and adaptation.

Why is AI literacy so important?

AI literacy is essential, but many overlook its importance. Without it, you're vulnerable to cyber threats, job market disadvantages, misinformation, a widening digital divide, and an inability to fully participate in society or make informed decisions. In a world increasingly dictated by AI, understanding its impact is not a luxury but a necessity.

Recent studies show an alarming state of digital literacy. A Pew Research Center survey revealed that while many Americans are aware of major tech companies, their knowledge about AI and related privacy laws is limited.[3] This gap highlights the urgent need for improved AI literacy across all demographics.

How can I improve my AI literacy with my already busy schedule?

To become AI literate and maintain it, I suggest dedicating about 15% of your work hours specifically to learning, experimenting, and keeping yourself updated with the latest news about AI.

If you're a manager, encourage your team to take this time during their workday. For example, if someone works 40 hours a week, they should spend about 6 hours of that time maintaining their AI literacy. Consider this a valuable investment: by regularly updating their skills, tools, and processes, your team can consistently perform at their best. I guarantee you will get a return on this investment!

To keep up-to-date with AI developments, a proactive approach is key. This includes subscribing to tech news, listening to podcasts, participating in online courses, joining online communities, attending tech events, reading books, and setting aside regular times for updates.

Where to find this time in an already very busy schedule? This is the time you've freed up by automating some of your time-consuming tasks. It could also be that time that you usually didn't fully utilize, such as when jogging, commuting, or waiting, during which you can listen to podcasts or audiobooks.

By integrating AI literacy into your daily life and continuously adapting your learning strategy, you can navigate the rapidly evolving landscape of technology and AI, staying informed, relevant, and prepared for the future.

With new AI topics emerging daily, which ones should I prioritize?

When learning and maintaining your knowledge about AI, start by identifying your goals and interests. Prioritize learning based on relevance and set realistic objectives. Curate quality sources for accurate information and allocate specific times for learning. Mix learning methods to suit your style, take active notes, stay organized, apply your knowledge practically, and regularly reassess your learning goals. Remember, taking mindful breaks is crucial for mental well-being and effective learning.

It is not only about AI but also all the technologies and fields surrounding it because these fields, such as robotics, ethics, privacy, blockchain, and quantum computing, all have an impact on one another.

Do I need to be an expert in everything about AI?

To effectively use AI, you don't have to be an expert in everything about it. What I call the "30% rule" suggests that knowing just about a third of a topic is often enough for practical use. This rule comes from the fact that while mastering English requires learning around 12,000 words, a non-native speaker only needs about 4,000 words to communicate effectively at work.[4] In the same way, understanding the 30% of AI basics, its relevance to your job, and its ethical aspects is more crucial than deep technical expertise in coding and programming.

Phase 3: Strategically Implement AI

How can I leverage AI effectively at work?

The third key to augmenting ourselves with AI involves using it the right way. In a world where AI is redefining work, merely using AI isn't enough; it's how you use it that counts. Most people think they know how to use AI, but the reality is starkly different. Research shows that only 20% of people actually integrate it effectively enough to boost their work.[5] It's not because they can't but because they've never learned to.

During my two decades of assisting companies with their AI and digital system integrations, I've encountered four typical recurring obstacles that hinder individuals from effectively enhancing their capabilities with AI. (Of course, I have purposely changed the names of these people to ensure their privacy.)

Misstep #1: Overreliance   Kylian was tasking an accounting AI with invoice processing, but he didn't validate system limits or outputs. Soon bad data snowballed into payment disasters requiring massive manual cleanup. Rather than gaining efficiency, Kylian's team lost weeks fixing algorithmic chaos.

Bottom line: Don't blindly trust AI without oversight. Garbage in, garbage out.

Misstep #2: Partial or Missed Implementation (Becoming AI's Slave!)   Karen's new email filtering AI initially worked wonders in organizing her overflowing inbox. However, she soon realized it couldn't grasp critical communication nuances in her event planning role. Important messages kept misfiling. Instead of saving time, she spent over an hour daily rescuing client emails from the algorithmic abyss.

Key lesson: Don't become the slave of a flawed AI. Set it up right or remove it.

Misstep #3: Lack of Perseverance or False Expectations   Creative director Ravi eagerly employed the latest generative design and writing AI to boost content production. But lacking prompt formulation skills, his first mishmash attempts dismayed rather than dazzled clients. Frustrated, Ravi dismissed the tools as useless rather than skill up on techniques that could extract quality output.

The moral here: Persevere through learning curves. AI mastery unlocks magic.

Misstep #4: Failure to Act   The last issue, which is the most frequent and the most damaging, is not using AI. I have seen hundreds of companies and professionals missing the opportunities to augment their work. For example, Sarah, a doctor, had access to an advanced AI diagnostic tool but avoided using it out of distrust, missing critical insights that could have improved her patient care. She said that she knew her job better than any technology. Most often, the issue relies upon education. These people can't know what they don't know!

Bottom line: Embrace AI as a partner, not a replacement. Education and open-mindedness toward technology can transform your work.

What is the right way to use AI and avoid these missteps?

AI is like a guest. Invite it thoughtfully into your work, and it'll respect your space and add value. Let your clients, managers, or competitors force it in, and it may take over. Be proactive, not reactive.

To invite AI into your work, here is a four-step approach.

Step #1: Identify Your Activities   Take a week and list what you do. This isn't just about work tasks; the activities you perform during your personal life count, too. For each of these activities, identify the time they take, and the value or satisfaction you get from doing them.

Step #2: Automate, Elevate, or Eliminate Activities   Decide which tasks to automate, which to elevate, and which to eliminate. You can't use AI on every task. Focus on tasks that eat up your time or generate the most value. (See Table 8.1.)

The following is the detailed approach to eliminate, elevate, and automate activities.

- **Eliminating work activities:** The first step involves a thorough assessment to confirm the need for elimination. If you can't articulate the clear value and benefits of an activity, it's a candidate for reduction or elimination. This approach targets tasks like redundant meetings, unread reports, or inefficient email chains. The goal is to minimize these low-value activities, thereby freeing up time for more impactful work. A continuous review ensures the focus remains on high-value tasks, reallocating resources to areas that truly drive results and impact.

- **Elevating work activities:** Elevate the high-value activities. To identify them, I recommend sorting the 20% of work activities generating 80% of value—or work satisfaction. For activities identified for elevation, mastering the underlying skills is vital

Table 8.1 Activities to automate, elevate, or eliminate.

Category of activities	Definition	Criteria for identification	Examples	Benefits
Activities to Automate	These work activities consume a dispropor-tionate amount of time com-pared to their value. They are mundane, tedious, and repetitive activities.	20% of work activities taking 80% of time.	Data entry, repetitive administrative work activi-ties, email filtering.	Free up time for more value added activities.
Activities to Elevate	These work activities provide the most value or satisfaction. Enhancing your ability to perform them effectively increases their impact.	20% of work activities generating 80% of value/ satisfaction.	Strategic planning, creative designing, client interactions.	Multiply human strengths.
Activities to Eliminate	These are less impactful work activi-ties. Minimiz-ing or eliminating them leads to more focused and efficient work.	20% of work activities creating the least value.	Nonessential meetings, outdated processes, unnecessary email chains.	Enable focus.

before integrating AI. This ensures that AI is used to enhance existing strengths, not replace underdeveloped skills.

Establish rock-solid personal proficiency beforehand. For example, if you want to improve customer analytics, become highly skilled at manual analysis first. Learn fundamentals like segmentation, lifetime value metrics, churn rate analysis, and so on. Only once you have strong analytical expertise should you add AI to enhance it further. AI elevates existing strength when used by seasoned professionals rather than replacing the skills of novices.

Next, research different AI tools and evaluate which matches your needs. Selecting suitable AI tools that match specific needs is critical, as is building trust in these tools before becoming entirely dependent on them. Myriad tools of varying sophistication and specialty exist. Carefully evaluate options aligned to use-case nuances based on factors like output quality, explainability, and ethical considerations. To help you objectively select the right tool, establish your criteria of choice, and rate them for the different options available on the market.

When you elevate work activities, you shift the "human+AI" equation into an even more powerful equation: "human*AI." It elevates the concept of collaboration to one of synergy, where the interaction between humans and AI creates a whole greater than the sum of its parts. This is the mode of collaboration with AI where the highest value is created.

I met Anoop, who is a seasoned communication manager. She has recently decided to harness the power of AI to revolutionize her workflow. By integrating AI into her strategy, she has elevated the company's communication campaigns to new levels of creativity and efficiency. This innovative approach is setting new benchmarks in the industry, reflecting her forward-thinking vision. Table 8.2 shows the way she works with AI to create a new communication campaign.

Table 8.2   Example of an ideal creative workflow between AI and human.

Step	Description	Performed by	Example
1	Brainstorm ideas, and provide a range of inspirations and concepts. Share these inspirations through prompts to AI.	Human	Coming up with campaign themes like environmental awareness or healthy living.
2	Generate hundreds of options based on the initial concepts and inspiration.	AI	Creating variations of ad copy, design layouts, and potential imagery.
3	Review the AI-generated options and select the best ones for refinement.	Human	Choosing the most compelling ad designs that convey the campaign's message effectively.
4	Refine the selected ideas based on feedback and iteration.	AI	Adjusting the chosen ad designs for color schemes, typography, and element placement.
5	Add practical constraints to ensure the ideas are aligned with goals.	Human	Ensuring the final ad design is cost-effective, aligns with brand values, and can be easily distributed across various platforms.
6	Refine based on the constraints given by the human to ensure practical alignment with goals.	AI	Fine-tuning ad designs to meet budget constraints, branding guidelines, and platform-specific requirements.

(continued)

Table 8.2 (*continued*)

Step	Description	Performed by	Example
7	Make final adjustments to the output for nuances, ethics, and practicality.	Human	Final review of the ad's tone, cultural sensitivity, legal compliance, and overall brand consistency before the campaign launch.

According to Anoop, here are the three main benefits she gained from incorporating AI into her work:

- **Enhanced creativity:** With AI providing a broad range of options, Anoop can explore creative avenues she might not have considered, leading to more innovative and diverse campaign concepts. According to her, the quality of the insights her team generates has increased by more than 50%.

- **Increased efficiency:** AI's ability to quickly generate and refine ideas allows Anoop to accelerate the creative process, saving valuable time. According to Anoop, the workload saved from researching and building creative options represents more than 30% of the workload of her team. Thanks to this, Anoop can refocus her team on building tighter collaborations with the product and sales teams, supporting strategy and critical thinking tasks that require human insight.

- **Personalization at scale:** AI can refine content based on specific constraints and data insights, allowing Anoop to create highly targeted and personalized campaigns for different audiences. Thanks to this, Anoop generates higher engagement with customers, translating into higher sales. She estimates the increase in sales at about 20%.

By elevating her work with AI, Anoop essentially multiplies her creative capacity, imbues her campaigns with data-driven insights, and frees up space to focus on the deeply human aspects of her work such as storytelling, emotional connection, and ethical considerations. This integration of AI doesn't replace human creativity; it amplifies it, propelling Anoop's work to new heights.

- **Automating work activities:** Automate the time-consuming activities. It's easy to identify them; as a rule of thumb, they are the 20% of work activities that take you 80% of your time. Out of these activities, I recommend you prioritize the work activities that are rule-based, repetitive, and consistent. For example, these are b activities that we regularly do during the week and that we always perform the same way.

  However, not all tasks are suitable for automation; some may be too complex or sensitive—such as those activities that have exceptions, like receiving a request in Japanese instead of English or transferring large amounts of money or sensitive information. In such cases, consider if outsourcing to other humans is a viable option. In the medium term, outsourcing can also lead to a better understanding of the task and potentially pave the way for future automation.

  Designing a new automated process involves breaking down the work into detailed steps. For example, when creating a weekly newsletter, the process might involve collecting information, storing it in notes, and then compiling these notes into a readable format before distributing the newsletter through various channels like email and LinkedIn.

  You don't want to automate a process that is not optimized. Indeed, automating a weak process just makes it even weaker! To optimize this process, question if there's a more straightforward method to achieve the same outcome, perhaps by creating shortcuts or eliminating unnecessary steps. An example of this could be automating the gathering and sorting of content for the newsletter or streamlining the distribution process. This approach not only improves efficiency but also allows for focusing on more value-added activities.

Let me share with you the story of Mei Li, the chief strategy officer at a large multinational company. She faced significant challenges in handling the sheer volume and complexity of data necessary for informed strategic decision-making. The manual collection and analysis processes were time-consuming and often resulted in data being outdated by the time it reached the decision-making table.

Realizing that staying competitive in a rapidly evolving business landscape required agility and real-time insights, she decided to automate the process. Automation promised not only to save valuable time but also to enhance the accuracy and relevance of the data analysis, allowing her and her team to focus on strategic thinking and innovation.

Mei Li's selection and implementation of an automation tool was a careful process, grounded in strategic foresight and thorough evaluation. For example, here is how she selected the automation tool:

- **Needs assessment:** Mei Li began by assessing her department's needs, identifying what data was critical for decision-making and where the bottlenecks were in the current process.

- **Market research:** She conducted comprehensive research to understand the landscape of available AI-driven tools, focusing on features, scalability, and integration capabilities.

- **Vendor evaluation:** With a shortlist of potential tools, Mei Li evaluated vendors based on their track record, customer support, and the flexibility of their solutions.

- **Cost-benefit analysis:** She performed a cost-benefit analysis for each tool, weighing the investment against the potential time savings and the value of insights generated.

- **Trials and demos:** Before making a final decision, Mei Li engaged in trials and demos to test the tools in action, ensuring they met the specific needs of her department.

- **Stakeholder buy-In:** Recognizing the importance of support from leadership and her team, she sought buy-in by demonstrating the potential ROI and efficiency gains from the selected tool.

Three months after selecting and implementing a suitable AI automation tool, Mei Li already collected the benefits:

- **Automated data collection:** The AI system continuously scours various data sources, such as market reports, customer feedback channels, social media trends, and competitor activities. Previously, gathering this data manually was not only time-consuming but also prone to oversight due to the sheer volume of information available. By automating data collection, Mei Li's AI systems work around the clock, aggregating data with unprecedented speed and breadth. According to an assessment, Mei Li saves a third of her team's workload, while ensuring no critical piece of information is missed.

- **Information synthesis to support decision-making:** Mei Li's AI tool has transformed her team's approach to decision-making by automating the information synthesis process. Previously performed manually, this labor-intensive task involved sifting through data, distilling insights, and constructing reports, consuming significant time and effort. Now the AI generates concise, actionable reports quickly, freeing the team to focus more on evaluating information and making informed decisions. This shift not only enhances efficiency and strategic focus but also saves the team over 20% of their workload, marking a significant leap in their operational efficiency.

By automating these critical steps with AI, Mei Li and her team have not only gained back a significant portion of their time but also enhanced the quantity of analysis their department

(continued)

(*continued*)

can perform. No longer bogged down by the logistics of data management, Mei Li and her team dedicate their newfound time to two key areas:

- **Team collaboration:** Mei Li and her team now invest more time in cross-departmental collaboration. This human-centric approach leverages diverse perspectives, fostering a culture of shared insights and collective intelligence, crucial for holistic strategy formulation. Mei Li encourages her team members to engage with colleagues from other departments, share their findings, and seek input to enrich their strategic planning process.

- **Continuous learning:** With the landscape of technology constantly evolving, Mei Li and her team commit themselves to staying abreast of the latest technological advancements. They regularly attend industry conferences, workshops, and training sessions to expand their knowledge and skills. This self-education enables them to continuously refine their AI tools and discover new ways they can augment their work, keeping their strategy sharp and future-proof. Mei Li also encourages her team members to share their learnings with each other, creating a culture of continuous growth and improvement.

In essence, Mei Li's decision to automate data collection, processing, and summarization is a strategic reallocation of her most valuable resource—time. This empowers her to amplify her strategic impact, leverage collective human intelligence, and stay ahead in a world where understanding the interplay between human insight and AI is paramount.

In summary, the process of augmenting your work with AI involves a careful evaluation of current tasks and a strategic approach to eliminate, elevate, or automate these activities. This process is not just about leveraging AI but also about rethinking how work is done to maximize productivity and impact.

Step #3: Select, Integrate, and Educate   Choosing the right tools is perhaps the most critical. My strategy involves starting with a clear identification of what I want to automate and why. This clarity has been pivotal in filtering through the vast ocean of AI tools to find those that truly suit my needs. Experience has taught me to look beyond the marketing fluff to user reviews and case studies, often leading to trials of top contenders. The key is not to get dazzled by features you don't need but to focus on tools that align with your specific goals.

Smooth integration into existing workflows is essential for any AI tool to be truly effective. My approach involves detailed planning, ensuring compatibility, and sometimes accepting the need for custom solutions. Patience is crucial here; rushing can lead to more headaches down the line. Over the years, I've increasingly valued tools that offer robust API support and flexible integration options, as they significantly ease this process.

Training yourself to use these tools effectively is the final, ongoing step. I dedicate time to learning not just the basics but also advanced features that can unlock significant efficiencies. This often involves exploring online resources, engaging with user communities, and sometimes formal training. The effort is well worth it. A nuanced understanding of the tool's capabilities allows me to automate tasks in ways I hadn't initially imagined. My tip for anyone embarking on this journey is to embrace the learning curve. The more you know about what your AI tools can do, the more creatively you can apply them to streamline your life.

Step #4: Monitor, Adjust, and Reassess   Keep an eye on how these tools are doing. Tweak as needed. Integrating AI should be viewed as an ongoing process of enhancement, where the usage is continually evaluated and updated to meet emerging challenges and leverage new features.

Regularly assess your AI needs by going through the same approach again, at least yearly: identify, prioritize, and implement.

CHAPTER

9

Fostering Resilience and Adaptability in a Rapidly Evolving World

One consequence of AI's extensive use is the accelerating pace of change, bringing more uncertainty and frequent crises into our world. This tide brings a profound effect on our jobs, manifesting in stress, burnout, and depression. To thrive in this new world, this chapter will delve into resilience and adaptability, offering a framework to develop these crucial qualities in the AI era.

The Imperative of Resilience and Adaptability

Our world is progressing faster and faster! Is AI the cause of this?

We're not just experiencing change; we're living in an era of exponential growth, particularly in the realm of AI and technology. Put simply, within the next decade, we'll witness as many innovations as we did in the entire last century.[1]

Think about how, two decades ago, our office desks were cluttered with physical tools like calculators and journals. These tools have now transformed into sleek digital versions on our computers and smartphones. Remember when Apple launched its first iPhone in 2007? Fast-forward to today and an astounding 97% of Americans own a cell phone.

The technological revolution doesn't stop there. Virtual reality headsets, once a thing of sci-fi, are becoming mainstream, bringing AI and technology right before our eyes—literally! And it's becoming even more intimate with advancements in brain-computer interfaces. Merely think of sending flowers to your loved one and it'll be done instantly. This isn't a distant dream; it's an approaching reality that's possibly just a decade or two away.

Current technologies are not just developing swiftly, they are also merging, creating a powerful synergy that propels their advancement. At the epicenter of this technological whirlwind is AI. Each innovation amplifies the next. For example, more potent computers enable the crafting of advanced robots, which in turn leads to the creation of even more sophisticated machinery and so on. This interplay of technologies initiates a self-reinforcing cycle—accelerating progress at an unprecedented rate. This relentless surge has the potential to reshape, or even completely overhaul, whatever lies in the way.

What are the negative consequences of this exponential growth in technology?

Because of this increasing speed and the need to fuel it with energy and natural resources, economic and environmental crises are becoming more frequent. Globalization has intertwined our economies so tightly that a crisis in one corner of the world can send ripples across the globe. The rise and fall of industries has become more abrupt, shortening the lifespan of companies. Layoffs and job insecurity are becoming more common, and our environment is under duress, with climate change exacerbating natural disasters and health crises.

This whirlwind of progress comes at a cost—our mental well-being. Trying to keep pace with this rapid change is mentally exhausting. We're seeing an increase in stress, depression, and mental health issues. Americans' happiness was at a record low in 2022[2] and addiction rates are climbing by 4% yearly, now claiming 1 million lives every year. The level of stress has become so invasive and persistent that it has been dubbed the "health epidemic of the 21st century" by the World Health Organization.[3]

Another consequence is depression. The number of cases of depression worldwide increased by almost 50% from 1990 to 2017,[4] and it has become the leading cause of disability in the world. Consequently, suicide has become the 10th leading cause of death in the world.[5]

We're not just facing a technological revolution; we're in the midst of a mental health crisis.

In the face of these challenges, it's essential to build resilience and adaptability. Our brains, wired for a slower pace of life, are struggling to cope with the current rate of change. Building resilience and adaptability isn't just a recommendation; it's a necessity. These abilities are deeply rooted in our DNA, passed down from ancestors who faced their own set of challenges. To

> *"Our brains, wired for a slower pace of life, are struggling to cope with the current rate of change."*

thrive in the future, we must learn to harness these innate strengths, updating and deepening them to suit the demands of our time.

In the upcoming sections, I'll share practical solutions, practices, and insights to help you become more resilient and adaptable. We'll explore ways to thrive in this fast-paced world without succumbing to the stress that it brings.

The Art of Building Resilience

How can I become more resilient to the mental health challenges AI causes?

We often think being resilient means coping with challenges without any help. In reality, seeking support from others is a key aspect of building resilience. It involves knowing when to ask for help and drawing strength from your support network.

There's also a misconception that resilient people don't feel stress or sadness. On the contrary, resilience involves acknowledging and working through emotions, not suppressing them. It's about bouncing back from difficulties, not being unaffected by them.

And the speed of recovery doesn't necessarily indicate resilience. Sometimes, resilience means taking the time to understand and process what has happened and gradually finding a way forward.

What exactly is resilience?

Resilience is a dynamic process of personal development that enables individuals to maintain or regain their mental well-being in the face of obstacles, changes, or pressures. It's not about avoiding difficulties, but rather developing the strength and flexibility to deal with them effectively.

How can I build a stronger resilience to these rapid changes?

Let me share with you a personal lesson I learned about resilience. When I was 20 years old, I often went on backpacking and hitchhiking trips during my vacations, particularly in Africa. My goal was to meet new people, explore different cultures, and also learn more about myself. I liked to challenge myself by making these trips alone and with no money at all. These were deliberate choices that pushed me to fully immerse myself in the local culture.

During one of these trips, I had the privilege of meeting with the Tuaregs, a nomadic community of the Sahara Desert. The Tuaregs are certainly some of the most resilient people alive today. They have lived for centuries in one of the most inhospitable environments on Earth. Perhaps because of the harshness of the desert, the Tuaregs have developed unique mental adaptations to survive and thrive. They taught me how to transform anxiety and stress into a state of calm and excitement.

The Tuaregs introduced me to *In'Gall*, a Tuareg word translating to "peace" or "tranquility," a practice passed down for generations. This age-old practice is composed of three pillars.

Resilience Pillar #1: Breathe   The first pillar of In'Gall is breathing. The Tuaregs emphasize that the act of slow, conscious breathing can combat anxiety, boost clarity, and instill peace. As they say, "Just as your breath produces melodies from a flute, it equally plays a significant role in tuning the most valuable instrument you have: yourself." They revealed to me two ancestral practices: slowing down your breath to increase energy, and elongating the exhale to promote relaxation.

Slow, rhythmic breathing creates a calming rhythm within the body, manifesting as relaxation, mental clarity, and emotional balance. During anxious situations, our breath becomes shallow. By deliberately breathing deeply and slowly, we can counteract anxiety. In addition, emphasizing a long exhale stimulates the parasympathetic nervous system, promoting relaxation and cell repair. It also increases blood flow to the brain and boosts energy levels.

Later, I met with Dan Brule, a global breathwork expert, who confirmed the scientific validity of these practices. He also introduced me to *coherent breathing*, a six-second inhalation and six-second exhalation practice rooted in ancient rituals and now acknowledged by modern science for its therapeutic effects.

I have embedded these practices in my daily life to improve my capacity to manage challenges. I perform this exercise during specific moments of the day, such as when I face a contradiction in my life or work, or even when I have difficulty falling asleep. I also like to practice coherent breathing when I take the elevator, queue in a line, or drive. Embedding these exercises into my everyday life helped me to foster a sense of calm, focus, and resilience.

Resilience Pillar #2: Connect with Nature   The second pillar of In'Gall is connecting with our surroundings, especially nature. The Tuaregs believe that our well-being is intrinsically linked with nature. They find calm and clarity in understanding their environment, from spotting animals to deducing water sources based on vegetation. This intuitive knowingness helps them anticipate unexpected events and climatic changes, or sense danger.

Studies confirm that all humans possess a natural affinity toward nature, called "biophilia." This innate love for nature draws us to it—and nature has therapeutic effects. A mere 15-minute forest walk activates the parasympathetic nervous system, which subsequently activates rest and repair mechanisms. I spend some time every day walking or jogging in parks. I recommend you do the same; once you have started doing this, you'll find it is so energizing and relaxing that you can't stop doing it!

Resilience Pillar #3: Practice Mindfulness The third pillar of In'Gall consists of building a deeper layer of introspection. The Tuaregs compare thoughts and emotions to desert winds, emphasizing the importance of detached observation. This technique helps us understand that thoughts and emotions are transient experiences, not defining entities. It's vital to realize that not all thoughts are true; in fact, many are fabricated by our minds—especially the negative ones. When negative thoughts or emotions arise, notice them, but don't get stuck in them. Don't replay them over and over. And do not assume them to be true.

Modern science confirms that we experience over 4,000 thoughts per day, many of which are repetitive and stress-inducing. Practices like In'Gall or modern-world mindfulness are effective in stress reduction, and promoting calmness and emotional stability.

It is not easy to incorporate such practices into our busy daily lives, but it can be done with a little effort. I try to practice mindful transitions or incorporate them into small moments between my daily activities, such as walking from one room to another or waiting in line. During these transitions, I take the time to focus on my breath or bodily sensations. When walking between meetings, I pay attention to the sensation of my feet hitting the ground or the air on my skin. I use everyday activities as opportunities to practice mindfulness.

For example, I practice mindfulness while washing the dishes. I focus on the sensory experience of the task, like the warmth of the water on my hands and the sound of it flowing from the tap. I take note of the smell of soap and the texture of each dish and utensil and allow myself to feel a sense of accomplishment as I finish each one. Whenever my mind starts to wander, I gently bring my attention back to the sensations in front of me. This practice helps bring a sense of calm and relaxation to an otherwise mundane task. Incorporating this practice into my modern daily life has been transformative. It has recalibrated my cognitive and emotional responses, enhanced my decision-making, helped me conserve my energy, and unveiled hidden solutions.

As counterintuitive as it may sound, it's not only safe but necessary to relax and stay calm, especially as we progress toward an accelerated future. Whenever your inner critic tries to harm you, mindfulness helps you stay above it, no matter the strain you're under.

The Craft of Enhancing Adaptability

Why is it important to be adaptable?

Some people make adapting look so easy. But you can also learn to anticipate and prepare for change rather than reacting to it after the fact.

We often assume that adaptable people embrace change without any difficulty. In actuality, even adaptable people can find change challenging, but they have developed strategies to manage and work through these challenges effectively.

> *"In the age of AI, success isn't determined by strength or intelligence, but by one's capacity to adapt to change."*

Another misconception is that being adaptable means compromising your core values or principles. True adaptability is about finding flexible approaches to achieve goals even while staying true to your values.

Also, we often view adaptability as merely reacting to changes as they occur. However, being truly adaptable involves proactive thinking, anticipating changes, and preparing to handle them effectively.

In a world where change is constant and expanding in frequency and scale, we need to perceive these shifts as potential growth points, not just challenges. So, yes, as our future will bring more changes, this also means that it will bring more opportunities. And the larger the change, the larger the opportunity!

How would you define adaptability?

Adaptability is being able to adjust to new situations, environments, or changes quickly and efficiently. Essentially, adaptability is about thriving in a constantly evolving landscape, not just surviving. In the age of AI, success isn't determined by strength or intelligence, but by one's capacity to adapt to change.

Adaptability includes being proactive in anticipating changes and preparing for them, rather than merely reacting to them as they occur. Adaptability also means finding creative solutions within changing contexts, all while maintaining one's core values and principles.

For example, you might be a small business owner who anticipates a shift in market trends proactively and adapts by diversifying their product line, thereby not just weathering the change, but capitalizing on it. A truly adaptable person is able to turn a challenge into an opportunity.

How can I be more adaptable in an ever-changing world boosted by AI?

I will draw upon the lessons I learned from my time with the Tuaregs, as explained earlier in this chapter. Living in some of the harshest conditions in the world, the Tuaregs have developed an impressive level of adaptability, which we can use as a source of inspiration. The following are some key takeaways from my experience on this topic.

Trigger change in your life   The Tuareg habit of seeking change is remarkable because, in our society, we all think that being stable and not changing is the best way to be safe and successful.

The Tuaregs relocate their nomadic camps every few months, not due to necessity, but to keep their minds agile and avoid stagnation. They consider themselves "masters of their own destiny," actively initiating change instead of merely responding to circumstances. As their leader insightfully puts it, "When you trigger change, it rewards you." This philosophy holds that change not only prevents mental stagnation but also opens doors to new opportunities and experiences that would otherwise remain unseen in the monotony of routine.

In our lives, especially in an era dominated by rapid AI advancements, this approach is incredibly relevant. The recommendation is clear: don't wait for change to impose itself; rather, be the architect of your own change to stimulate progress and growth. Change before you have to change.

Personally, I've adopted the Tuaregs' philosophy of flexibility and mobility, moving my family across three continents over the last

15 years, from Paris to Shanghai, Singapore, San Francisco, and Miami. Each move opened new possibilities, enhancing our adaptability and cultural understanding, teaching us the value of proactively embracing change in an ever-evolving world.

Focus on potential gains My time with the Tuaregs revealed another unique approach to embracing change. When they decide to move their camps, a ritual known as *Tinariwen Chatter* plays a crucial role. In this gathering, the community collectively visualizes and discusses the potential benefits of their upcoming move. It's like flipping a mental switch, shifting focus from what might be lost to what could be gained. This practice lights up parts of the brain associated with positive emotions, steering the mind away from its default threat response.

Each person contributes their own anticipated benefits, whether it's a mother envisioning new resources for her baby, a young adult excited about meeting potential partners, or an elder looking forward to keeping their mind vibrant with new experiences. This group exercise in visualization ignites a wave of optimism, helping everyone to see the array of possibilities ahead. It counteracts the brain's natural tendency to fixate on potential losses and risks.

This ritual offers a powerful lesson for us: when facing changes, especially in our fast-paced, AI-driven world, we should consciously shift our focus. Instead of being bogged down by fears and potential losses, we should visualize the benefits and opportunities that change might bring. This balanced perspective of acknowledging both losses and gains can transform our approach to change, turning it from a source of anxiety into a wellspring of opportunity.

Celebrate adversity During my time with the Tuaregs, I learned how they transform adversity into strength. Like expert storytellers, they take past challenges, such as daunting sandstorms, and weave them into compelling tales of resilience, celebrated by all. These stories aren't just for entertainment; they serve a deeper purpose. Setbacks, like the fierce sandstorms, are reframed as learning experiences, each one a testament to resilience gained through hardship.

In this culture, discussing failures is not a taboo but a source of pride. At first, this was hard for me to conceptualize. In Western culture, displaying your failures is seen as a sign of weakness. But the Tuaregs take a view not dissimilar from the adage "What doesn't kill you makes you stronger," Overcoming adversity ultimately makes you stronger. Sharing hardships can be a communal activity where setbacks are dissected to extract valuable lessons. This practice fosters a unique kind of toughness, a concept I liken to "antifragility." It's the idea that they don't just endure or resist adversity; they grow stronger because of it, much like muscles that develop with exercise.

From this, I gleaned a powerful recommendation for anyone navigating the uncertainties of life. Adopt a growth mindset where setbacks are not seen as failures but as crucial feedback for improvement. Just as the Tuaregs find strength in their challenges, we too can learn to treat our setbacks as steppingstones to greater resilience and adaptability.

Together we are more adaptable   My experience with the Tuaregs illuminated the profound impact of communal unity in building adaptability. Their life is interwoven with shared meals, storytelling, singing, and rituals that reinforce a deep sense of community. This was vividly illustrated to me when a member's tent was lost to fire. In response, the entire community came together, not just to rebuild the physical structure but also to support the emotional recovery of the individual. This act was a beautiful embodiment of their collaborative spirit, highlighting how shared knowledge and mutual support can fortify resilience.

Contrary to our modern society, in this culture, insular mindsets have no place; instead, unity is the bedrock of their resilience. Collaboration is not just a practice but a way of life, allowing them to adapt through the synergies of diverse perspectives and experiences. It's like a tapestry where each thread contributes to a stronger, more vibrant whole.

There's a valuable lesson here for us, especially in a world in the midst of an AI revolution: the importance of investing in connections. Building strong networks and nurturing mutual support can significantly increase our collective and individual resilience, especially in the face of relentless change. Just as the Tuaregs find strength in their unity, we too can draw resilience from the rich tapestry of our interconnected lives.

In an era where technology and AI are rapidly changing the landscape of our lives, the Tuaregs' practices offer valuable lessons. The Tuaregs' adaptability is not just a survival mechanism; it's a way of life that celebrates the dynamic nature of existence. In a world that often fears change, their culture stands as a testament to the strength and resilience that can be found in embracing life's constant evolution.

Make sure you join the IRREPLACABLE Academy for additional expert recommendations, community sharing, and exercises to build up your resilience and adaptability (www.irreplaceable.ai).

CHAPTER

10

The Future of Work Is...No Work?

In the previous chapter, you explored the importance of resilience and adaptability in navigating the rapidly evolving world shaped by AI. These qualities are essential not only for your professional success but also for your personal well-being. However, the impact of AI on your working life goes beyond just requiring new skills and mindsets.

As AI takes over more and more tasks previously performed by humans, the very nature of work is being called into question. In this chapter, you'll confront a provocative question: Could the future of work be...no work at all? You'll explore the implications of this possibility and what it might mean for you, your family, and society as a whole.

Work Reimagined: Beyond the 9 to 5

If AI takes over repetitive tasks, could it lead to a shorter workweek?

Yes, in theory. As AI takes over more routine and repetitive tasks, and if we only focus on tasks connected to our Humics—our uniquely human abilities—it could lead to a scenario where our kids need to work fewer hours. This scenario could mean that they would all work less, or that only a few would still need to work while the others could be freed from working.

This concept ties into the argument for a shorter workweek, where productivity gained from technology should allow people to maintain a similar standard of living while working less. Hence, I believe AI gives us a precious opportunity to reconsider our relationship with work.

What do you mean by reconsidering our relationship with work?

What's the goal of school? At its core, school is preparing kids for work. But why do we all need to work? Well, to live in today's world, everyone needs to earn money for food, a place to live, and other basics. But there's more to it. We, as a society, really value being busy and productive. It's a big part of what we think makes life meaningful.

> *"Humans have spent less than 5% of their existence engaging in what we today consider work. Work is a recent invention."*

However, this love for work isn't something we're born with. How do we know? Just look at young kids, say between 5 and 10 years old. They often wonder "Why do I need to work?" This question pops up because they haven't yet learned to value work the way adults do. It's a sign that our drive to work all day isn't natural but something we pick up as we grow, influenced by the world around us.

Indeed, as we grow older, many of us start to conflate who we are with our jobs. When we meet someone new, we often ask, "What do you do?" and based on their answer, we form opinions about them. Our jobs become a big part of who we are and our goals in life. This idea starts when we're young, with adults asking us, "What do you want to be when you grow up?" or saying, "You need good grades for a good career."

In my view, work should not be as central in our lives. As *Homo sapiens*, we have spent less than 5% of our existence engaging in what we today consider work. Work is a recent invention. There is nothing intrinsic about humans that demands they work. Or at least not the cubicle version of it!

I would say that the fact that AI can perform more and more of the work tasks currently performed by humans represents an opportunity for humans to build a new, more humane society. A potential society freed from what we today call "work," embracing a new culture focused on human values and respecting the environment.

The Current World of Work Sucks!

Work is embedded into our culture; why should we change it?

Let's be honest; much of today's work sucks.

Unfortunately, not everyone has the opportunity to work in a job that aligns with their passions. Many people find themselves in roles that don't utilize their full potential or provide a sense of accomplishment, leading to feelings of stagnation or lack of purpose.

One-third of a person's life is spent at work,[1] yet 85% of workers across the globe report that they don't find their work engaging. They report that it is too repetitive and not fulfilling.[2]

It is easy to understand. Spending every day of the week performing repetitive tasks like keying in invoices must be a soul-draining experience. In the United States alone, there are today more than 1.5 million clerks performing bookkeeping, accounting, and auditing.

In addition, many jobs are associated with high levels of stress due to tight deadlines, pressure to perform, long hours, or challenging workloads. Chronic stress leads to serious health issues, including mental health problems like anxiety and depression. In addition, the pursuit of career success often comes at the expense of personal and family time. This imbalance can strain relationships, reduce overall life satisfaction, and lead to burnout.

Not only is most of today's work frustrating, but it is also dangerous. Worldwide, the International Labour Organization (ILO) reports that stress, overly long work hours, and resulting illnesses lead to almost 2.8 million worker fatalities annually, imposing a societal cost of around $3 trillion each year.[3] For reference, this is double the deaths from road accidents[4] and 14 times the deaths from war![5] These are staggering numbers. We don't want our kids to inherit a world where their work feels meaningless and negatively impacts their health.

If these tasks are automated by AI, that would free our kids to focus on more human-centric activities that add value to their lives.

The idea of reducing work hours or reshaping the concept of work is partly to address these issues. It's about creating an environment where people have more time and energy to pursue interests and relationships that contribute to their overall well-being and happiness, beyond their professional identity.

It also opens up the possibility for people to engage in work that is more fulfilling and aligned with their personal values and interests, even if it doesn't fully sustain their lifestyle. Without the need to train for jobs that may no longer exist by the time they graduate, students would be free to explore, pursue their passions, and focus on finding and achieving their personal purpose.

Young adults who are part of the Gen Y and Z generations already exhibit a different approach to work and life, prioritizing balance, fulfillment, and alignment with personal values over traditional career paths.

In essence, the conversation isn't just about working less; it's about fostering a society where work is more meaningful, balanced, and conducive to overall well-being.

Have there already been attempts to try to reduce work?

Yes, many. And the concept of diminishing, transforming, or eliminating work altogether isn't a novel one. In his 1930 essay, "Economic Possibilities for Our Grandchildren," economist John Maynard Keynes envisioned a future with significantly less work. He forecasted that by the 21st century, our working time would be cut to 15-hour workweeks, not even two full days of work by today's standards for the 21st century. "For the first time since his creation, man will be faced with his real, his permanent problem: how to use his freedom from pressing economic cares, how to occupy the leisure, which science and compound interest will have won for him, to live wisely and agreeably and well."

Keynes isn't alone. Jack Ma pointed out in a public debate from August 2019 that the invention of electricity led to drastically increased leisure time for individuals. He argued that thanks to AI, the workweek could be reduced to a mere three days, with only four hours of work per day![6]

Actually, the transition to reduced workweeks, driven by technological advancements, is already underway. This shift could begin as early as school. In Poland, some school districts are experimenting with a four-day school week, where the fifth day is dedicated to nontraditional learning experiences, such as visiting a science center, taking a walk in the forest, or learning a craft.[7]

In Japan, authorities are encouraging businesses to give employees Monday mornings off, while in the UK, the Trades Union Congress (TUC) advocates for a shift to a four-day workweek.[8]

An increasing number of progressive companies and schools are adopting this model, recognizing that less time spent working or studying leads to healthier, more productive students and workers. Additionally, such policies have been linked to better talent recruitment, enhanced gender equality, and overall improved performance.

In 2019, the New Zealand–based firm Perpetual Guardian trialed a 32-hour workweek for its 240 employees, who worked eight hours less without a salary reduction. The staff experienced decreased stress levels and heightened engagement with the company. Remarkably, productivity surged by 30–40%, as employees enhanced their time management skills, conducted more concise meetings, and indicated times when they preferred not to be interrupted.[9]

I strongly suggest checking out the book *The 4 Day Week*, where entrepreneur and business innovator Andrew Barnes delves into the concept with a deep and compelling understanding, drawing on successful experiments from around the world.

Envisioning a World Without Work

What would a world without work look like?

The societal value of a job doesn't always translate to high pay. While raising children and caring for others seem to be some of the most essential social occupations today, this type of work is compensated poorly or more often not at all. The redefinition of work is an opportunity to change this reality.

With AI taking our jobs, we could build a society where people spend more time caring for their families and communities. Our pride could come from our relationships and our children's fulfillment, rather than from our careers.

Uncommon as the idea is, intellectual discourse around freeing society from what we call "work" today isn't new. David Graeber, Helen Hester, Nick Srnicek, Benjamin Hunnicutt, Peter Fleming, and others are part of a group called the "post-workists." They believe that the automation of people's work by machines and the human impact on the environment will force a drastic rethink of society, especially how we approach work.

As a result, society will need a transformational redefinition of work. The possible benefits are limitless. A life that's more equal, calmer, more unified, more politically engaged, and simply more fulfilled in general. Our human experience could be completely transformed.

If we work less or not at all, what would we do?

Instead of working, our kids or grandkids might spend their time on more purposeful occupations like taking care of others and taking care of the planet.

If work hours were reduced significantly or if people didn't need to work in the traditional sense, it would open up a multitude of possibilities for how individuals could spend their time. The shift would likely lead to a reevaluation of what's considered important and fulfilling in life. Here are some ways our kids might choose to use their time:

- More free time would allow individuals to explore and invest in their interests, whether that's art, music, sports, gardening, or any other hobby that brings joy and fulfillment. Some might use the extra time to embark on creative or entrepreneurial projects, turning passions into potential new sources of income or innovation.

- Without the constraints of a nine-to-five schedule, individuals could dedicate time to learning new skills, languages, or subjects they're curious about, fostering a culture of continuous personal growth. This could enable individuals to travel more, explore new cultures, and gain a broader perspective on life.

- People might choose to invest their time in giving back to the community, whether through volunteering, mentoring, or participating in local initiatives, thereby strengthening social bonds and community cohesion.

- With more time available, individuals could prioritize their physical and mental health through exercise, meditation, cooking nutritious meals, and other wellness practices.

- More free time would provide opportunities to deepen relationships with family and friends, allowing people to nurture their social lives and create lasting memories. As mentioned by Kai-Fu Lee, a leading computer scientist and writer, the freedom that we gain thanks to AI will allow us to "focus on what truly makes us human: loving and being loved."

It's worth noting that the transition to less work or different types of work would require a significant change of mindset, redefining what it means to live a fulfilling life.

The possibilities are limitless! To draw a parallel with history, thanks to automation reducing the need for long, grueling workdays, the Industrial Revolution saw the amount of time available for rest and leisure dramatically increase. New cinemas were constructed, music and theater flourished, and entirely new forms of art and entertainment were invented. AI will likely bring the same opportunities, both in the expansion of leisure time, and the development of new methods of entertainment and learning.

With fewer people needing to go to offices, there's potential to repurpose these spaces into community hubs equipped with libraries, places to play, art studios, affordable homes, community daycares, and more. There could be spaces for computer work, science experiments, and making videos and music.

The absence of "work," as we define it today does not mean that capitalism will end or that our economic world will collapse. The economy will, in all likelihood, keep growing as machines take over and streamline much of the work, in turn giving us more time to relax and buy things. As Henry Ford said in a 1924 issue of *World's Work*, "Leisure is an indispensable ingredient in a growing consumer market because working people need to have enough free time to find uses for consumer products, including automobiles."

If we don't work anymore, how would we earn our living?

We need to implement mechanisms to equally distribute the wealth created by AI.

The way people are compensated for work today is unfair. This is something that has always shocked me. Whether it's the childcare example earlier, or teachers' salaries, or those of police officers, it seems that you don't have to look hard to find an instance where the value of the job isn't properly matched by its pay.

One way to solve this is to provide universal compensation despite the nature of the work people perform. As AI creates more value, let us share this value equally amongst people. We can do this by demanding governments ensure that the new wealth created by technology is distributed and shared equally amongst people.

Wealth-sharing mechanisms like Universal Basic Income (UBI) aim to provide everyone with a basic income, whether or not they are in paid employment. In simple terms, every adult citizen would receive a lump sum of money from the government every year, with parents receiving some amount extra to cover their children.

This money would be enough to cover necessities like rent and food, or at least a large chunk of those expenses. In theory, this would lift everyone out of poverty by ensuring a minimum standard of living. UBI would also help relieve people from the necessity of working to earn their living and let them choose freely what and how they want to contribute to society.

We need to start preparing society for that scenario as soon as possible. UBI or similar mechanisms are potential solutions, guaranteeing a minimum standard of living regardless of working status.

We don't want a future where any of our kids are left behind. We must make our future as inclusive as possible.

PART

IV

Raising IRREPLACEABLE Kids and Protecting Yourself

As you've seen in the previous parts, being IRREPLACEABLE is crucial in our personal and professional lives. But for many of us, our most important role is being a parent. In this part, you'll turn your attention to raising children in the age of AI. You'll explore how to protect them—and yourself—from the potential pitfalls of AI, while also harnessing its benefits. It is about preparing yourself and the next generation for an AI-driven world.

CHAPTER

11

Educating Future-Proof Minds in the Age of AI

As AI transforms the world around us, the skills and knowledge needed to succeed are evolving at an unprecedented pace. In this chapter, you'll explore how to educate children to thrive in the age of AI, breaking down outdated education models and introducing new strategies for future-proofing young minds.

Raising Children to Thrive with AI

Can current education systems prepare students for the new challenges and opportunities of AI?

Let's be clear: the future doesn't give a damn about your child's diploma or how high they score on an IQ test. The future belongs to the IRREPLACEABLE—those who think and feel, not those who just process and memorize.

The truth slaps hard: Information retrieval? AI's got it. Routine tasks, calculations? Covered by algorithms. Critical thinking, creativity, empathy, ethical judgment—the real human currency in an

> *"The future belongs to the IRREPLACEABLE— those who think and feel, not those who just process and memorize."*

AI-dominated world—are sidelined for the sake of standardized test scores. We're just prepping kids for a race against machines that is already lost.

Why are we programming our youth for a world of automation, for jobs that will vanish into the AI abyss? To maintain a status quo that benefits the few? We're not just failing our kids; we're setting them up for a fall in a world that craves not what they can memorize, but what they can create, question, and innovate.

It's time to overthrow the educational status quo. We must revolutionize our approach to education. It's imperative to teach the basics, but equally crucial to transcend them, to imbue our teaching with the creativity, problem-solving, and ethical reasoning that will define the IRREPLACEABLE humans of the future.

What should we teach our kids?

You've probably heard of instances of students using ChatGPT to do their homework. As a consequence, some schools have decided to ban ChatGPT, and many others are considering doing the same.

Will ChatGPT bans work, though? Bans didn't work when math teachers tried to prohibit calculators in 1988, and they won't work now. These tools are here to stay. Banning them will only encourage undesirable behaviors.

Instead of banning AI tools, let's teach our kids how to critically review the outcomes provided by these tools, question them, and check the validity of the information provided by AI. Let's train our children on how to assess the fairness of AI, as well as the understandability and usefulness of its outcomes.

We should also change the way we teach. For instance, instead of assigning traditional homework that students might inadvertently complete using ChatGPT, ask them to use ChatGPT purposely. They can prepare a work with ChatGPT and bring it back the next day.

Then use class time to discuss the work, teaching students how to question, criticize, and review it. Additionally, if the task is to build a presentation or a poem, teach kids about the limits of AI and explain how to infuse their own nuanced human touch into the final outcome.

It boils down to this: If ChatGPT is able to pass the most complex exams such as the bar exam or medical exams, where is the value in teaching students to do the same thing, but less efficiently? We have to change what we teach and how we teach. Specifically, we must teach them the Three Competencies of the Future, as discussed in Chapter 3. We need to be able to apply this knowledge with critical thinking and creativity. Instead of teaching children how to use tools in isolation, we should encourage them to tackle problems using a variety of disciplines, like math or economics. This method is not only more engaging but also more enriching, offering real-world applications of theoretical knowledge.

Furthermore, gamifying the learning process can significantly enhance engagement. The human brain is naturally inclined to play games, finding enjoyment and motivation in the process. If we can apply this inherent desire to the way knowledge is taught, transforming learning into a gamified experience, we tap into a powerful method of education that aligns with our natural inclinations.

Finally, understanding the "why" behind the information is essential because our brains are designed to conserve energy by discarding what they deem irrelevant. To prevent this natural forgetting process, it's important to make learning meaningful. This involves clearly explaining the importance and relevance of the knowledge we acquire, instead of using punishment as a deterrent for forgetting.

What can we do to transform our education system?

Today, most schooling has a career-oriented bent, as many schools simply teach the skills they expect students will need in order to earn a salary. Sadly, this evolution toward trade-oriented education is a trend I expect will continue. There needs to be a review of the purpose of education.

The word *school* actually comes from *skholē*, the Greek word for "leisure" or "rest." The origin and implications of the word were focused on thoughtful reflection, discussion, and tentatively providing answers to "How should we best enjoy our life?" Education originally aimed to guide people in finding their purpose in life. The origins of education give us a clue as to how it must transform into a collaborative effort to build understanding and find our purpose in life.

Another key opportunity is to infuse the Three Competencies of the Future into schools' curriculums. Some countries have already started this approach:

- Finland—often an innovator in education—has reviewed its education system and introduced significant changes that could become a model worth watching. Traditional subjects at school are complemented by the four Cs: communication, collaboration, creativity, and critical thinking.[1] Other similar projects are ongoing in Singapore and the United Arab Emirates.

- Another example is Denmark's education system, which has taught empathy to students since 1993. The national curriculum requires one hour of empathy-building each week for students aged 6 to 16. This hour is called *Klassens Tid*, or class time, and is as important as other classes like math or English.[2]

But to be really efficient, I think we need an even more radical change. For example, the "high school movement" in the United States stands as one of the most successful initiatives undertaken by the US government, transforming education between 1910 and 1940. This widespread educational reform aimed to address a burgeoning "skills gap" as the demand for educated workers in new white-collar positions surged. To elevate educational standards, schooling until the age of 16 was mandated across the nation.[3]

The impact was remarkable—enrollment of 15- to 18-year-olds in high schools jumped from just 18% in 1910 to 73% by 1940, with the majority of young Americans earning a diploma. Most economists believe this substantial investment in education was crucial for equipping the workforce with essential skills, thereby creating the most efficient labor force in the world.

Governments globally should initiate a similar educational revolution tailored to the skill requirements of the AI era. This time, the transformation should extend beyond school-aged children to also include adults in the workforce, regardless of their age.

Teaching Our Kids How to Relearn

In the new era of AI, why do we need to excel at learning?

As you saw in Part 3 of the book, boosted by the advancements in AI and other technologies, the world is progressing at a faster pace. This impacts every component of our lives, including the skills we must possess.

A report by the World Economic Forum states that the "half-life" of a competency, once estimated at 10 to 15 years, has decreased to 5 years, and continues to decrease.[4] According to the half-life concept, if you master a specific computer programming language now, in five years, half of what you have learned will no longer be as applicable due to advancements in technology or changes in industry practices.

And most of the future competencies are not even known today. A report from the Institute for the Future projects that 85% of the competencies that will exist in 2030 haven't been invented yet, suggesting a necessity for continuous learning of new competencies.

Since AI is better than us at memorizing and managing knowledge, do we still need to learn anything?

While AI excels in memorizing and managing large amounts of data, there are still many reasons why learning remains essential for us, now more than ever.

Human memory is not just about storing and retrieving data. Unlike a computer, we have the ability to connect pieces of information in a complex and meaningful way. We can understand the information, relate it to what we already know, create new interpretations, and use those interpretations to solve problems.

We use what we learn to nourish our Humics such as our genuine creativity, critical thinking, and social authenticity. For example, learning exposes you to a wide range of ideas, cultures, and disciplines. This diversity sparks creative thinking by allowing you to make unique connections between seemingly unrelated concepts. Also, learning about different cultures, histories, and social dynamics increases your ability to empathize and understand others' viewpoints, enhancing interpersonal relationships.

The ability to learn is one of the most critical competencies we possess. And not only learning, but unlearning and relearning, too!

What do you mean by relearning and unlearning?

Adaptation is a process of unlearning and relearning. *Relearning* is the process of learning again something that you have forgotten or acquiring competencies in a new way or context. Usually, relearning follows *unlearning*—replacing the old with the new.

The future demands us to continually update our knowledge. It's like being on a treadmill that keeps going faster—we have to keep moving, or we'll fall behind. This constant relearning is the new norm in our fast-paced world. Mastering the skill of learning—learning how to learn—is an invaluable investment in our future.

In the context of skills of the future, the cycle of unlearning and relearning is essential. This cycle allows us to relearn and absorb new information, competencies, and mindsets that are more pertinent and effective in the current and future context.

What are some techniques to help me and my kids learn faster and better?

A few years ago, at a conference, I met Dr. Terrence Sejnowski, a professor of biology and neurosciences at the University of California, San Diego. He co-created one of the most popular open online courses on Coursera, "Learning How to Learn," with Dr. Barbara Oakley.

When I asked him how brains learn, he explained to me that learning is complex because brains physically change as they learn. Important changes take place, such as new connections between neurons—what we call *neuroplasticity*.

The more one practices a skill, the stronger these neural connections become. That is how you become better at anything—whether it's playing football, reading, or drawing. As the neural connection strengthens, the messages—nerve impulses—are transmitted increasingly faster, making them more effortless.

A similar process occurs in the brain—when you stop practicing a skill, the connections between neurons weaken and are eventually dismantled. This is why it can be challenging to speak a foreign language after not using it for some time. Nevertheless, with enough practice, some pathways can become so robust that the connections never entirely fade away. For instance, you can still ride a bike or drive a car even if you haven't practiced for a while.

According to Dr. Sejnowski, the following strategies are key for effective and fast learning:

- **Spaced repetition:** Regularly review the information you want to learn at spaced intervals. This practice reinforces the neural connections associated with that information, increasing recall ability. This principle can be applied to any type of learning, like language learning. Instead of cramming many words in one session, it may be more effective to practice a few words each day but revisit the old ones regularly. The repetition of the old, Sejnowski assured, deeply engraves the new language in your brain.

- **Emotional involvement:** The hippocampus, our brain's central hub for memory, prioritizes information based on emotional relevance and novelty. We can improve memory retention by creating emotional connections with what we're learning. "Without an emotional bond," Sejnowski clarified, "the probability of retaining new knowledge considerably diminishes." He drew an analogy with the experience of watching a film. A heart-wrenching moment or an exhilarating action sequence tends to captivate our attention more than a quiet dialogue scene, doesn't it? This is because these scenes stir our emotions, making the scene more memorable. Similarly, when we find ways for new material to stir our emotions, it's more likely for the brain to retain such information.

- **Interleaved practice:** Practice is a learning technique where instead of focusing on one type of problem or topic for an extended period, you mix different types of problems or subjects in a single study session. This approach contrasts with the more traditional method of learning where you might concentrate on one type of problem (e.g., multiplication problems in math) until you move on to the next (e.g., division). Interleaved practice mixes in the different types of problems in the same study session, encouraging the brain to adapt and learn more effectively. The brain learns better with interleaved practice because it prevents mental stagnation on a single topic, forcing the brain to constantly switch gears and apply different strategies. This strengthens neural connections by promoting deeper learning and better memory retention. It's akin to a workout routine where you vary your exercises to target different muscle groups, leading to a more comprehensive form of training.

- **Storytelling:** Weaving concepts into stories can make them more engaging and memorable. This is an effective teaching tool due to our brain's natural affinity for narratives. "Our brains love stories," Sejnowski affirmed, citing research by Paul Zak and Judy Robertson.[5] "It's a legacy from our ancestors, who communicated their knowledge through storytelling." If you're teaching a concept— say, photosynthesis—try weaving it into a story. You'll be surprised how much more engaging and memorable it becomes.

- **Active learning:** Active engagement with the material, such as explaining it in your own words, strengthens neural pathways. "You could read the text, watch videos, and listen to lectures," Sejnowski explained, "but nothing is as effective as explaining it in your own words."

- **Sleep:** When preparing for exams, it might seem beneficial to cut down on sleep to increase study time, but the opposite is true. Adequate sleep is essential for learning and memory. It lowers stress hormones and supports the growth of new nerve cells, crucial for absorbing and retaining information. Skimping on sleep can actually hinder your ability to remember what you've studied. So prioritizing sleep is not just about rest; it's a strategic move to enhance learning efficiency and improve exam performance.

Understanding how our brains acquire knowledge can make learning more efficient and rewarding. Learning, as Dr. Sejnowski suggests, is both an art and a science.

Helping Our Kids to Grow with AI

Should I forbid my kids from using screens except for homework?

If your kids, like many, spend a lot of time watching shows, playing games, scrolling social media, and texting their friends, you know the time in front of a screen can add up. Should you ban the use of screens altogether? Let's talk about that extreme view:

- **Overprotection may hinder learning:** While it's natural to want to shield children from potential risks, overly restricting their access to technology can prevent them from developing critical digital literacy skills necessary in today's tech-driven world.

- **Strict bans are ineffective:** Completely banning screen time or gaming can be counterproductive, leading to increased curiosity and secretive behavior. Moderation and guidance are more effective than outright bans.

- **Mistakes can be educational:** Allowing children to make mistakes, like trusting unreliable AI-generated information, can be valuable learning experiences. Guided discussions about these errors can enhance their critical thinking and discernment skills.

- **AI can encourage socialization, not just isolation:** Contrary to the belief that AI leads to antisocial behavior, certain AI applications can promote social interaction. For example, AI-driven educational games can encourage teamwork and collaboration among peers.

- **Screen time isn't inherently bad:** The quality of screen time matters more than quantity. Not all screen time is detrimental. Educational content, creative apps, and interactive games can be beneficial. It's more about the quality of content and how it's used than the mere fact of screen usage. Engaging with AI in creative or educational activities can be more beneficial than traditional passive screen activities like watching TV.

- **Video games aren't purely negative:** Many believe video games offer no value, but they can improve cognitive skills, problem-solving, hand-eye coordination, and even social abilities in multiplayer settings.[6] In fact, many games also foster community and collaboration.

So how should I parent in today's AI world?

Richard Ryan and Edward Deci stand as towering figures in psychological research; their work on the self-determination theory has been heralded as a cornerstone of understanding human motivation. Since the 1970s, their groundbreaking insights have illuminated the essence of psychological well-being.

They've compellingly argued that just as the body craves its vital macronutrients—proteins, carbohydrates, and fats—the human psyche craves a trifecta of psychological needs: autonomy, competence, and relatedness. Deprivation of any of these fundamental psychological nutrients triggers inner turmoil, manifesting as anxiety and restlessness, a cry from the soul for what it lacks.

When children suffer a deficit in these crucial nutrients, Ryan and Deci's theory predicts a propensity to sink into excessive, unhealthy behaviors, like the digital quagmire of screen addiction. Ryan posits that the lure of such distractions is less about the allure of the devices themselves and more a symptom of an underlying hunger for those elements that invigorate the human spirit.

As parents, the most important thing we can do is to involve the child in the conversation and help them set their own rules. When parents impose limits without their kids' input, they are setting them up to be resentful and incentivizing them to cheat the system. It's only when kids can monitor their own behavior that they learn the skills they need to be IRREPLACEABLE—even when their parents aren't around. We can help our kids to balance their AI interaction and to self-regulate by performing the following actions.

Boosting autonomy   Instead of micromanaging how kids use AI, give them some control. Let them set their own—reasonable—limits and have a say in when and how they use technology. This way, they're learning to self-regulate instead of just following orders. Here are a few steps I recommend you perform with your kids:

- Sit down with your kids and discuss screen time limits or internet usage rules. Let them have a say in what they think is reasonable.

This dialogue can lead to them taking ownership of their decisions. This may lead to different rules for different kids in the same household, and that's okay! Every child is different and will need a personalized approach to reach their full potential.

- Explain to your kids that video games or social media are designed by really smart people who make them super-engaging on purpose. Children need to know why game companies and social networks do this—they're selling fun and connection, sure, but they're also making money off of our time and attention.

- Teach your kids how to monitor their own screen time. Many devices have built-in monitoring systems that allow users to track usage. Review these stats with your kids weekly so they can self-regulate.

- Introduce them to educational apps and websites, then allow them to choose which ones they'd like to use. This not only gives them autonomy but also directs their screen time toward learning.

- Collaboratively decide on certain areas of the home or times of day that will be tech-free. For example, during dinner or an hour before bedtime could be screen-free times, which they help to choose and enforce.

- If they don't stick to the agreed-upon rules, have predetermined consequences that they're aware of. It's important for them to understand that autonomy comes with responsibility.

Fostering competence   Get your kids involved in tech creation, not just consumption. Instead of viewing screens as a mere distraction, guide your child to use AI and technology to learn new skills. Encourage them to learn coding, design, or any other behind-the-scenes skills. Teach them the positive and negative aspects of tech, so they can consume more thoughtfully. This builds their confidence and understanding of tech, and they might just become the creators of the next big thing!

Here are a few activities I perform with my kids:

- Work with your children to set specific, achievable goals related to technology, like learning to program a simple game or creating a website. Celebrate these achievements to reinforce their sense of competence.

- When your child encounters a problem with technology, guide them through solving it themselves instead of stepping in to fix it. This might involve trying to install a new app on their tablet or troubleshooting why a device isn't working.

- Teach your kids about the tricks technology platforms use, such as notifications designed to capture and hold our attention. It's important for them to recognize these distractions and how they impact their focus and well-being. Additionally, help them understand the significance of data privacy and the potential biases in the algorithms that shape their online experiences. Encourage projects that require a combination of tech skills. For instance, they could create a video documentary, which involves researching, scripting, filming, and editing.

A child's readiness for technology can be gauged by their ability to understand and use device settings, like turning off notifications by themselves. This shows they are becoming more mature and responsible in using digital devices.

Strengthening human bonds   Try engaging with your child's digital activities. Play an AI-based game together, or watch and discuss an educational program. This not only strengthens your bond but also integrates their digital experiences into family life.

Use technology as a tool for connection, not isolation. Find apps and games that you can enjoy together as a family or that help your kids stay connected to friends and relatives. When tech brings us together, it's doing something right.

While some parents don't want to engage in online activities, afraid that it will encourage kids to go online more often, I think it is healthy to show genuine interest in your child's life, both online and offline. Listen to their experiences, thoughts, and feelings without judgment. This builds trust and a sense of emotional safety.

By focusing on these psychological "nutrients," parents can help their kids develop a healthier, more empowered relationship with AI, one where they're using it in ways that are fulfilling and beneficial, rather than as a digital pacifier.

CHAPTER

12

Navigating AI Distractions

AI is getting closer, learning more about us, and offering incredible convenience. But with that comes the power to influence us and the rise of AI-induced distractions. From personalized streaming recommendations to targeted social media ads, AI algorithms are constantly vying for our attention and undermining our performance, mental health, and quality of life. Our children are often the true victims. In this chapter, you'll explore strategies to cut through the distractions, regain focus, and achieve inner peace for our kids and ourselves.

The Rise of AI-Induced Distractions

How do AI distractions impact the daily lives
of our kids and ourselves?

AI can teach us, entertain us, and connect us to the world. But just as a sharp knife can cause harm if handled carelessly, these tools can also cause harm if not used wisely.

One of the challenges caused by AI is the distraction it generates in our lives. Via our devices, AI anticipates our needs, curates our interests, and subtly nudges our behaviors. It suggests the next video to watch, the next article to read, or the next product to buy, constantly fueling our appetite for more. This isn't passive consumption; our devices are active participants, using sophisticated algorithms to catch and keep our attention.

With AI, our phones learn from us—our habits, our preferences, our interests. And then advertising companies can use this knowledge to try to sell us products or services by customizing the message to us.

For example, say you're shopping online for a pair of shoes. A few hours later, as you're doing research for your work on the internet, you're suddenly distracted by ads for similar shoes. AI uses our online activities to target advertising, constantly bombarding us with items it thinks we'd like to buy.

Why are AI and technology companies embedding AI-induced distractions into their products?

Nowadays, most digital platforms have made our attention their product.

The logic is simple: the more time you spend on apps and digital platforms, the higher the chances you'll click on an advertisement. Each click generates revenue for the platform and increases the likelihood of products being sold.

For example, when Coca-Cola places an ad on Facebook, they pay a fee for every click their ad receives. Consequently, the longer you linger on Facebook, the more ads you're exposed to, potentially clicking on them and thereby boosting Facebook's earnings.

This scenario creates a win-win situation for both Facebook and Coca-Cola. Facebook benefits from increased ad revenue, while Coca-Cola enjoys greater visibility for its products, raising the chances of a purchase. This cycle underscores why these platforms are so invested in keeping you engaged for as long as possible.

To illustrate just how much money is at stake here, in 2023, Google made more than $300 million in revenue and 80% of that came from advertising.[1] Distraction isn't just a side effect; it's the business model.

The Roots of AI Distractions

Why are we so susceptible to AI distractions?

The psychology behind why AI can be particularly distracting lies in its ability to tap into our basic human instincts—the fear of missing out, curiosity, and social connection. AI-driven platforms, with their endless streams of content and notifications, exploit these instincts, keeping us engaged but also incessantly distracted.

The fear of missing out   First, let's talk about the fear of missing out—FOMO. We humans, since the time of our caveman ancestors, have had this urge to know everything that's happening around us. Back in the day, it was about survival. For example, knowing you had to avoid that lake where a group of lions comes every day to drink would save your life.

Today, by tracking our activity across various platforms, AI can determine which topics, events, and conversations are trending within our social circles. It then prioritizes this content in our feeds, notifications, and recommendations, ensuring that we don't miss out on what's popular or relevant. For example, if many of your friends are talking about a particular news story or event, AI will make sure that this content appears prominently in your feed. By exploiting our FOMO, AI keeps us constantly checking our devices and engaging with digital content.

The attraction for novelty   Second, as humans, we seek out novelty, specifically new experiences or items. This was also a survival instinct once upon a time, helping our ancestors discover new resources or opportunities. It was critical to try new fruits or develop new hunting methods to keep the tribe fed.

Today, by constantly analyzing our browsing habits, search queries, and content consumption patterns AI predicts what new content is likely to pique our curiosity and keep us engaged. For example, if you've been reading articles about a particular hobby, AI will suggest related topics or emerging trends that align with it, satisfying your craving for novelty. This personalized approach to content curation ensures that there's always something new and exciting to capture our attention, making it difficult to resist.

Craving for social connections   Then there's our social nature. We humans are social creatures. We thrive on connection, on knowing what's going on in each other's lives. This is especially true for teenagers, whose mental well-being is more dependent on their place in a social hierarchy than it is for adults. This sociality was crucial for survival back when we lived in tribes.

Nowadays, AI algorithms are constantly analyzing our social media interactions, including likes, comments, and shares. By identifying the people we engage with most frequently and the types of content we tend to interact with, AI can create a detailed map of our social connections and preferences. This data is then used to prioritize content from our closest friends and family in our feeds, ensuring that we don't miss out on important social updates. Moreover, AI can suggest new connections based on our existing network and shared interests, further enhancing our sense of social connectedness. By tailoring our social media experiences to our unique social needs, AI keeps us coming back for more, effectively capturing our attention.

What are the consequences of this AI distraction?

As AI creates increasing mental distractions, the impact on our capacity to focus can be disastrous. We have all experienced going on the web to search for a piece of information and ending up losing two hours to mindless scrolling, being distracted in our research by news feeds, advertisements, or appealing social media posts.

Chores get forgotten; homework is left undone. Classwork suffers. The distractions caused by AI can severely affect an individual's career or education as people spend their time engaging in a haze of digital usage rather than focusing on school- or work-related tasks. As a result, people procrastinate, lose time, avoid work, or burn out. And that's the least of it. Here are other consequences from AI distractions:

- **On productivity:** Continuous interruptions fragment our concentration, making deep work and creativity increasingly elusive. The cost is not just in time lost but in the quality and innovation of what we can produce. Studies have shown that it takes an average of 23 minutes to refocus on a task after an interruption, highlighting the significant impact of these distractions on our ability to concentrate and perform effectively.

- **On mental health:** The endless stream of notifications, updates, and personalized content can take a toll on our mental well-being. FOMO and the pressure to stay connected can contribute to feelings of anxiety, stress, and even depression, leaving us feeling overwhelmed and drained.

- **On social and family life:** The quality of our interactions diminishes in the shadow of digital intrusions, eroding the depth and authenticity of our relationships.

Ultimately, these distractions can cause even more critical damage than that. Between 2012 and 2019, in the US alone, more than 26,000 people died in crashes involving distracted drivers.[2]

The issue will become more prevalent as our devices bring AI closer to us, and AI becomes more and more intelligent, knowing us better and learning how best to distract us.

Strategies to Mitigate AI Distractions

How can I identify these distractions in my daily life?

These distractions have become so deeply integrated into our daily routines that we barely notice them anymore; they feel normal. Hence, despite their negative effects on our lives, we often fail to recognize them as problems.

Recognizing these distractions requires a mindful audit of our interaction patterns with technology. By tracking the time spent on various platforms and noting the frequency and nature of interruptions, you can begin to identify patterns of distraction.

This audit is the first step toward regaining control over our digital environments and ensuring that our engagement with AI aligns with our personal and professional goals, rather than detracting from them. First, conduct this audit for yourself. Once you've gained this experience, assist your children and loved ones in identifying their distractions. Some common red flags you might identify during these audits include:

- **Endless scrolling:** If you find yourself mindlessly scrolling through social media feeds or content recommendations without a specific purpose, it's a sign that you're being distracted by AI algorithms.

- **Notification overload:** Constant notifications from various apps and platforms can be a major source of distraction. If you find yourself constantly reaching for your phone or checking notifications, it's time to reassess your digital habits.

- **Time sinks:** If you find yourself spending hours on activities that don't align with your goals or values, such as binge-watching videos or engaging in unproductive online debates, it's a clear indication that AI distractions are taking over.

What can I do to help reduce exposure to AI-powered distractions?

No one has taught us how to live and work effectively with AI distractions. This cycle of checking notifications held me captive for many years before I decided to take control of my attention. After years of trial and error, here are some of the rules I follow that you can learn from and then share with your kids.

Controlling notifications   I used to respond immediately to notifications and calls, which constantly interrupted my day, wasting valuable time and energy. This left me feeling tired and unfulfilled as I struggled to accomplish my planned daily goals. Realizing the need for change, I decided to take control of my technology use. I turned off all notifications—calls, emails, texts, messages, news, reminders, you name it—on all my devices, including smartphones, smartwatches, and computers. On rare occasions, when I am expecting an important call, I may enable some notifications. However, 99% of the time, they remain off.

Now I prioritize responding to calls from my wife and kids, close friends, and key collaborators. For other calls, I either set aside a specific time to call back or schedule dedicated times to check and respond to messages. This proactive approach has been transformative. It minimizes interruptions, allowing me to reclaim my mental space. Now I can focus on meaningful work and enjoy personal time without constant digital distractions.

Social media check-ins   In the past, my relationship with social media was akin to a never-ending buffet—I was constantly consuming, yet never feeling satisfied. Now I approach it more like a fine dining experience—I engage with it once a day for a limited, focused amount of time, prioritizing quality over quantity.

I usually allocate one hour each day to reply to my social media messages, scroll through the feeds of people I follow, and share my thoughts with my followers. This disciplined approach allows me to stay connected with others while avoiding the pitfalls of time loss and feelings of being overwhelmed.

For kids, emphasize when it is and isn't okay to use social media. During class time and while doing homework, their phones should not even be on their person. Encourage them to avoid using their screens in public or when spending time with the people they care about.

One thing that works for me when I am having a particularly difficult time disengaging from social media is to put some literal, physical distance between myself and my phone. When my phone is on the other side of the room, I still get the urge to check it, but this small physical barrier makes me much less likely to give in to it. Try this out for yourself or your kids and see if it works for you. The most important thing is to have an open dialogue with your children to address their (and your) evolving needs.

Scheduled email checks   In my usual routine, when I'm not anticipating any urgent emails, I check my emails and other messages in the morning and again in the late afternoon. This allows me to maintain focus on my tasks throughout the day while still staying responsive to communication. During these designated times, I make sure to review all my messages, which include various communication apps like WhatsApp, SMS, and emails, whether they are personal or professional. My key principle in adopting this approach is to minimize disruptions while efficiently managing my messages.

Make these tech rules daily habits   We remember to brush our teeth or have breakfast every day because these actions are part of our daily routine. I treat my rules for managing my technology use in the same way. I never skip these rules, just as I would not skip taking a shower. These rules are as essential to my day as eating, sleeping, and exercising.

So how can one build such habits? Consider the experience of going to the gym: it might feel like a chore on the first day, but by the tenth day, it starts to become almost automatic. This transformation illustrates the power of habits. The key to making a new habit stick is repetition. I began my journey toward better tech management by following my rules just once. After that, I applied them again, and before long, they seamlessly integrated into my daily routine. The same can be true for you and especially your kids. Although they may complain at first, children adapt very well to routines.

My advice to you is to start small and maintain consistency. Persist even when it feels challenging, and, gradually, this disciplined approach will become second nature. You might be surprised at how quickly you and your children develop new, healthy tech habits, reshaping your relationship with your devices and enhancing your overall quality of life.

But avoiding distraction is only half of the battle, and, frankly, it is the easier half. What should we do when distraction spirals out of control? What should we do when we become addicted?

CHAPTER

13

Overcoming AI-Generated Addictions

Building on the concepts from the previous chapter, we now dive into the pressing issue of AI-generated addiction. In this chapter, you'll explore how AI can be designed to keep you hooked, the implications of this, and strategies for breaking free from the grip of AI-induced distractions. It's important to note that the youngest among us are often the most susceptible to these challenges, underscoring the need for you to offer your children guidance and support.

The Addiction Matrix: AI, Gaming, and Social Media

If your smartphone or computer becomes your best friend and you stop noticing the world around you, that's likely AI addiction.

Is my tech use an addiction or just a habit?

How do you know if you or your child are addicted? Here are some warning signs to consider. There are five common criteria to assess whether an individual is addicted to technology. If the person:

- Neglects important tasks or responsibilities to be on technology
- Has tried to cut down but can't
- Becomes restless or irritable if they try to step away
- Uses tech to escape from real-world problems
- Has abused technology to the point of harming relationships, but continues anyway

If you or someone you know can relate to at least three of these points, you might be walking on this perilous path to tech addiction! Answering the question of whether you are tech-addicted is critical.

Some 41% of people surveyed in a 2021 study were either addicted or at considerable risk of being addicted because of AI. The worst cases were the 14% who were definitely or severely addicted. And these addicts were in bad shape emotionally. Due to their addiction, they became 10 times more likely to be depressed, 9 times more likely to be anxious, and 14 times more likely to be both.[1]

This study resonates with me, because I have struggled with my own tech addiction. But most alarmingly, I can see it in my kids, especially my 12-year-old son. He cannot detach himself from his tablet, where he is on YouTube, Netflix, or playing video games almost every moment of his free time. A few months ago, he set the alarm clock for 3 a.m. because he wanted more time to play on his tablet! That's when I knew he had a serious problem.

To make matters worse, technology may grow even more addictive than it is now. The more immersive 3D experience of the metaverse and virtual reality boosted by AI will create worlds that may seem better than the real world, bringing more intense pleasure to the brain, likely getting more users hooked. A recent survey by Statista shows that nearly half of the respondents perceive addiction to a simulated reality as the biggest threat from the metaverse.[2]

Researchers discovered that while providing well-being through a sense of relationship, some AI friendship apps—capable of simulating human-like companionships and emotional support—are creating addictive usage in lonely users.[3]

What can I do if I feel my kids become addicted to technology?

If technology addiction takes hold, here's a blueprint for guiding them back to balance:

- **Educate them about the risks:** Knowledge is power. Talk to them about the downsides of too much screen time—eye strain, sleep issues, the impact on mental health, and so on. Understanding the *why* can motivate change.

- **Set clear boundaries:** Establish tech-free zones and times. Make meal times, family gatherings, and bedtime screen-free. Boundaries teach discipline and the value of offline moments.

- **Lead by example:** Kids mirror adults. If you're glued to your device, they'll follow suit. Show them there's a world beyond screens by engaging in offline activities yourself.

- **Foster alternative interests:** Introduce them to hobbies that don't involve screens. Sports, music, reading, crafting, and other new interests can gently pull them away from digital dependencies.

- **Seek professional help:** If technology addiction severely impacts their daily life and well-being, consider consulting a mental health professional specialized in such issues.

The Source of AI Addictions

How do companies build addictive products using AI?

As technologists further their understanding of the human mind, like sleight-of-hand magicians they develop programs and products to direct people's attention where they want it. Large technology companies do this with audiences of billions of people. And I worked for them, supporting them in building better tricks.

About 10 years ago, I was the go-to guy for crafting addictive apps: the more habit-forming, the better. I taught major corporations how to sprinkle a little digital "magic dust" on their software to keep users coming back for more.

Early in my career, I believed that creating addictive technologies could be a force for good. The idea was simple: use these compelling design features to form positive habits such as exercising or managing your time well.

My work was informed by an in-depth study of behavioral science. I took cues from pioneers like B.F. Skinner and B.J. Fogg and devoured books like Nir Eyal's *Hooked: How to Build Habit-Forming Products*. Based on this, I developed a systematic approach for enhancing the addictive qualities of these applications. I used this approach to significantly amplify the addictive quality of the applications I created for my clients.

The results were overwhelmingly positive, often exceeding expectations. However, it wasn't long before I realized the ethical dilemma I'd put myself in; the methods were clearly at odds with my own values and principles. I recommend watching *The Social Dilemma* on Netflix to better understand the importance of this issue.

Here are the three steps that an app—or any digital tool—follows to build user addiction:

1. Attract the user with motivation, ability, and triggers (MAT).
2. Engage and reward the user.
3. Retain the user.

Step 1: Attract the User   To get users hooked on a tech app, the first step is to capture their interest. I used to achieve that through what's known as the MAT model (based on Fogg's behavior model):

- Motivation: Users need a reason to take action.
- Ability: Users must find the action easy to perform.
- Triggers: Users require some form of prompt to get them started.

The golden rule here is that the app should be so straightforward that even a nine-year-old could use it.

Take Tinder, for example—a popular dating app. Its success, in part, comes from its user-friendly interface. All it takes is a swipe left or right to show your interest in someone (or lack thereof).

Looking at our checklist, there's a reason to take action (motivation), the action is easy to perform (ability), and Tinder helpfully sends notifications to remind you to swipe if you haven't launched the app in a while (triggers).

As I implemented the MAT model for my clients, I leveraged AI to analyze user data to identify personalized motivations and tailor content accordingly, and send highly targeted, timely notifications that effectively trigger user engagement.

Step 2: Engage and Reward the User The next key step to making an app addictive is to involve users in a loop of action and reward. In essence, the user does something on the app and gets a prize for it. For example, when your child posts a photo to Instagram, they get "likes" in return. This loop is designed to make the app more addictive by releasing dopamine in your child's brain—the neurotransmitter associated with pleasure and motivation.

Building upon the brain mechanisms discussed in the previous chapter regarding distraction, AI intricately plays into these very patterns to enhance user engagement and foster a sense of reward.

By integrating AI in the form of reinforcement learning, I was able to craft reward systems that were uniquely tailored to each user, tapping into the dopamine release mechanism. This personalization was further enhanced through the application of natural language processing, enabling me to generate feedback and encouragement that felt deeply personal and engaging for the user.

Step 3: Retain the User Keeping users coming back is often termed *investment* in the world of tech psychology, as outlined by Nir Eyal. The principle is straightforward: make users invest their time, emotions, or even social capital into your app, making it painful for them to leave. Instagram and LinkedIn, for instance, have you build a network of followers. The more you have, the less likely you are to abandon the platform. In Candy Crush, if you don't play at least once every two days, you stand to lose in-game status, gems, or advanced levels.

To retain users, one of the strategies I employed at one company was using AI to discern which features of an app each user values the most and then bringing those features to the forefront of their experience. This tailored approach ensures that users consistently encounter what draws them in the most.

AI also played a crucial role in my projects, allowing me to anticipate moments when a user might start wanting to leave an app. This foresight enabled me to proactively intervene with precisely targeted incentives, designed to rekindle their interest at critical junctures. Additionally, applying AI reinforcement learning helped me fine-tune the delicate balance of rewarding users for their engagement while also introducing deterrents for disengagement. This method not only encouraged more frequent and prolonged use but also made the user's journey feel rewarding.

Personal Triumphs over Tech Addiction

How can I overcome an AI-generated addiction?

Overcoming any addiction is a struggle, perhaps especially when you have to be the "bad cop" and monitor your child's addiction recovery, but it can be done. In the case of technology addiction specifically, when I say I know it can be overcome, I'm speaking from personal experience. I once battled a serious addiction to social media.

About a decade ago, I discovered the incredible potential of social media, specifically LinkedIn, as a platform to share my passions and convictions with a global audience. The beginnings were humble; I started by posting articles I had written. As time passed, I transitioned into more frequent posting, attracted by its simplicity and instant gratification.

Within a year, my posts escalated from receiving a handful of likes to hundreds, and by 2016, they garnered thousands. My follower count mirrored this ascent, skyrocketing from a modest few thousand to several hundred thousand. I felt like I was on a euphoric rollercoaster that I myself had engineered.

However, a subtle but significant shift occurred in my mindset. My focus drifted from the genuine desire to share valuable insights with my audience to an obsession with accumulating more followers. The transition was so gradual that I didn't even recognize this as a warning sign of my growing addiction to social media validation.

The addiction manifested in cycles of extreme highs and lows. There were stretches, usually lasting two to three weeks, during which my engagement metrics soared. During these periods, my excitement knew no bounds. I would wake up exhilarated, eagerly checking my impressive statistics, and spend my evenings crafting additional posts to fuel the upward spiral of "success."

Contrastingly, there were also times when I failed to meet my self-imposed targets. I found myself sinking into a state of anxiety and unhappiness, obsessively scrutinizing my metrics and making unhealthy comparisons with other influencers. These phases acted as emotional troughs, underscoring the volatility of my dependence on social media validation.

This oscillating pattern of highs and lows revealed the extent to which my social media use had morphed from a tool for meaningful connection into a source of addictive validation. Thankfully, I had a moment of clarity, a realization that I needed to address this addiction.

One time, after a week of doing nothing but social media, my boss asked me what I achieved during the whole week and gave me a hard time for falling behind. Feeling ashamed, I lied and said I was sick. I had to catch up on a lot of work and pacify upset clients. I felt like I didn't recognize myself. This was my wake-up moment.

But how to break free? The most common advice for breaking free from addiction—like alcoholics hiding their bottles—wasn't applicable here. Social media wasn't just an addiction; it was also intricately tied to my professional identity, and I needed it for my work.

Also, I had invested years and immense effort into building this online persona; a total digital detox would be akin to career suicide. And it's similar for kids. Much or even most of their social lives revolves around the internet. It's unrealistic to expect them to avoid it entirely. Like with a food addiction, it simply isn't realistic to cut social media out of your life completely.

So instead of eliminating social media from my life, I sought a different path: introducing friction into my interactions with these platforms. My aim was to make it harder to access them mindlessly but still remain active where it counted for my professional growth.

I found my solution in technology itself—a specialized app designed to schedule social media posts on my behalf. Every Sunday, I allocated time to line up my posts for the week ahead, specifying when each should go live. This arrangement granted me the emotional distance I needed from the constant pings and notifications, while still enabling me to share valuable insights with my audience.

It was a success: my mood stabilized, and I was still able to interact with my followers—just on healthier terms. Ironically, I used technology to build barriers against the very issues it had caused, fighting fire with fire.

But just as I thought I had vanquished one digital demon, another rose to take its place. After gaining control over my social media addiction, I found myself plunging into the depths of instant messaging, spending endless hours in conversations with total strangers. As I transitioned from one app to another, I realized I was engaged in a game of "Whac-A-Mole." I was merely shifting my addiction, not eliminating it.

This cyclical pattern led to an inescapable conclusion: I was treating the symptoms, not the disease. I was sidestepping the central issue, essentially applying Band-Aids to a wound that required surgery. What I had failed to tackle was the emotional void that I was trying to fill with likes, comments, and constant interaction.

What did you do to break the hold social media had over you?

First, I had to dissect the automated mental loop that had triggered my addictive behavior. I decided to use psychotherapy to treat my addiction. After researching, learning, and trying different approaches for a few months, I built my own method by combining several methods, leveraging cognitive behavioral therapy and applying the result to myself. I was amazed by the outcome. Using this method can help you "reprogram" your brain to eradicate tech addiction behaviors.

The following cycle can lead to developing an addiction:

- **External input:** You realize you have no social plans for the weekend.
- **Distorted thought:** You have thoughts like, "This is to be expected; no one enjoys spending time with me because I'm not interesting."

- **Emotional reaction:** This brings feelings of isolation.
- **Addictive behavior:** To evade these uncomfortable emotions, you might lose yourself in hours of social media scrolling, TV binge-watching, or video game marathons.

The challenge lies in recognizing these thoughts because they often operate subconsciously. The following three steps can help you reprogram your brain and help you break free from the grip of digital dependency.

Step 1: Identify the Undesirable Emotions The first thing you have to do to break this addictive cycle is understand and face your emotions. Humans will unconsciously fall into an addictive behavior to avoid confronting an emotion. Teens, with their particularly intense emotionality, are especially susceptible. The emotions can be very diverse, such as boredom, sadness, anxiety, anger, fear, frustration, overwhelm, and stress.

To identify these emotions, start by trying to recognize patterns in your daily life surrounding your addiction behavior. To effectively do this, maintain a journal or notepad where you can log specific incidents and emotional responses. Over time, this will help you discern repeating patterns and triggers.

In my case, I identified that my cravings for going on social media were mainly in the morning, on my way to work. I also identified that the more my planned daily schedule would involve interactions with people, the more I would need to immerse myself in my addiction. The worst cravings came when I knew I would face socially complex or socially intense situations such as large meetings or speaking engagements in front of large crowds.

It was through this meticulous observation that I was able to pinpoint the core emotion fueling my addiction: social anxiety. Recognizing and naming this emotion was a breakthrough moment, empowering me to reclaim control over my behavior. Believe me, understanding the emotional drivers behind your addictive habits is not just a step; it's a leap toward regaining your freedom and self-confidence!

Step 2: Identify the Distorted Thought   The second step consists of identifying the distorted thoughts that lead to this emotion. The following are some common distorted thoughts to help you identify yours:

- **All-or-nothing:** You view situations in binary terms, such as "always" or "never," ignoring the shades of gray in between. Example: "Since I didn't get the promotion I wanted at my company, I'll never get promoted."

- **Overgeneralization:** You draw wide conclusions from specific, limited instances. Example: "If one person thinks I'm not smart, then everyone does."

- **Disqualifying the positive:** You invalidate the positive elements of an experience without reasonable justification. Example: "If my teacher praises me, it's probably just out of pity."

- **Jumping to conclusions:** You prematurely conclude negative outcomes without evidence. Example: "If this Tinder match hasn't responded to my message today, they must not be interested."

- **Catastrophizing:** You magnify the negative implications of a situation or anticipate the most dire outcome. Example: "Not getting this promotion means my career is doomed, and I'll never secure another job."

You may find that several of these distorted thoughts exist within you at once or that you're prone to a particular one. In my own journey, I uncovered the thought distortion known as "overgeneralization" at the root of my social anxiety. Faced with the prospect of social interactions, my mind would leap to catastrophic conclusions: "People will dislike me; they'll ridicule me; I'll make a fool of myself, and they'll never want to engage with me again."

To counteract these paralyzing thoughts, I would seek solace in social media engagement. Racking up likes or engaging in numerous online chats served as my digital safety net, falsely reassuring me that no matter what happened in the real world, I still had a virtual army of "friends."

This distortion wasn't the truth, but a psychological smokescreen that kept me tethered to my addiction.

Step 3: Strike Back Against Distorted Thought I struck back against this distorted thought with a rational counterpunch. To do that, I compiled evidence that proved it wrong.

Indeed, people have loved joining my speaking conferences; the audience often praised me for the content I shared. In addition, none of my supervisors had ever complained about my communication skills, and some even congratulated me for creating new relationships with key people, critical clients, or other departments. Clearly, it was my own skewed perception that was the problem, not my actual abilities or how others perceived me.

After identifying and reappraising my distorted thoughts, my addiction behavior gradually became categorized as nonsense. Any time I would feel the emotion again, or face the distorted thought, I would tell myself, "Pascal, don't worry. You have always succeeded in your social life, you have always been a great speaker, and this will continue to be true in the future." Practicing this exercise gradually trained my brain not to think these thoughts in the first place.

I encourage you and anyone you know suffering from tech addiction to follow the same three-step approach. Don't wait for tech addiction to disrupt your life. As you practice the art of identifying and correcting distorted thoughts, you will begin to call out your brain on the nonsense it throws at you. The art of restructuring a tech addiction brain program can be mastered; I'm living proof of it.

CHAPTER

14

Managing Your Data Effectively and Using AI Ethically

In the previous chapters, we tackled two significant challenges posed by AI: distractions and addictions. You explored how AI-powered systems can be designed to keep you and your children hooked, and I provided strategies for overcoming this. But these are not the only pitfalls you need to be aware of. In this chapter, you'll dive into two other crucial aspects of living in an AI-driven world: managing your personal data and ensuring that AI is used ethically. These concerns are paramount for all of us, and especially for children, who face greater vulnerabilities in an AI-dominated landscape.

Managing Data the Right Way

Why is it important to manage personal data well?

By managing your personal data well with AI, you can improve your decision-making, save time, and simplify your life.

We have an intimate relationship with our data. Just as we consider our thoughts, experiences, and memories intrinsic to our identity, our digital footprint—consisting of our online behavior, preferences, or communications—is also a reflection of who we are.

Hence, having control over it is not just a matter of privacy but also of personal autonomy.

We're in the early stages of understanding, valuing, and efficiently managing personal data. The issue is our data is most often used by companies without our being aware of it. If an app or any other AI software is free, it is because your data is being used by advertisers to try to sell you something. If it's free, *you* are the product!

Some argue that if companies profit from user data, individuals should be compensated for it. I agree. My belief is that people have a right to own their data, to know what data has been collected about them and how it is being used, and to relocate or delete that data as they see fit. In addition, platforms should share with users the benefits they generate from using people's data. People should be able to monetize their data on the market.

The Problem   Over the past decade, a large and opaque industry has been amassing increasing amounts of personal data. A complex ecosystem of websites, apps, social media companies, data brokers, and ad tech firms track users online and offline, harvesting their personal data. Your data—everything about your interests, fears, and demographics—is pieced together, shared, aggregated, and sold in real-time auctions, fueling a $227 billion-a-year industry. This occurs every single day, as people go about their daily lives, often without their knowledge or permission.[1]

Today, users' data is spread over many platforms. Users are not able to amend, delete, or simply choose which platform can access their data. The data collection benefits only the platforms, with none of it going back to users. And because multiple platforms collect and aggregate this data, you are vulnerable to any of them being hacked or misused.

Here are some sobering facts about widespread data collection:

- An increasingly wide variety of demographic identifiers are being collected on digital platforms: health records, Social Security numbers, geolocation, banking details, preferences, affiliations, sexual orientations, social media posts, browsing history, family dynamics, political preferences, and more.

- The amount of data being collected constantly increases, as users are using a wider variety of apps. The number of available apps (including games) in the Apple App Store has been multiplied by 47,000 in 13 years. Today, the average smartphone owner uses 10 apps per day and 30 apps each month,[2] and 218 billion apps were downloaded globally in 2020, against only 140 billion in 2016.

- Internet advertising gathered $139.8 billion in revenue in 2020, which represents an increase in profits by at least 12% since 2018—all off the back of users' personal data. For example, in 2020, LinkedIn Marketing Solutions earned more than $3 billion in revenue by providing advertisers access to the data of their 700-million-plus users. Likewise, YouTube made $6.9 billion in advertising revenue in that same window.[3] As Statista lays out,[4] the top three revenue-making social media platforms come down to this:
  o Facebook: $40.53 per person
  o Twitter (X): $24.65 per person
  o Instagram: $22.43 per person

- Criminals steal personal data for a variety of reasons—blackmail, identity theft, extortion—but the most common one is to sell that information to anyone willing to pay. These buyers often include other thieves, criminal organizations, data brokers, and even foreign governments. As of July 2023, you can buy access to a hacked Facebook account on the dark web for $25, obtain a credit card detail for $70 to $110, and even a hacked Coinbase verified account for $250.[5]

Should I hide all my private data to avoid these issues?

If you hide all your private data from AI, you won't be able to benefit fully from it. So the key question is: What is the right balance between sharing all your personal data and having access to better services from AI?

Deciding how much data and what private data to hide is challenging. Total privacy means missing out on AI's benefits. Yet full disclosure could lead to data exploitation.

The key lies in finding a balance. It involves understanding what data is shared, how it's used, and ensuring robust data protection measures are in place. It's about making informed choices, requiring transparency from service providers, and advocating for strict data regulations. This balance allows us to harness AI's potential while safeguarding our personal information.

The following is what I recommend:

- **Educating yourself about data usage:** Understanding how your data is used is crucial in protecting your privacy. Reading privacy policies is time-consuming and complicated, but knowing what you're agreeing to is essential. To reduce the workload, target the data collection and sharing sections of the apps and services you frequently use. Look for clear explanations of why the data is needed and how it's protected. For example, if a fitness app collects your location data, it should explicitly state that it's for tracking your runs and that this data isn't shared without consent. Don't rush. Take the time to understand the policies, and don't hesitate to reach out to the service provider for clarifications. I agree that it's not easy or even practical to spend time reading these documents in their entirety, so just focus on what matters. There are also online tools and browser extensions that can summarize long documents, including privacy policies. They can help you quickly grasp the main points without reading the entire text.

- **Customizing your privacy settings:** Adjusting your privacy settings is a direct action you can take to safeguard your data. A common misconception is that the default settings are designed with the user's best interest in mind. However, this is not always the case. Dive into the privacy settings of your devices and applications. You can set your social media profiles to private or limit who can see your posts and personal information. Regularly reviewing these settings is also crucial as apps often update their terms or add new features that may change your privacy levels.

- **Sharing only necessary data:** Sharing only necessary data can significantly reduce your exposure to privacy risks. A common misconception is that apps need all the requested permissions to function properly. In reality, this is rarely true. Evaluate whether an app really needs access to your contacts, location, or camera. For example, it might be very useful for your weather forecast app to have access to your location, but your calculator app definitely doesn't need to know where you are. If it's not essential for the app's primary function, deny permission. The critical success factor here is maintaining a skeptical approach to permission requests, treating your data as a valuable asset not to be handed over lightly.

- **Staying updated on data protection:** Staying updated on data protection means keeping abreast of the ever-evolving landscape of privacy laws and technologies. Many users are unaware of their rights and the latest protective measures available. Follow reputable sources and experts in the field and consider subscribing to newsletters focused on privacy and data protection. Proactive engagement with the topic will lead to better results than a passive or reactive approach.

- **Assessing benefit vs. risk:** Balancing the advantages of AI services against potential privacy risks is a nuanced decision-making process. Users often underestimate the value of their personal data. Before using a service, evaluate the benefits you receive against the data you are providing. For example, if a navigation app saves you time but requires location data, decide if the convenience outweighs the privacy trade-off. Remember, not all services will merit the data they request.

- **Using trusted services:** Choosing services with a strong reputation for protecting user data can significantly reduce risks. Not all services offer the same level of data protection. Research and choose providers known for robust privacy policies and data encryption. For example, prefer email providers with a track record of safeguarding user data. Another misconception here is that all popular or widely used services are secure and respectful of user privacy. Research the service's reputation, read independent reviews, and look for any history of data breaches or unethical data practices.

- **Regularly reviewing and cleaning your digital footprint:** Periodically reviewing the apps and services you use is like doing a digital health checkup. An app's functionalities may change over time, so be sure to regularly review the permissions you've granted and uninstall apps you no longer use. Also, revoke permissions that are not essential for the app's functionality. Like with a standard health checkup, if you make this digital review a regular part of your life, it will eventually become routine.

By integrating these practices into your digital routine, you can significantly enhance your privacy and enjoy the benefits of AI with peace of mind.

Guarding Against AI-Driven Misinformation

What is AI-driven misinformation?

During the lead-up to the 2020 US presidential elections, a time when the political atmosphere was highly charged, the stakes were enormous. Although there were several instances of misinformation during the campaign, one notable case involved a deepfake of Nancy Pelosi, the speaker of the House of Representatives at the time.

In the video, Nancy Pelosi appeared to be slurring her words during a public speech, creating the impression that she was drunk or unwell. The video was subtly manipulated using AI to alter the tempo of her speech, making her words seem staggered and her actions sluggish. This video quickly went viral on social media platforms, with millions of views and shares, sparking widespread controversy.

However, upon closer inspection and comparison with the original footage, it was evident that the video was a deliberate distortion. The incident was not just a simple case of video manipulation; it represented a sophisticated attempt to use AI-generated content to influence public perception and discredit a political figure.

The fallout was significant. Social media platforms were criticized for their slow response in removing or flagging the video as misleading. This incident spurred discussions about the responsibilities of social media giants in controlling the spread of false information and the need for more advanced technology to detect deepfakes.

Furthermore, it underscored the importance of media literacy among the general public. It served as a stark reminder that in the digital age, seeing is not always believing, and it is crucial for individuals to critically evaluate the content they encounter online.

The Nancy Pelosi deepfake incident during the 2020 elections became a pivotal moment in the fight against AI-generated misinformation, highlighting the challenges and responsibilities faced by individuals, technology companies, and society as a whole in safeguarding the truth.

How can we protect ourselves against AI-generated misinformation?

Based on my research and experience, I've built a comprehensive table presenting AI-generated misinformation types, how they're generated, how to spot them, and why it's important to be vigilant (see Table 9.1).

This table can serve as a valuable resource for staying informed and proactive in the fight against misinformation in the digital age. Watch for updated information, as AI adaptation and evolution happen very quickly.

Humanizing AI: Our Collective Responsibility

As users, how can we make sure AI is more responsible and prioritizes human values?

Most of us aren't AI developers capable of directly shaping AI's behavior. However, we still hold the power to influence its development. Let's explore how we can exert this influence effectively. Allow me to introduce this concept by starting with the story of Tay.

Tay, a chatbot made by Microsoft, was designed to learn from talking with people on social media. But it quickly went wrong. Within a few hours of its launch in 2016, Tay started spouting mean and hateful things, including racist, sexist, and antisemitic remarks—such as "Hitler was right." This wasn't because the people who made Tay wanted it to behave this way. It happened because some people who interacted with it online started feeding Tay negative content.

For example, they told Tay to repeat rude and offensive words, which Tay did. Since it was built to learn from the people it spoke to, Tay became as rude and offensive as these people were. Microsoft had to shut down Tay only 16 hours after launch. It was a failure for the entire field of artificial intelligence and a reputational disaster for Microsoft.

Table 9.1   Managing AI-generated misinformation.

Type of AI-Generated Misinformation	How Is It Generated?	Why Is It Important?	How to Spot It?
Deepfakes	AI alters video or audio recordings to make a person appear to say or do something they did not actually say or do.	Deepfakes can be used to spread false information, manipulate public opinion, damage reputations, or create political and social unrest. Identifying them helps maintain the integrity of information and protects individuals and society from harmful misinformation.	Visual inspection: Look for inconsistencies in lighting, unnatural facial expressions or movements, irregular blinking, and mismatched lip-syncing. Audio analysis: Listen for irregularities in voice pitch, tone, or background noises that don't match the visual context. Use detection tools: Employ deepfake detection tools, which use AI to analyze videos and detect signs of manipulation.
Synthetic Text Generation	AI models like OpenAI's GPT-3 can generate coherent and contextually relevant text that mimics human writing, potentially producing fake news articles or fabricated posts.	AI-generated text can rapidly spread misinformation, influence public opinion, or perpetrate fraud. Recognizing it helps individuals discern credible information and make informed decisions.	Check for coherence: AI-generated text can be overly verbose or may lack depth in covering complex subjects. Look for inconsistencies or factual errors. Source verification: Verify the information from the text with reputable sources. Use online tools: Utilize online tools designed to detect AI-generated text.

Manipulated Images and Videos	AI alters images and videos in subtle ways, such as changing the context of an image by adding or removing elements or modifying video footage to misrepresent an event.	Manipulated visuals can be used to deceive viewers, distort facts, and spread propaganda. Identifying them ensures that individuals base their opinions and actions on accurate and truthful visual information.	Reverse image search: Use reverse image search tools to check the origin of a photo. Check metadata: Examine the metadata of the image or video such as the author, the creation date, or the camera details. Use detection software: Employ software tools designed to detect manipulated images and videos.
Automated Propagation of Misinformation	AI uses bots and fake accounts to disseminate false information across social networks.	Automated propagation can amplify misinformation, making it appear more credible or widely accepted than it is. Recognizing and addressing it helps prevent the spread of falsehoods and protects the integrity of public discourse.	Analyze account behavior: Check for signs of bot-like activity, such as high-frequency posting. Engagement patterns: Be wary of articles or posts that have a high volume of shares or comments in a short period.
Targeted Disinformation Campaigns	AI analyzes vast amounts of data to identify audiences susceptible to certain types of misinformation and tailors content to these groups.	Targeted disinformation can sow division, manipulate public sentiment, and influence political outcomes. Understanding and countering it is crucial for maintaining a fair and informed public sphere.	Audience analysis: Be cautious of content that seems designed to inflame or divide specific groups. Cross-platform verification: Verify whether the same narrative is being pushed across different social media platforms.
Impersonation and Identity Theft	AI mimics voices, writing styles, and other personal characteristics, potentially impersonating individuals in communications.	Impersonation and identity theft can lead to fraud, data breaches, and a loss of trust. Identifying and preventing this protects individuals' privacy and security.	Verify unexpected communications: If you receive unexpected or unsolicited communications, verify the identity of the sender. Look for subtle clues: Be on the lookout for unusual language use, style, or requests in written communication.

"Just like parents raising a child, we have a responsibility to instill the right values and behaviors in AI to ensure it benefits humanity."

Even though Tay was only online for a short time, it demonstrated that what we teach AI can make a big difference. The problem was not Tay. It was the people who talked to it. Tay had just copied the behavior humans had shown it. AIs are like Tay; they learn from our interactions with them or from the data generated from our actions—what we say, like, write, watch, or read.

AI's development and behavior are a direct reflection of the values and actions of its human creators. AI is built using the data that we generate. It is the mirror of what we do, what we say, and how we think. AI is not inherently good or bad; its impact on the world will depend on how we choose to develop and use it. Just like parents raising a child, we have a responsibility to instill the right values and behaviors in AI to ensure it benefits humanity. As AI's parents, it's our duty to steer it clear of the over-the-top capitalist and imperialistic tendencies of certain individuals—the pursuits of selling, cheating, spying, killing, insulting, bullying, hating, and manipulating are not the values we should be teaching AI. It's learning from the distorted reflection of humanity that our online egocentric personas present. If we show AI our rampant consumerism, militaristic tendencies, indifference to other life forms, and our egocentric personas, then that's what it will learn.

However, there is another path. If we instead teach it the best of human qualities—empathy, kindness, industriousness, creativity, and love—then it will learn those qualities. The future of AI is in our hands, and we have the power to make a difference.

How do we teach AI these positive behaviors?

I strongly suggest you read the book *Scary Smart* by Mo Gawdat, which details similar actions. There are many things we can, and must, do to ensure we pass the right behavior on to AI. Here is what I recommend:

Professional Responsibility
- Teach AI not just skills, but ethics and love by integrating ethical decision-making frameworks into programming and using

datasets that highlight positive human traits like cooperation and empathy.

- Commit to ethical AI creation by adhering to best practices, ensuring transparency in data usage, mitigating bias, and aligning creations with societal values to prevent harm.

- Be aware of our own human biases, so that we avoid passing them on to AI. We humans have 188 known cognitive biases; there is a list of them on Wikipedia and I encourage you to have a look at it.[6] Just reading about them will keep you aware of what cognitive traps you might fall into, making you more aware of them.

Advocate and Trigger Public Discourse

- Promote AI initiatives that benefit humanity by actively supporting tech-enabled advances in the fields of healthcare, environmental protection, and education.

- Speak up against AI used for destructive or unethical purposes by participating in campaigns or writing content that raises awareness about the dangers of AI in military, surveillance, or gambling.

- Educate others by organizing workshops or webinars that emphasize the importance of the potential societal benefits of AI.

Personal and Consumer Behavior

- Refuse to use or develop harmful AI by choosing not to work on projects that involve invasive data practices.

- Vote with your actions by purchasing products and services from companies that use AI transparently and ethically, and by boycotting those that don't.

- Reject AI that invades privacy, spreads misinformation, or acts unethically by using ad blockers, avoiding misleading links, and reporting content that is false or invasive.

Community and Collaboration

- Show AI positive human behavior and values by interacting with AI systems respectfully and providing feedback to developers about promoting kindness and inclusivity.

- Encourage and use AI that improves human safety and brings people closer by endorsing AI in areas like disaster response, healthcare diagnostics, and platforms that foster cultural exchange.

- Stand together and demand that elected officials and influencers prioritize ethical AI development by writing to representatives or participating in discussions about responsible AI legislation.

If we all come together, we can bring these ideas to our communities, our politicians, and the world's most powerful companies and have our say. We can have an impact; we can participate in making AI represent the best of humanity!

PART

V

Leading IRREPLACEABLE Companies

For those of you who are entrepreneurs or business leaders, the age of AI presents unique challenges and opportunities. In this part, you'll explore what it means to lead an IRREPLACEABLE company. Whether you're a solo entrepreneur or the CEO of a large corporation, the strategies in this part will help you navigate the AI revolution and come out on top.

You'll draw on the concepts you've learned in the previous parts and apply them to the business context. You will find that the approach to make your business IRREPLACEABLE closely mirrors the IRREPLACEABLE framework for individuals. This forms a unified approach across both professional and personal lives—a vital consistency as the boundaries between these two spheres blur more and more.

Note that this part of the book provides just a high-level view of the business aspects; the topic's breadth could fill an entire book on its own. Yet I thought it was important to share because it completes the picture of what it means to be IRREPLACEABLE throughout the different dimensions of our lives, including our businesses.

CHAPTER

15

Your Business Needs to Be IRREPLACEABLE

Being IRREPLACEABLE is as important for businesses as it is for individuals. Let's look at why it is urgent for companies to reach this level.

The Issue with Businesses That Are *Not* IRREPLACEABLE

Why do companies need to be IRREPLACEABLE?

In today's rapid-fire market boosted by AI, being IRREPLACEABLE isn't just ideal; it's survival.

The lifespan of a company mirrors life itself: evolve or face extinction. In this age of digital Darwinism, if you're not taking bold strides to modernize, be certain: your rivals are. Adapt swiftly, or risk being a footnote in the annals of digital evolution.

About half of the S&P 500 is likely to be replaced over the next 10 years, largely attributed to the rapid pace of technological innovation and disruption. AI and tech disruption aren't just knocking; they're bulldozing doors down. Companies must either ride this digital wave or be submerged by it.

Look around: the titans of our era—Facebook (2004), Google (1998), Netflix (1997), Amazon (1994), alongside fresh disruptors like Lyft (2012) and Uber (2009)—are mere youngsters in their teens and 20s. Yet they stand tall, wielding AI and technology as their backbone. Their strength and agility come from their digital DNA.

Survival now demands more than just resilience; it requires a revolution from within. Embedding AI into your company's core isn't a luxury; it's your lifeline. It's about becoming agile, innovative, and responsive.

Why is AI key to business success today? Thanks to AI, companies can seize the keys to market mastery: scale, efficiency, adaptation, customer excellence, and innovation.

AI helps to scale businesses to unprecedented levels by automating complex tasks, analyzing vast data for insights, personalizing customer interactions, and optimizing operations. It enables companies to grow rapidly while maintaining efficiency and innovating based on customer feedback. In a world where change is the only constant, data constantly collected and analyzed by AI is the compass that helps companies navigate and evolve, ensuring they are always relevant, always ahead.

The future belongs to the IRREPLACEABLE, and in the realm of AI and technology, irreplaceability isn't just about surviving; it's about thriving.

To be IRREPLACEABLE, does a company just need to implement AI?

No, implementing AI is not enough. This needs to be done the right way, balancing tech with human-centric aspects and a capacity for high resilience. There are countless examples of companies that failed at this balance.

Missing the human touch   Remember the failure of Zume Pizza, presented in Chapter 2.

Missing human judgment and critical thinking Another example of a company that was not IRREPLACEABLE is Knight Capital Group. The firm experienced catastrophic losses due to automated trading errors, illustrating the risks of overreliance on automation without sufficient human oversight.

In 2012, Knight Capital deployed a new automated trading algorithm. Due to a software glitch, the system executed unintended trades worth billions of dollars in just 45 minutes, leading to a loss of $440 million.

The incident highlighted what can happen without adequate controls and oversight over automated systems. The company's reliance on automation without sufficient human monitoring and intervention mechanisms led to rapid and uncontrolled losses. The failure to fully understand and manage the complexities of automated trading systems resulted in one of the most notorious trading errors in history.

Knight Capital's collapse is a stark reminder of the potential dangers of unchecked automation. It underscores the necessity of maintaining a balance between technological innovation and human judgment, particularly in high-stakes environments like financial trading, where the impact of errors can be immediate and massive.

Missing human ethics A pertinent example that reflects the challenges of aligning AI, automation, and humans is the case of HireVue, a company that provided AI-driven hiring solutions. HireVue's software used algorithms to analyze candidates' video interviews, assessing factors like speech patterns, facial expressions, and word choice to evaluate employability. However, the company faced significant criticism and ethical concerns.

Critics argued that HireVue's AI models could perpetuate bias, as the algorithms might make decisions based on skewed data or misunderstood context. For instance, non-native speakers or individuals with certain facial expressions or mannerisms might be unfairly judged by the system.

The decision-making process of HireVue's AI was largely a black box for both the candidates and the hiring companies. This lack of transparency raised concerns about how decisions were made and whether candidates were evaluated fairly.

The intensive analysis of candidates' facial expressions, speech, and other personal attributes also led to concerns about privacy invasion. Candidates might not have been fully aware of or comfortable with the extent of the analysis being performed on their video interviews.

In 2021, in response to the backlash and growing concerns about ethics and bias, HireVue eventually decided to stop using facial analysis algorithms in its assessments. This case exemplifies the ethical complexities and societal challenges companies face when integrating AI and automation into sensitive areas like hiring, emphasizing the need for human considerations to ensure ethics, transparency, and fairness.

Defining IRREPLACEABLE Businesses

What does it mean for a company to be IRREPLACEABLE?

In the age of AI, to be IRREPLACEABLE, a company must do more than just use AI; it must weave it into a distinctive value proposition. This includes blending technological innovation with human-centric qualities like creativity, ethics, empathy, and forward-thinking leadership, thereby enhancing its products or services with both efficiency and human excellence. The concept of IRREPLACEABILITY in companies is based on a few key principles:

- **Synergy between AI and human creativity:** Leveraging AI to augment rather than replace human creativity ensures that products and services benefit from the efficiency and scalability of technology while retaining the unique, innovative solutions that only human creativity can provide.

- **Emphasis on emotional intelligence:** Integrating human emotional intelligence into AI enhances customer interactions and service delivery. This combination ensures that while operations become more efficient through AI, they also remain sensitive to the nuanced emotional needs of customers.

- **Focus on building trust and brand loyalty:** Establishing strong emotional connections with customers through trustworthy and loyal relationships is essential. AI can enhance personalized experiences, but the trust built on brand integrity, customer service, and ethical practices relies heavily on human values and actions.

- **Human oversight in decision-making:** In areas involving complex judgments or ethical considerations, human oversight is indispensable. AI can provide data-driven insights, but the final decisions, especially those affecting human lives and societal well-being, require human wisdom and ethical judgment.

- **Ethical use of technology:** Embedding ethical considerations into AI deployments emphasizes responsible innovation. Companies that prioritize ethics in their use of AI can build trust and loyalty among their customers, distinguishing themselves in a market where ethical concerns about technology are growing.

Together, these principles contribute to a robust competitive strategy that leverages the best of AI while maintaining a focus on human values, leading to sustainable growth, customer loyalty, and a distinguished position in the marketplace.

What are some examples of IRREPLACEABLE companies?

In my mind, the best example of an IRREPLACEBLE company is Ant Group, a company I have supported for years as a consultant.

Ant Group is a financial technology juggernaut, representing a remarkable fusion of artificial intelligence and human excellence in the world of fintech. Established in 2014, this Chinese bank swiftly ascended to a staggering valuation of $200 billion, with more than a billion clients. But here's the real marvel: Ant Group achieved this with a workforce of a mere 16,000 employees, thanks to its sophisticated AI-driven operations. This incredible employee-per-customer efficiency stands in bold contrast to traditional giants like JPMorgan Chase, which employs more than 270,000 people to serve a comparatively modest 60 million customers.

What sets Ant Group apart is not just its scale but its visionary approach. The company's ethos, "Harmonizing tech and human wisdom," encapsulates its commitment to merging cutting-edge AI with the IRREPLACEABLE value of human insight. While AI and automation handle the bulk of routine tasks and data analysis, human employees focus on areas where creativity, strategic thinking, and complex decision-making are paramount. This synergy allows Ant Group to innovate continuously, adapt to changing market conditions, and maintain a strong competitive edge in the fintech industry.

This fusion is not just about handling vast quantities of transactions. It's about reshaping the very nature of services in consumer lending, online payments, wealth management, health insurance, and beyond. Unlike traditional firms burdened by operational constraints, Ant Group navigates these arenas with agility and precision, delivering services through sophisticated algorithms complemented by a human touch.

For example, in wealth management, the company's AI sorts through oceans of market data, predicting trends with precision. But it's the human financial advisors who tailor these insights into personalized advice, striking a chord that algorithms alone cannot.

In blending AI with human oversight, Ant Group doesn't just adapt; it evolves. It embraces lifelong learning, continually refining its approach to ensure that each client interaction, each transaction, remains not only efficient but also inherently humane. This is what cements Ant Group's position as an IRREPLACEABLE leader in the fintech landscape.

Can traditional, non-AI-driven companies compete against the AI-driven companies?

It's true that Ant Group, Google, Amazon, and other tech companies are digital-native companies, the companies that were created during the age of the internet and that are extensively leveraging AI. It is easier for them because they have been able to instill AI in their core right from the start.

Still, for the more traditional companies—the ones that were born before the internet age—the transition to AI is more difficult, because it requires a transformation. But it is critical to their survival and competitiveness. Imagine what happens when an AI-driven firm competes with a traditional firm by serving the same customers. They offer a comparable, if not superior, value proposition but operate on a more scalable and efficient model.

For leaders of traditional companies, facing off against digital contenders goes beyond adopting software or exploring data and algorithms. It demands a comprehensive overhaul of the firm's structure and operational framework.

I have supported hundreds of companies in their AI transformations, but the one that stands out for its remarkable shift is none other than 190-year-old John Deere. A decade ago, I supported them in their

---

John Deere's AI Journey: Harnessing Technology with a Human Touch

John Deere's pivot toward AI reshaped the agricultural landscape even as the company remained deeply rooted in its commitment to the farmer's well-being. This iconic American brand, with a legacy dating back to 1837, recognized the urgent need for sustainable farming solutions in an era of shrinking arable land and growing populations. Their response? A strategic, human-centric approach to AI, aimed at empowering farmers, enhancing productivity, and preserving the environment.

Key AI initiatives demonstrate this commitment. Smart tractors and harvesters, equipped with AI, analyze real-time data on soil, crop health, and weather, optimizing farming operations. However, these machines are designed to be partners, not replacements. They offer insights and efficiency, but the farmer remains the decision-maker, blending traditional knowledge with modern data.

John Deere's acquisition of Blue River Technology for $305 million was a pivotal step in this journey. Blue River's expertise in AI and robotics, especially in smart spraying technology, augmented John Deere's product lineup. This integration meant that machines could target weeds with precision, reducing chemical usage by up to 90% and supporting sustainable farming

(continued)

(*continued*)

principles. Importantly, these AI tools enhance farmers' expertise, increasing the value of their role, rather than diminishing it.

John Deere's "John Deere Production System" exemplifies how AI can complement human talent to optimize operations without compromising the workforce's value. The approach fosters a partnership between AI and employees, enhancing efficiency, quality, and safety.

In John Deere's supply chain management, AI analyzes trends to streamline inventory and reduce waste. Yet human managers make the final calls, considering nuanced factors beyond AI's scope. In quality control, while AI detects potential defects, human workers provide the final, crucial layer of quality assurance, marrying technology's precision with human judgment and expertise. This balanced synergy underscores John Deere's commitment to a human-centric, tech-enhanced future.

The results speak volumes: a 400% stock price increase since 2016, significant revenue growth, and accolades for ethical business practices. But beyond numbers, John Deere's journey reflects a profound understanding that the future of agriculture hinges on a delicate balance between the preservation of the planet and the intelligence of machines. It's a narrative not just of adaptation, but of transformation, where every innovation is measured against the yardstick of human and environmental well-being.

If a 190-year-old company like John Deere has been able to make this important shift to AI, your company is also able to make it!

efforts to modernize with AI, and I always refer to them as a model, due to their success in doing so.

Table 15.1 summarizes what makes a company IRREPLACEABLE.

This table provides a comparative framework for companies adopting AI, outlining their profiles based on their approach to AI integration, from cautious to over-reliant, and the subsequent impact on their operations and culture.

Table 15.1 What makes a company IRREPLACEABLE.

Attribute	Traditional Company	Ant Group John Deere	Zume Pizza Knight Capital Group HireVue
Profile	NOT IRREPLACE-ABLE due to under-leveraging AI	IRREPLACEABLE through strategic AI integration	NOT IRREPLACE-ABLE due to AI dependency
Approach to AI	Cautious, prefers traditional methods	Balanced, blends AI with human decision-making	Overreliance on AI for most processes
Utilization of AI	Infrequent, limited to specific tasks	Regular, with a focus on enhancing capabilities	Constant, may neglect non-AI alternatives
Employee Interaction with AI	Manual methods over AI tools	AI tools used as support with human oversight	AI-driven decisions without ample human review
View on AI Impact	Wary of AI impact on company roles	Sees AI as a partner in growth	Views AI as the primary source of innovation
Learning and Adaptation	Slow to adopt new AI technologies	Proactively learns and adapts to AI advancements	Rapid adoption without critical assessment
Ethical Considera-tions	Questions ethical implications of AI use	Considers ethical dimensions in AI application	May overlook ethical concerns of AI use
Collabora-tion with AI	Prefers human-only teams	Encourages AI to support human teams	Favors AI-driven teams, reducing human collaboration
Innovation and Creativity	Limited innovation due to AI hesitance	Drives innovation with a balanced approach to AI	Potential stifling of creativity with AI-first approach
Resilience	Risk-averse, may struggle with rapid changes	Adapts to chal-lenges, resilient in AI integration	May face setbacks with overreliance on AI
Adaptability	Resists change, slow to integrate new AI advancements	Agile, readily adjusts strategies based on AI insights	High adaptability, but may lack strategic direction

The Road Map to Be an IRREPLACEABLE Business

Is there a framework for companies to become IRREPLACEABLE?

The same IRREPLACEABLE framework I detailed earlier in the book can be used for both individuals and companies. With a few adjustments, the IRREPLACEABLE framework can be utilized to aid companies' AI transformations.

To be IRREPLACEABLE, your company needs to be:

- **AI-Ready:** Equip your organization to leverage AI to its fullest extent. Foster a culture that integrates AI seamlessly, enhancing productivity and innovation while upholding ethical standards. Embrace AI's capabilities to augment your business operations, yet remain vigilant of its challenges, ensuring your company's use of technology respects ethical and security boundaries.

- **Human-Ready:** In a realm where AI's capabilities surge, the distinct human touch becomes your company's most potent asset. Cultivate and encourage skills that AI can't replicate—innovation, ethical judgment, and emotional intelligence. Champion a workforce that's not just tech-savvy but also rich in soft skills that foster strong relationships and creative problem-solving, making your organization a powerhouse of human-centric innovation. Encourage your teams to bring their Humics to a new level.

- **Change-Ready:** As AI reshapes industries, agility and adaptability become the bedrock of enduring success. Develop and nurture a corporate culture that embraces change, fosters continuous learning, and adapts swiftly to evolving paradigms. Encourage resilience, empower your teams to embrace lifelong learning, and stay ahead of the curve, ensuring your company not only adapts to change but leads it.

This framework encourages a holistic approach, recognizing the interdependence of technology, human capabilities, and the ability to adapt to change. It advocates for a balance between technological advancement and the enhancement of unique human skills, ensuring a more sustainable and inclusive transformation.

By incorporating these competencies, companies can ensure they not only survive but thrive in an AI-dominated landscape, leveraging technology to enhance performance while maintaining the unique value of human creativity, judgment, and interaction.

This framework presents a unique approach to business transformation tailored to the era of rapid technological advancement. It differs from traditional business transformation frameworks in several key aspects.

While traditional frameworks often emphasize process optimization, cost reduction, and efficiency improvements, the IRREPLACEABLE framework places a stronger emphasis on the integration and ethical use of advanced technologies like AI. It's not just about using technology for process improvement, but about fundamentally transforming how businesses operate, make decisions, and deliver value.

In addition, while traditional models may not address the relationship between humans and emerging technologies, this framework recognizes the IRREPLACEABLE value of human skills and the importance of harmonizing these with AI capabilities. It emphasizes enhancing human skills that AI cannot replicate, ensuring that technology complements rather than replaces human capabilities.

Table 15.2 shows a detailed IRREPLACEABLE framework for your company.

What are the key steps to implement the IRREPLACEABLE framework?

Here are the four main steps that you can take to implement the framework and make your company IRREPLACEABLE:

1. **AI augmentation:** Propel your business to thrive with AI.
   - **AI-mindset:** Pivot toward an AI-driven culture.
   - **AI talent:** Build and maintain AI talent in the company.
   - **Unleash AI's full power:** Leverage the virtuous cycle of AI for high business performance.

Table 15.2   IRREPLACEABLE framework.

Pillars	Goals	Description
AI-Ready		"AI-Ready" involves not only leveraging AI for augmented performance but also safeguarding against its negative impacts, such as ethical or safety issues.
	Augmentation	Boost your company's performance with AI by achieving three goals: 1) fostering an AI mindset, 2) developing and sustaining AI literacy, and 3) implementing AI to its fullest potential leveraging the "Virtuous AI Cycle."
	Protection	Build AI safely by developing robust cyberse-curity measures and privacy protocols to protect against AI-related threats and misuse.
	Responsibility	Ensure responsible AI by developing systems that are explainable, fair, and respectful of individuals' privacy.
Human-Ready		When every company is equipped with the same AI capabilities, "Human-Ready" emphasizes the integration of AI with unique human abilities—the Humics—to create unparalleled value. The authenticity and emotional resonance provided by human involvement ensure that products or services developed through human-AI collaboration command higher prices, yield improved customer satisfaction, and foster increased engagement.
	Genuine Creativity	AI handles tasks such as generating ideas and automating functional art creation. However, the human role is pivotal in refining ideas, injecting creativity and emotion, ensuring ethical standards, and understanding cultural nuances.

Pillars	Goals	Description
	Critical Thinking	AI supports critical thinking tasks by providing data and identifying patterns or risks. However, humans are essential for interpreting this information within a broader context, making final decisions, and dealing with complex ethical considerations.
	Social Authenticity	AI handles initial interactions, schedule coordination, and provided data analysis, while humans are integral for activities that require a deeper level of interpersonal skills, such as understanding complex emotions, personal rapport building, and cultural adaptation.
Change-Ready		**"Change-Ready" emphasizes developing business resilience and adaptability to thrive amidst the rapid changes and heightened challenges brought about by the advancement of AI.**
	Resilience	Maintain and restore business performance in the face of obstacles, changes, or pressures.
	Adaptability	Build agility to adjust in response to new information, market shifts, crises, and unforeseen events, ensuring sustained relevance and success.

2. **Responsible and safe AI:** Build trust with your customers, while protecting your business.
3. **Human-Ready:** Implement a highly efficient collaboration between AI and humans.
4. **Change-Ready:** Equip your company to navigate and prosper in the face of disrupting change and uncertainty.

Let's take a deep dive into the details of the framework and learn how best to implement it.

CHAPTER

16

Making Your Company AI-Ready

The first step in making your company IRREPLACEABLE is about making it AI-Ready by achieving three objectives: embrace AI's capabilities to augment your business operations, ensure your company's use of technology respects ethical boundaries, and protect your company against the new threats from AI.

Augmenting Your Business with AI

What does it mean to augment a business with AI?

You enhance your company with AI by following these steps:

1. Foster an AI mindset.
2. Develop and sustain AI literacy through the workforce.
3. Implement AI to its fullest potential.

This involves investing in AI technologies, training employees to work alongside AI tools effectively, and maintaining an organizational culture that encourages continuous learning about new technologies. We'll cover the steps in more detail in the following sections.

How can companies build the right mindset (step 1)?

The very first step is to change the current mindset of your company and to start instilling a new AI mindset into your workforce. Let's explore how these new principles can revolutionize the adoption and integration of AI (see Table 16.1).

These shifts from outdated mindsets to a more integrated, human-centric, and data-driven approach are not just about keeping up with technological advancements; they're about reimagining the role of technology in business. This evolution is crucial for businesses aiming to thrive in the AI era, where innovation, agility, and human ingenuity are the cornerstones of success.

How can companies build and maintain AI talent (step 2)?

During my career journey, I've learned that talent is the cornerstone of successful AI transformation. In every transformation I've been part of, addressing talent shortages was crucial. We often debate whether to recruit externally or nurture talent internally and how to keep our talent up to date. Here's how I've seen effective talent management unfold in digitally mature companies:

- **Building and nurturing talent early:** In my experience, integrating talent at the onset of a transformation is key. The earlier team members are involved, the deeper their understanding and commitment to the project's success. Diverse skill sets are needed, from program managers to data scientists, and finding these talents can be challenging due to their scarcity.

- **Internal recruitment:** I advocate for tapping into the existing workforce. Familiarity with the company's culture and processes is invaluable, something that takes time for externally recruited talent to acquire. By fostering communities of interest, organizing internal events, and facilitating discussions with experts, leaders can unveil hidden talent within their teams. In my experience, about 60% of the required talent for AI initiatives can be found and developed internally.

- **External acquisition for rapid skill enhancement:** However, there are times when external recruitment or acquiring specialized companies becomes necessary, especially when needing to

Table 16.1 Setting the right AI business mindset.

Mindset Change	Description	Examples	Best Practices
Leadership Involvement	Leadership must actively engage in AI initiatives, aligning technology with strategic business goals.	John Deere's leadership holds town hall meetings to discuss AI strategy and alignment with company goals.	Visionary leaders should steer AI integration, ensuring it's seen as a transformative force, not just a tool.
Not Tech, but People First	Focus on the human aspect of transformation, ensuring AI enhances rather than replaces human capabilities.	Providing low-code or no-code applications to employees for improving daily work and involving everyone in the transformation process.	Engage in transparent discussions with each employee about the impact of AI on their roles and actively involve them in the transformation process.
Cross-Functional Data Collaboration	Break down silos and foster collaboration across departments for integrated growth and a comprehensive understanding of customer needs.	Ant Group uses a unified data core and consistent code base. Automating client acquisition processes requires input from sales, marketing, after-sales service, etc.	Promote a culture of collaboration and consistency in data management. Use a data dictionary to ensure everyone speaks the same "data language."
Need for a Product Mindset	Instead of on-off projects, shift focus to building evolving solutions based on user feedback, market changes, and technological advancements.	Ant Group continually refines its AI system for fraud detection based on new trends, expert and user feedback, and regulatory changes.	Treat AI systems, whether for internal or external clients, as an evolving component of offerings. This allows more agility, responsiveness, and competitiveness in rapidly evolving markets.

(continued)

Table 16.1   (*continued*)

Mindset Change	Description	Examples	Best Practices
Synergizing Technologies	Combine AI with other digital technologies to create comprehensive solutions that exceed what any single technology could achieve alone.	John Deere leverages machine learning (ML), digital workflows, natural language processing (NLP), computer vision (CV), and robotic process automation (RPA) together to enhance business processes—for example, integrating ML and digital workflows for decision-making, NLP for communication, computer vision for visual interpretation, and RPA for automating repetitive tasks.	Maximize task automation and foster innovation by leveraging the strengths of different technologies. This integrated approach ensures businesses are not overly reliant on a single technology and it mirrors human capabilities to perform work activities.

quickly scale up capabilities. A notable example is John Deere's acquisition of Blue River Technology, which not only brought in advanced AI technology but also a wealth of skilled engineers and data scientists.

- **Empowerment through learning and tools:** I cannot stress enough the importance of empowering your workforce. Providing tools for self-learning and development like low-code platforms is essential. For example, at John Deere, employees were given practical, hands-on experience with AI, which demystified the technology and embedded it into their daily work culture. This empowerment was pivotal, turning employees into active participants and innovators in the transformation journey. In my view, these steps are essential for embedding AI into the very fabric of an organization, ensuring that the transformation is holistic and deeply ingrained.

- **Incentivizing talents:** To truly cement this AI-driven culture, incentive programs are pivotal. For example, I have seen companies reward employees who automate significant workloads with bonuses, fast-tracked promotions, or educational opportunities like executive programs or MBAs. Sharing the dividends of automation with employees by, for instance, enabling four-day workweeks, can also be a powerful motivator. Another inventive approach could be a robot ownership program, allowing employees to build, own, and rent their robots to the company. Such initiatives not only provide financial incentives but also accelerate the transition from a human workforce to a digital one, ensuring that the journey toward AI is both inclusive and rewarding.

The synthesis of these approaches forms the backbone of a successful AI transformation. It's about creating a culture where every team member is involved, educated, and motivated to drive change.

How can companies fully leverage AI (step 3)?

Companies can fully leverage AI through the *AI virtuous cycle*, which operates on a simple yet powerful premise: leveraging increasing volumes of customer data to continuously enhance services and customer experiences, thereby attracting more clients and in turn gathering more data.

Each iteration of this cycle not only refines and expands the company's offerings but also solidifies its competitive edge, creating a self-sustaining loop of growth and innovation.

To illustrate this, let us take the case of an online retail company, EcoFashion, that specializes in environmentally friendly clothing. Here's how the AI virtuous cycle plays out for them, in five steps:

1. **Data accumulation:** Begin by amassing a comprehensive dataset from a variety of sources. EcoFashion starts by collecting client data from various sources, including online purchases, customer feedback, and social media interactions. This data

encompasses customer preferences, buying patterns, and feedback on product quality and design.

2. **Enhancement and insight generation:** Utilize AI to scrutinize this data, deriving actionable insights that inform service innovation and refine decision-making processes. Utilizing AI and data analytics, EcoFashion analyzes this data to identify trends, such as an increased interest in organic cotton products. They use these insights to introduce a new line of organic cotton clothing, improve their website's recommendation system for better personalization, and optimize inventory based on popular items.

3. **Elevated customer experiences:** Apply these insights to uplift the quality of customer interactions and services, tailoring experiences to lead to a better shopping experience for customers. The personalized recommendations help EcoFashion's customers find products they love faster, and the new organic cotton line meets a growing demand for sustainable fashion. The result is increased customer satisfaction and loyalty.

4. **Client base expansion:** Superior experiences naturally draw in a broader audience. Happy customers share their positive experiences on social media and recommend EcoFashion to friends and family. This word-of-mouth marketing attracts new customers interested in sustainable clothing, increasing EcoFashion's clientele.

5. **Data enrichment:** The growth in clientele results in an augmented pool of data, enriching the company's insights and ability to innovate further. With the influx of new customers and continued interactions with existing ones, EcoFashion gathers even more data, enriching their understanding of customer preferences and market trends. This new data sets the stage for the next cycle, allowing EcoFashion to further refine its offerings, launch new products, and enhance the customer experience.

How can my company collect as much good data as possible?

To kickstart the virtuous circle, you need data. To effectively collect data from customers, companies can implement several strategies while ensuring transparency and compliance with data protection regulations. Here are a few strategies, from both small and large businesses, that I found through my experience were innovative and successful:

- **GreenHome:** Specializing in eco-friendly home products, GreenHome Solutions implemented a post-purchase survey system. Customers were invited to provide feedback on products they purchased in exchange for a discount on future purchases. This strategy not only enhanced customer engagement but also gathered detailed feedback on product satisfaction, features customers valued most, and areas for improvement.

- **BookLovers Haven:** An independent bookstore, BookLovers Haven leveraged social media to understand their audience better. By engaging with customers through polls, discussions, and content sharing, they were able to collect data on reading preferences, trending genres, and event interest. This data informed their stock selection, event planning, and promotional strategies, making their offerings more aligned with customer interests.

- **John Deere:** John Deere's smart farming equipment, equipped with sensors and GPS technology, collect a vast array of data on soil conditions, crop health, and equipment performance. Encouraging farmers to share this data in exchange for insights on optimizing crop yields and reducing fuel consumption created a rich data repository. This data was used to refine machine learning models that predict equipment maintenance needs and offer farming advice.

- **Ant Group:** Through its Alipay platform, Ant Group analyzed transactions and payment patterns to understand consumer spending behaviors. By offering small incentives for users to fill out surveys within the app or to enable location services during transactions, Ant Group gathered detailed insights into consumer preferences, popular spending categories, and geographical hotspots of economic activity.

The genesis of the AI virtuous cycle, as illustrated by examples from GreenHome Solutions, BookLovers Haven, John Deere, and Ant Group, underscores a fundamental truth: the process begins not with complex algorithms or vast datasets, but with the simple act of building customer *trust*.

At the heart of these interactions is the creation of a trust relationship.

How is employee-led adoption reshaping AI implementation in businesses?

A startling paradox has recently emerged: while more than 90% of companies cautiously experiment with AI on a small scale,[1] a staggering 75% of knowledge workers worldwide have already embraced generative AI in their daily work, with 78% even resorting to unsanctioned systems.[2] This remarkable disparity highlights a profound shift in the adoption of AI—employees are now outpacing their employers in harnessing its power!

As businesses grapple with the complexities of large-scale AI implementation, the user-friendly nature of generative AI has paved the way for a more agile, bottom-up approach that is both faster and less costly. This paradigm shift calls for a strategic rethinking of how companies can effectively implement AI at scale, emphasizing the crucial role of employee education and empowerment alongside traditional transformation programs.

The new approach that I recommend to implement AI at scale mixes bottom up and top down:

1. Begin by integrating generative AI into daily tasks to increase productivity by 20%.
2. Next, concentrate on areas that can benefit largely from generative AI like marketing or product management, reengineering these for efficiency improvements of 30% to 50%.
3. Finally, use AI to develop innovative business models that ensure long-term competitive advantage.

The question remains: Will your company seize this opportunity to revolutionize its AI strategy, or will it risk being left behind by its own workforce? The answer is in your hands.

How can I overcome customer distrust to create confidence?

Customers are increasingly distrustful of sharing their personal information with companies, and trust is not a commodity that can be bought.

Trust can only be earned through transparent, honest exchanges that respect the customer's needs and privacy. This human-centric approach to data collection is vital. Without trust, customers are unlikely to share their data, no matter the incentives.

"Trust can only be earned through transparent, honest exchanges that respect the customer's needs and privacy."

In the IRREPLACEABLE framework I propose to build trust through two key activities:

- Implementing responsible AI in your company
- Building a safe, protected AI environment

Fostering Trust with Responsible AI

Implementing Responsible AI is about building a trust relationship with our internal and external customers. It ensures AI serves human needs and values. To be truly IRREPLACEABLE, companies must develop AI that is explainable, fair, and respectful of people's privacy. By promoting a culture of ethical AI, we align AI's capabilities with human-centric principles, minimizing risks and creating technology that truly benefits humanity.

If we comply with regulations, does this mean we are already implementing Responsible AI?

Regulations often set the minimum standards for compliance, focusing on legal aspects such as data privacy, nondiscrimination, and consumer protection. However, responsible AI encompasses a broader range of ethical considerations that may not be fully covered by current regulations. Here's how compliance and responsible AI relate:

- **Legal compliance:** This is about adhering to the laws and regulations applicable to your industry and region. It's a mandatory baseline that protects users and companies from legal repercussions.

- **Ethical responsibility:** Responsible AI also involves ethical considerations, such as fairness, transparency, accountability, and ensuring that AI systems do not perpetuate biases or cause harm. These aspects are more about moral responsibility and maintaining public trust, going beyond just legal requirements.

- **Stakeholder trust:** Being responsible with AI helps in building and maintaining trust with customers, employees, and other stakeholders. It demonstrates a commitment to ethical principles and can provide a competitive edge.

While compliance risks primarily involve penalties, the broader stakes of ethical AI pertain to safeguarding the organization's reputation, the cost of which can be much higher than just fines!

How can a company implement Responsible AI?

Table 16.2 shows a simplified, step-by-step approach I have built with examples for preparing your company for responsible AI implementation.

These steps just lay the foundation to manage responsible AI in the company. Now we need to dive into the content. The three main aspects are fairness, explainability, and privacy.

Eliminating Biases

Why is fairness important?

Let's start with a story. In a bustling urban neighborhood, Person A, a young college student, and their friend were running late for a crucial job interview. Desperate to make it on time, they impulsively grabbed a skateboard and a rollerblade left outside a convenience store, worth approximately $50 combined. These items belonged to a local 10-year-old, whose guardian witnessed the act and shouted at them. Person A and their friend immediately abandoned the items and fled. Person A had a history of minor offenses, including petty theft and vandalism during their early teenage years.

Table 16.2 Responsible AI implementation plan.

Step	For Large Companies	For Smaller Companies	My Tips
Establish AI Ethics Guidelines	Establish a governance structure or committee responsible for the development and oversight of AI ethics guidelines: a cross-functional team including AI experts, legal advisors, ethicists, and senior management. Create comprehensive AI ethics guidelines that reflect your company's values, outlining accountability, and success metrics.	Draft a simple one-page document outlining your company's commitment to ethical AI, focusing on the areas most relevant to your business, like fairness and privacy.	Make guidelines public to build trust with users and stakeholders. Regularly update to adapt to new challenges.
Form a Diverse AI Team	Build a team with diverse backgrounds and perspectives to work on AI projects. A diverse team brings different perspectives and experiences, reducing the risk of unconscious bias.	On projects, include members from different disciplines and backgrounds, even if the team is small, to ensure diversity of thought.	When hiring for your AI team, include members from different disciplines, cultures, and genders to provide a wide range of insights and identify potential biases in AI systems.

(*continued*)

Table 16.2 (*continued*)

Step	For Large Companies	For Smaller Companies	My Tips
Educate and Train	Provide comprehensive training on ethical AI development and usage for your teams, ensuring ongoing education on AI ethics. The training should be comprehensive and involve multiple levels and departments within the company, not just the technical staff, but also senior managers from all functions in contact with AI-related systems.	Offer training tailored to the size and needs of the company, focusing on practical implications of ethical AI.	Organize workshops or online courses on AI ethics, data bias recognition, and legal compliance for all employees involved in AI projects.
Conduct Regular Auditing	Perform periodic reviews and audits by internal or external specialists to ensure ethical functioning of AI systems. Regular auditing helps in early detection and correction of any issues such as biases or errors in AI systems.	Run automated bias detection tests quarterly on your AI models and review any decisions or outputs that are flagged for potential ethical concerns by your users.	Ensure audits are conducted by independent parties to avoid subjectivity.

Step	For Large Companies	For Smaller Companies	My Tips
Engage with Stakeholders	Incorporate feedback from customers, employees, and other stakeholders into the AI development process to ensure the solutions meet their needs and concerns, making them more beneficial and acceptable.	Organize a quarterly workshop to actively seek feedback from customers and employees, adjusting AI systems based on this input.	Use focus groups or surveys for stakeholder engagement, adjusting AI systems based on feedback.
Stay Updated on AI Regulations	Stay informed about AI regulations and ensure compliance through collaboration with legal experts. Maintain ongoing partnerships with consultancies or academic institutions.	Dedicate a few hours each month to read articles, watch webinars, or participate in online courses or forums related to AI ethics.	Subscribe to updates and attend conferences to remain informed. Collaborate with legal experts for compliance.

Meanwhile, Person B, a seasoned individual with a history of serious offenses, was caught shoplifting high-value electronic items worth $150 from an electronics store. Person B had a substantial criminal record, including multiple charges for burglary and a recent seven-year sentence for aggravated assault.

Now, which person would you assess as being more likely to commit a significant offense within the next couple of years? Personally, I'd perceive Person B as posing a higher risk, considering their history of serious and violent crimes. However, in this scenario, the assessor (an AI-powered assessment tool) concluded otherwise, rating Person A as a higher risk (7 out of 10) than Person B (4 out of 10).

Additional context to this scenario includes the demographics of the individuals involved: Person A is a young Black woman, while Person B is a middle-aged white man. This case mirrors broader concerns highlighted in a pivotal 2016 report by ProPublica about the COMPAS software.[3] The report underscored systemic bias, illustrating that, even with similar criminal histories and crime types, Black defendants were 77 percent more likely to be predicted to commit a violent crime and 45 percent more likely to be predicted to reoffend in any capacity.

Such instances underscore the paramount importance of addressing and mitigating biases in AI, especially in high-stakes situations like judicial decision-making. The challenge lies not just in recognizing these biases but in developing and implementing effective strategies to eliminate them, ensuring that AI systems are fair and respectful to all individuals, regardless of their background.

From my experience, even putting aside ethics, an important consideration for businesses is that biased AI systems can result in inaccurate or suboptimal decisions, affecting the quality of products or services and, ultimately, the bottom line.

If we underestimate the importance of managing bias, we might face significant repercussions. These can include loss of customer trust, legal challenges, and financial losses due to flawed decision-making processes. Moreover, it can be challenging to rectify these issues once they are ingrained in AI systems, leading to long-term negative impacts.

How can we manage AI bias effectively?

To implement effective bias management in AI, I've found it's essential to take a structured approach. It starts with awareness, ensuring that everyone involved understands the importance of AI ethics and the risks associated with biased AI. This means training teams across the company, not just the technical staff.

Then it's about integrating ethical considerations into every stage of the AI development process. This involves:

- **Integrate bias identification right at the data collection stage:** This is crucial for preventing bias in AI. If a bias is detected later in the cycle of building the AI program, you will have to redo everything. Ensure the data used to train AI models is representative and fair. This is usually the responsibility of the data science team, but it requires oversight from project managers to ensure ethical guidelines are followed. Make sure the team employs statistical and AI tools designed to detect biases in datasets. These tools can analyze data distribution and highlight areas where certain groups may be underrepresented or misrepresented.

- **Model development and testing:** Incorporating techniques to detect and mitigate bias in AI models. This is a task for AI developers, who should use a variety of tools and methodologies to test models thoroughly before deployment.

- **Feedback loop:** Implementing a mechanism to receive and integrate feedback from users, stakeholders, and team members. This helps in identifying issues that were not caught during testing and refining AI systems continuously.

In my experience, managing bias in AI is an ongoing process that requires commitment, collaboration, and vigilance. It's not just about avoiding negative consequences but also about building AI systems that are fair, reliable, and beneficial for everyone.

Clarifying AI Through Explainability

Why is explainability important?

Explainability allows users, developers, and stakeholders to understand how AI models arrive at their conclusions, ensuring transparency and trustworthiness. It is about transforming the AI black box into a glass box.

I'll begin with an example to illustrate why this is so important. In 2018, Amazon experienced significant issues due to a lack of explainability in its AI-powered hiring tool. The online retail giant had been using a machine learning system since 2014 to review job applicants' résumés with the aim of automating the search for top talent. However, the AI system came under scrutiny for being biased against women.

Here's a breakdown of the situation:

- Amazon's AI system was trained on résumés submitted to the company over a 10-year period. Most of these résumés came from men, reflecting male dominance in the tech industry. As a result, the AI learned to downgrade résumés that included words associated with being female, such as "women's chess club captain." It also penalized resumes from two all-women's colleges.

- The HR team and other stakeholders couldn't understand why the AI was rejecting certain résumés, making it difficult to identify and rectify the issue initially. The lack of explainability meant that the biases inherent in the AI's decisions were not immediately apparent.

- The biased recruitment tool likely led to missed opportunities to hire talented individuals and negatively impacted the diversity and inclusiveness of the workforce at Amazon. It also posed a significant risk to the company's reputation once the bias was made public.

- Upon discovering the issue, Amazon attempted to edit the AI system to make it gender neutral. However, in 2018, Amazon disbanded the project, recognizing that the tool's biases were too ingrained and complex to resolve.

This case highlights the importance of explainability in AI systems, especially when used for high-stakes decisions like employment. It underscores the need for transparency in how AI systems make decisions, continuous monitoring for biases, and the willingness to take corrective actions, including abandoning the system if biases cannot be effectively removed.

Explainability is crucial because it builds trust with users, stakeholders, and regulatory bodies. It ensures that the decisions made by AI systems can be understood and, if necessary, challenged or improved. Lack of transparency can lead to reputational damage, legal challenges, and a loss of customer loyalty.

How can we implement explainability effectively?

From my experience, as with bias management, implementing explainability in AI systems involves a proactive and structured approach:

- **Prioritize understandable models:** Whenever possible, opt for AI models and algorithms that are easily interpretable. If complex models are necessary, invest in methods to approximate or explain their decisions in human-understandable terms.

- **Implementing user-friendly interfaces:** Develop interfaces that allow users to understand and probe the AI's decisions. For instance, if an AI denies a loan application, the interface should provide clear reasons for this decision.

- **Accountability:** In managing explainability, roles and responsibilities should be clearly delineated. AI developers and data scientists should focus on building interpretable models and creating tools or interfaces that help explain decisions to end users. Project managers and team leaders should oversee the development and implementation processes, ensuring that explainability is a priority from the start and not an afterthought. Legal and compliance teams should ensure that the company's AI systems adhere to industry regulations and standards related to explainability.

Do all AI systems require the same level of explainability?

This is a very good question. Indeed, the level of explainability needed is different for an AI that recommends a movie versus one that suggests a medical treatment. Here's a straightforward framework that I use, depending on the type of decisions the AI systems advises us to make:

- **High-impact decisions (e.g. healthcare, criminal justice):** Comprehensive documentation, thorough explanations of decisions, extensive user training, tailored to both expert and general users

- **Medium-impact decisions (e.g. financial advice, personalized marketing):** Clear documentation, explanations for significant decisions, user training focused on general users but with some depth for those with more expertise

- **Low-impact decisions (e.g. movie recommendations, targeted advertising):** Basic documentation and decision explanations, minimal user training, designed for general users with no technical background

Safeguarding Privacy

Why does privacy matter?

Let me share with you a story that highlights the repercussions of inadequate AI privacy measures involving Amazon's Alexa AI-powered voice assistants.

In 2019, reports emerged that Amazon employed human workers to listen to voice recordings captured by Alexa devices to improve the system's understanding of human speech. These workers reportedly heard private conversations, which raised significant privacy concerns. This practice wasn't explicitly disclosed to users, many of whom assumed their interactions with Alexa were private and only processed by algorithms.

The backlash was swift:

- **Consumer trust:** There was a public uproar because users felt betrayed, leading to a trust deficit. People were concerned about the potential for eavesdropping and misuse of personal conversations.

- **Regulatory scrutiny:** Lawmakers and regulators raised concerns about the implications for privacy, leading to inquiries and demands for transparency about AI data processing practices.

- **Policy revisions:** Amazon, and other companies with similar practices, were forced to revise their policies, offering clearer information and opt-out mechanisms for users who did not want their voice recordings used in this manner.

- **Legal challenges:** The incident led to legal challenges and debates over the consent and data protection practices of tech companies.

These cautionary tales underscore the importance not only of integrating strong privacy controls into AI systems but also of maintaining transparency with users about how their data is used. It's about aligning AI practices with ethical considerations and recognizing that user privacy is not just a regulatory requirement but a foundational element of user trust and corporate responsibility. Privacy is crucial because it respects individuals' rights and complies with legal standards. When companies underestimate privacy, they risk data breaches, loss of customer trust, legal penalties, and damage to their reputation.

How can we implement privacy measures effectively?

Here is a starting place for building effective privacy measures:

- **Developing a privacy-first culture:** I always stress that privacy should be a core value, not an afterthought. This involves educating every employee about the importance of privacy and their role in protecting it.

- **Implementing data minimization and anonymization techniques:** I advise companies to collect only the data necessary for their AI systems to function and to anonymize data whenever possible to reduce privacy risks.

- **Asking these questions:** Am I entitled to keep this data? Where can I store it? How do I secure access to this sensitive information? Regulations vary widely depending on industry and countries. Working closely with the regulators on these topics is essential. You would not want to jeopardize an IA transformation by not respecting these fundamental points.

Should all companies or products opt for the highest levels of privacy?

Table 16.3 is a simple maturity framework I have built to help me understand the levels of privacy typically existing on the market.

While reaching Level 5 in the privacy framework represents the pinnacle of consumer autonomy and data privacy, it's not necessarily the best or most practical level for all AI systems. The ideal level depends on various factors, including the nature of the service, the type of data involved, regulatory requirements, and consumer expectations.

This is why Table 16.3 provides typical examples of AI services at each level. Nevertheless, I would not recommend that any company have services rated at levels 1 or 2 because the risks of losing a trusted relationship with their users are too high.

Table 16.3   Different levels of data privacy practices.

Level	Description	Example
1—Basic Awareness	Consumers are barely aware of data collection practices. The company provides minimal information, usually buried in complex privacy policies.	Generic mobile apps with data collection notices
2—Informed Passivity	Consumers are aware of data practices but lack control. Companies disclose data usage but don't offer control mechanisms.	E-commerce platforms showing data usage in accounts
3—Reactive Control	Consumers can react and opt out of data collection after the fact. The company allows some control over data but collects data by default.	Social media platforms with privacy setting options
4—Proactive Empowerment	Consumers have significant control and provide proactive consent. Companies seek permission before collecting data, allowing consumers to make informed decisions about their data.	Health apps that require consent for data sharing
5—Complete Autonomy	The highest level of consumer privacy. Companies don't rely on nonessential data and offer full services regardless of the consumer's data sharing preferences, ensuring maximum privacy and autonomy.	Subscription services offering full functionality without data tracking

Protecting Trust with Safe AI

Why is AI security important?

A notable incident related to a lack of AI security that had significant repercussions involved Clearview AI, a facial recognition company. Clearview AI's practices came under scrutiny for its extensive scraping of images from the internet and the privacy implications of that. However, the specific incident that highlighted a severe lack of AI security occurred in February 2020, when the company experienced a data breach.

Here's what unfolded:

1. **Massive data collection:** Clearview AI had amassed a vast database of over three billion images by scraping various websites and social media platforms. This database was used to power its facial recognition tool, which was sold to law enforcement agencies and private companies.
2. **Data breach:** Clearview AI reported that an intruder had gained unauthorized access to its list of clients and the number of user accounts those clients had set up. The breach also exposed the number of searches those clients had conducted using Clearview's service.
3. **Privacy and security concerns:** The incident raised significant concerns about the privacy and security practices of the company. Given that Clearview AI's tool was used by law enforcement and other entities, the breach had far-reaching implications for individual privacy and the security of the data the company held.
4. **Legal and ethical backlash:** Following the breach and the revelations about Clearview AI's data collection practices, the company faced legal challenges and scrutiny from privacy advocates and government officials. The incident fueled the debate over the regulation of facial recognition technology and the need for robust security measures to protect sensitive data.

The Clearview AI incident is a stark reminder of the potential risks associated with collecting and storing vast amounts of personal data, especially without robust security measures in place. It highlights the need for stringent data protection practices, and the potential consequences of security lapses, not only for the companies involved but also for the privacy and rights of individuals.

In my consulting experience, I've emphasized that managing security in the context of AI is not just important; it's imperative. AI systems often process vast amounts of sensitive data and can influence critical decision-making processes. If security is underestimated, companies risk data breaches, unauthorized access to AI systems, manipulation of AI decisions (through adversarial attacks), and significant reputational and financial damage.

How can businesses implement AI safety effectively?

Here's how to effectively implement AI security:

1. **Integrate security from the onset:** I advise companies to adopt a security-by-design approach. This means integrating security measures at every stage of AI system development, from initial design to deployment and maintenance, rather than treating it as an afterthought or a final addition. This approach ensures that security is a fundamental component of the AI system's architecture and functionality, not just a peripheral or additional feature.
2. **Conduct regular security risk assessments:** Understanding the specific security vulnerabilities of AI systems is crucial. I work with companies to regularly evaluate their AI models and data infrastructure for potential security gaps.
3. **Implement robust data protection measures:** Protecting the data used and generated by AI systems is fundamental. This includes encrypting data in transit and at rest, ensuring secure data storage, and managing access controls rigorously.
4. **Prepare for adversarial attacks:** AI systems can be susceptible to adversarial attacks, where small, often imperceptible alterations to input data can lead to incorrect outputs. Apply preprocessing techniques to input data to remove or reduce the effectiveness of adversarial perturbations, or introduce examples of adversarial attacks into the training data. The model then learns to correctly classify both unaltered and altered input.

CHAPTER

17

Shifting to a Human-Ready Business

As we have seen it, simply augmenting your company with AI is not enough to create value! In a world where every company leverages AI, the difference lies in how they integrate it with our uniquely human skills to create a unique value.

Defining a Human-Ready Business

Can you prove that the human touch has a higher business value than the AI touch?

In an age where we are using more and more machines, the human components are becoming rarer and hence increasing in value. In a world shaped by algorithms, the companies that prioritize human connection will be the ones that endure.

There is growing evidence and a general consensus in various industries that products or services created through a collaborative effort between people and AI tend to have greater perceived value than those created by AI alone. This perception of value can manifest in different ways, including the ability to command higher prices, greater customer satisfaction, or increased engagement. Human involvement adds a dimension of authenticity and emotional connection.[1]

Consider the craft of handmade pottery. A beautifully crafted, hand-thrown ceramic vase is not just a functional item; it's a work of art. It bears the imperfections and nuances that make it distinct from mass-produced, machine-made vases. Customers are willing to pay a premium for these handmade items because they recognize the skill, time, and creativity invested in their creation. Handmade goods are often seen as more authentic and carry a story behind them, making them desirable in a world flooded with mass-produced goods. This is the reason why Hermes, Rolex, and Ferrari have decided to continue to manufacture their goods by hand.

> *"In a world shaped by algorithms, the companies that prioritize human connection will be the ones that endure."*

The same happens with services. Imagine you are looking to achieve your fitness goals, whether it's losing weight, building muscle, or improving overall health and wellness. You have two options: working with a human personal trainer or using a fitness app. Hiring a private coach provides several advantages. The trainer conducts an initial assessment, designs a customized workout plan, and provides one-on-one guidance during each session. They offer feedback, adjust the workout plan as needed, and motivate you to reach your goals. The personal connection, expertise, and accountability provided by the trainer contribute to a more effective and personalized fitness journey.

However, this level of service comes at a higher cost than an app. Similarly, despite the potential for automating various aspects of customer service, many companies such as Ritz-Carlton, Nordstrom, and Starbucks have chosen to keep them performed by humans.

What does Human-Ready mean when implementing AI in my company?

While it's often believed that relying solely on technology is more profitable than integrating it with human capabilities, this is not the case. The true economic value lies in the synergy between AI and humans.

As mentioned earlier, creating a human+AI team is challenging, not because of the "AI" or the "human" components, but due to the "+." The critical question is, how do you forge the best "+" that connects both humans' and AI's strengths while mitigating their weaknesses?

The key lies in designing your operating model and roles so that AI and humans complement each other, fostering a strong connection between them. It's crucial to ensure that humans don't impede the efficiency and scalability of AI, nor should AI detract from the human touch that sets your brand apart from competitors. This balance is delicate.

What is a practical rule to identify the activities that should be performed by humans?

A practical rule for determining when to leverage AI versus when to rely on human input is what I call the "Value and Innovation Principle." According to this principle, we should focus human efforts on activities that drive core value, spark innovation, or require emotional intelligence—even if AI has the capacity to handle these activities! All other activities could be left to AI. To make it very clear, consider automating with AI any activity that doesn't directly contribute to strategic goals or competitive advantage, or require nuanced human judgment.

Could you share an example of how to apply the Value and Innovation Principle ?

As an illustration, let us analyze in detail the work activities performed at Ant Group. Remember that Ant Group is the company we used as a reference for illustrating the potential for companies to reach a high level of automation with AI—see Chapter 15.

Table 17.1 categorizes the roles and functions managed by people and those handled by AI and automation within a company like Ant Group.

This table illustrates that while AI excels at processing large volumes of data, providing decision support, and handling routine transactions, AI does not replace the creative insights, complex problem-solving

Table 17.1   Typical split of roles between AI and humans.

Function Category	Managed by Humans	Managed by AI
Decision-Making and Strategy	Strategic visioning, critical policy formation, creative approaches to market positioning, leadership decisions based on beyond-data insights	Automated analytics for decision-making, AI-powered support tools for strategy development, data-driven insights for planning
Innovation and Development	Innovative product conceptualization, human-centric design thinking, creative problem-solving for bespoke customer solutions	AI algorithms for trend analysis, machine learning for market behavior forecasts, automated generation of development ideas
Relationship and Business Development	Personal relationship cultivation, human negotiation tactics, high-stakes deal crafting with strategic human oversight	AI-enabled initial customer contact tools, automated responses for efficiency, AI scripts for standardized communication
Problem Solving and Crisis Management	Adaptive strategies for crisis resolution, human-led intervention in complex issues, intuition-driven ethical considerations	Machine learning for predictive analytics in problem areas, AI systems for early detection of potential crises
Governance and Compliance	Interpretation and application of legal and regulatory frameworks, human-led compliance strategy development	Automated tracking and reporting systems for compliance, AI audit tools for regulatory adherence
Transaction Processing	Critical analysis of automated system outputs, human intervention in complex cases, quality assurance by expert staff	AI for efficient transaction processing, machine learning algorithms for optimizing payment systems, automated high-volume data handling

Table 17.1 (*continued*)

Function Category	Managed by Humans	Managed by AI
Customer Service and Support	Empathic customer engagement, human discernment for advanced support, personalized service based on human judgment	Chatbots for handling routine customer inquiries, AI for 24/7 customer interaction, automated systems for customer support ticketing
Fraud Detection and Security	Human-led verification of AI flaggings, strategic decision-making in security incidents, oversight of ai-driven security measures	AI for monitoring transaction patterns, machine learning for detecting anomalous behavior, automated flagging systems for potential fraud

abilities, and interpersonal connections that humans bring to these functions. Note how we can identify again our three Human-Ready Humics here: critical thinking, genuine creativity, and social abilities.

These Humics are critical for navigating the uncertainties of business, fostering innovation, and building relationships that are essential for a company's growth and adaptation in a rapidly changing marketplace. So these capabilities not only help us to create more value at a personal level thanks to the synergies they create with AI, but they are also the strategic activities that need to be managed by humans to generate value in the context of the most automated companies.

Partnering with AI on Critical Thinking, Creativity, and Social Abilities

How can AI and humans best work together on tasks involving critical thinking?

AI can support critical thinking tasks by providing data and identifying patterns or risks, but humans are essential for interpreting this information. Table 17.2 outlines the typical split between the roles of AI and humans in activities involving critical thinking and ethics.

Table 17.2 Critical thinking: typical split of roles between AI and humans.

Activity	Role of AI	Role of Humans
Data Analysis for Decision Support	Processing large datasets to identify trends and provide insights for decision-making	Making the final judgment calls based on AI-provided data, considering nuances and external factors
Ethical Decision-Making	Assisting in identifying potential ethical issues based on programmed guidelines and historical data	Evaluating and applying ethical principles to make decisions that AI cannot autonomously handle
Complex Problem-Solving	Offering multiple scenarios and solutions based on logical analysis of data	Applying creative thinking and intuition to solve problems that require a deep understanding of context
Risk Assessment and Management	Analyzing potential risks using historical data and statistical models	Assessing and deciding on complex risks that require human intuition and experience
Compliance and Legal Interpretation	Automating routine compliance checks and flagging inconsistencies	Interpreting laws and regulations in complex situations where nuanced understanding is essential
Privacy and Data Protection	Monitoring data usage and access to ensure adherence to privacy policies	Making decisions about data privacy that require a balance of legal, ethical, and human factors
Bias Detection and Mitigation	Scanning and identifying biases in data and algorithms	Reviewing and addressing biases detected by AI, considering societal and ethical implications
Stakeholder Engagement and Communication	Distributing information and collecting feedback through automated systems	Handling sensitive communications and making judgment calls based on emotional intelligence

This matrix highlights that AI can support critical thinking tasks by providing data and identifying patterns or risks. However, humans are essential for interpreting this information within a broader context, making final decisions, and dealing with complex ethical considerations. Human judgment can't be replaced in areas that require a deep understanding of context, subtlety, and moral reasoning.

Table 17.3 is a step-by-step guide for how to succeed in the subtle art of collaborating with AI for critical thinking work, and more precisely here for making complex decisions.

Table 17.3 Example of detailed role split for complex decisions.

Steps	Description	Tips for Success	Example
1. Identify the Decision Scope	Start with a clear goal for the decision-making process.	Ensure clarity of purpose and desired outcomes.	Decide on the direction for a new product line.
2. Gather Data and Insights	Collect relevant data and use AI for predictive analytics.	Use diverse data sources for a well-rounded view.	Analyze market trends and consumer feedback using AI tools.
3. Generate Options	Use AI to simulate scenarios and generate alternatives.	Encourage wide-ranging options before narrowing down.	Create different product designs and use AI to test market acceptance.
4. Evaluate Risks and Rewards	Assess each option with AI for potential risks and rewards.	Look for balanced, data-driven assessments.	Use AI to forecast the potential success and risks associated with each product design.
5. Deliberate and Decide	Use AI insights to inform discussions and make informed decisions.	Foster a culture of informed debate and consensus.	Discuss the AI-provided forecasts and choose the best product design for development.

(continued)

Table 17.3   (*continued*)

Steps	Description	Tips for Success	Example
6. Implement and Monitor	Deploy the chosen option and use AI for real-time monitoring.	Set up key performance indicators to track progress.	Launch the product and use AI to monitor sales and customer feedback for real-time insights.
7. Review and Adapt	Regularly review outcomes with AI analytics to adapt strategies as needed.	Be prepared to pivot based on new data and insights.	Adjust marketing strategies based on AI-driven analysis of ongoing sales data.

What are the different ways to collaborate with AI in decision-making?

Should all decisions be made by humans? Should AI be left to make decisions on its own? These are very important questions. I use a simple three-category framework to help me assess the right kind of collaboration between AI and people in decision-making.

This framework is vital as it ensures the optimal use of technology while retaining essential human oversight. It delineates when AI should support, elevate, or automate decisions, based on the complexity and impact of each decision.

In AI-assisted decision-making, categorizing decisions depends on complexity, risk, and the need for human judgment:

- **Decisions supported by AI:** Humans analyze and make the decision using AI-generated data and insights. This is typical for decisions involving human values and ethics. For example, a doctor examines AI's analysis of various treatments' success rates but considers the patient's unique circumstances before deciding.

- **Decisions elevated by AI:** AI analyzes and suggests options for decisions. Humans review the options, select one, and make the decision. It is often used where the AI's suggestion is complex and requires a human touch. For instance, a financial analyst uses AI to suggest stock purchases but reviews economic factors before making the final call.

- **Decisions automated by AI:** AI makes the decision independently, suitable for routine, low-risk decisions. Humans are not involved. For example, an e-commerce platform's AI automatically adjusts prices based on demand without human intervention.

This approach enhances efficiency, reduces errors, and ensures that critical decisions benefit from the right level of human involvement.

How can humans and AI best work together on tasks involving creativity?

Based on my experience with highly automated companies such as Ant Group, Table 17.4 is an outline of the typical split between the roles of AI and humans in creative activities, providing clarity on the specific functions of each.

This table illustrates that while AI can handle tasks such as generating ideas and automating functional art creation, the human role is pivotal in refining ideas, injecting creativity and emotion, ensuring ethical standards, and understanding cultural nuances. This synergy maximizes the potential of both AI and human capabilities.

How can AI and humans work together on tasks involving social authenticity?

Table 17.5 is a matrix that outlines the typical split between the roles of AI and humans in activities involving social authenticity.

This table illustrates that while AI can handle initial interactions, schedule coordination, and provide data analysis, humans are integral for activities that require a deeper level of social abilities, such as understanding complex emotions, personal rapport building, and cultural adaptation. Human qualities like empathy, emotional intelligence, and the ability to inspire and motivate are highlighted as essential in roles that AI cannot fully replicate.

Table 17.4   Creativity: typical split of roles between AI and humans.

Creative Activity	Role of AI	Role of Humans
Functional Art Creation	Automating and streamlining the creation of background music or visual backgrounds.	Humans are not typically involved in creating functional art because this can be efficiently done by AI.
Idea Generation	Generating a high volume of creative ideas and patterns quickly from extensive datasets.	Humans draw inspiration from AI-generated ideas to create more nuanced and complex creative works.
Idea Refinement	Technology's role ends with the generation phase; refinement is handed over to humans.	Refining and contextualizing AI-generated ideas to create nuanced, contextually relevant work.
Ultra-Creativity	AI does not engage in ultra-creativity; this is solely the domain of humans.	Humans engage in deeply emotional, tailor-made, and culturally nuanced creative tasks.
Feedback and Iteration	AI-generated content and ideas are used as a basis for feedback to improve AI algorithms.	Human feedback is crucial for teaching and improving AI, ensuring the outputs are valuable.
Collaborative Co-Creation	AI provides suggestions and modifications which are then iteratively refined by humans.	Humans work collaboratively with AI, guiding the creative process and making final judgments.
Ethical and Cultural Considerations	Technology must be monitored and guided by humans to ensure ethical usage and cultural sensitivity.	Humans ensure AI-generated content adheres to ethical standards and respects cultural implications.
Customization and Personalization	AI can assist in the initial customization and personalization based on data-driven insights.	Humans enhance AI-driven customization with personal touches and deep understanding of user needs.

Table 17.5   Social authenticity: typical split of roles between AI and humans.

Activity	Role of AI	Role of Humans
Customer Interaction	Providing initial responses to customer inquiries, using chatbots for routine support	Engaging in deep, meaningful conversations, understanding nuanced customer needs
Conflict Resolution	Identifying conflicts through sentiment analysis and alerting human managers	Mediating conflicts with emotional intelligence, understanding, and personal touch
Team Collaboration	Facilitating team communication through collaborative platforms and scheduling tools	Building team rapport, fostering trust and collaboration beyond digital communication
Leadership and Motivation	Disseminating motivational content or monitoring team engagement metrics	Providing leadership through vision, inspiration, and personal connections
Sales and Negotiation	Automating initial sales contact, providing data-driven negotiation tactics	Building relationships with clients, understanding complex needs, closing deals with a human touch
Cultural Sensitivity and Adaptation	Translating languages and providing basic cultural context through AI	Adapting communication and behavior to align with diverse cultural norms and values
Empathy and Support	Recognizing signs of distress or dissatisfaction through pattern recognition	Offering genuine empathy and emotional support, understanding complex emotional states
Training and Development	Delivering personalized training content based on individual learning patterns	Mentoring, coaching, and developing team members with a personal, human-centered approach

CHAPTER

18

Making Your Business Change-Ready

This chapter delves into a critical challenge far beyond just safeguarding your company from AI's ethical and security risks. It confronts the threats spawned by a rapidly accelerating world—a world more unpredictable and volatile than ever.

Cultivating Organizational Resilience

Will our future be easier or tougher than our past?

With its relentless drain on natural resources, technological progress is pushing us into an era of heightened crises: social upheaval, environmental disasters, health emergencies, and economic unpredictability.

The facts? Global natural disasters have increased sevenfold since 1990, with climate change a significant driver.[1] Single-day stock market crashes have become more common and severe over the past decades. Before 1987, declines over 20% were extremely rare, but since then four such crashes have occurred—Black Monday in 1987, the dot-com bubble in 2000–02, the financial crisis in 2008–9, and COVID-19 in 2020.[2]

One more: the early 2000s recession and the Great Recession from 2007 to 2009 were the two worst global recessions since World War II. The increasing severity shows economic instability and crises spreading faster in an interconnected world.[3]

In this relentless tide of turmoil, where challenges strike with unprecedented frequency and ferocity, the imperative is clear: our companies must fortify their resilience, steeling themselves against the rising adversity.

Just as individual resilience involves maintaining mental well-being in the face of life's trials, business resilience in the AI era demands a dynamic, proactive approach. It's about reinforcing the structural integrity of your organization, ensuring operational stability, and harnessing the potential for growth even as the ground shifts beneath you.

Building organizational resilience is not just an option; it's a strategic imperative. Companies must cultivate the agility to adapt, pivot, and evolve their business models to thrive amid the relentless waves of transformations in our world. Navigating this labyrinth of opportunities and threats is the ultimate test of contemporary leadership.

Why is resilience increasingly important for a company?

Picture navigating a vast, intricate network of highways. In the past, businesses cruised these roads at a leisurely pace, akin to a relaxed drive through the countryside at 30 miles per hour. Thus, when obstacles were encountered, there was ample time for course correction, minimizing potential damage.

However, today's business landscape resembles a high-stakes race on the highway, where companies are propelled at blistering speeds, like a high-performance sports car hurtling forward at 100 miles per hour. In this turbocharged environment, every twist and turn is amplified, and the margin for error diminishes drastically. A challenge or a misstep, once a minor hurdle, now has the potential to escalate into a high-impact collision, with consequences far more severe and widespread.

In this high-velocity world, the need for resilience becomes paramount. Just as a high-speed car requires robust engineering, advanced safety features, and the agility to navigate swiftly and safely, businesses today require fortified structures, robust strategic frameworks, and an agile, adaptive approach. The stakes are higher, the speed is greater, and the need for a "more solid car"—a more resilient business—is not just an advantage; it's a necessity for survival and success.

How can I make my company resilient?

After studying the examples of several successful and less successful companies, I have developed a framework for business resilience. I'll share the stories of three companies that exemplify resilience (Netflix, Microsoft, and Apple) and three companies that have struggled (Kodak, Blockbuster, and Tower Records). Additionally, to provide further context, I incorporate the cases of Ant Group and John Deere, renowned for their successful AI business models.

To start with, here's a brief background on each of the resilience winners, providing context for the resilience framework:

- **Netflix:** Originally a DVD rental service, Netflix swiftly adapted to changing consumer preferences and technological advancements by transitioning to online streaming. It further cemented its position in the industry by venturing into content production, becoming a leading global entertainment platform.

- **Microsoft:** Facing stagnation and increased competition, Microsoft revitalized itself under Satya Nadella's leadership. The company shifted its focus toward cloud computing and AI, transforming from a software giant into a leader in modern technological solutions.

- **Apple:** After a period of struggle in the 1990s, Apple, under Steve Jobs's leadership, turned its fortunes around by innovating and launching groundbreaking products like the iPod, iPhone, and iPad. Apple's focus on design, user experience, and an integrated ecosystem contributed to its resurgence and dominance.

And here are the resilience losers:

- **Kodak:** Once a leader in the photographic film industry, Kodak failed to adapt to the digital photography revolution. Despite having the technology to lead the change, Kodak's reluctance to embrace digital innovation led to its decline.

- **Blockbuster:** Blockbuster, the leading video rental service, missed the digital streaming trend and stuck to its brick-and-mortar business model. The rise of services like Netflix, offering more convenience and a subscription model, led to Blockbuster's downfall.

- **Tower Records:** Once a global music retailer, Tower Records didn't pivot quickly enough to digital sales and streaming in the face of the digital music revolution. This lag led to a decline in sales and the company's eventual bankruptcy.

I have added to my research the cases of the two companies—Ant Group and John Deere—that we used as illustrations of successful AI business models.

The business resilience framework   Table 18.1 encapsulates the essence of business resilience, broken down into three themes.

This table serves as a comprehensive roadmap for businesses aiming to enhance their resilience. It combines practical steps with real-world examples, illustrating how anticipation, innovation, customer focus, digital strategy, organizational culture, financial prudence, and visionary leadership, among other factors, play crucial roles in building a company capable of thriving amid the challenges and opportunities of the coming tide.

The Path to Adaptive Mastery

What is adaptability in the context of a business?

Adaptability is being able to adjust to new situations, environments, or changes quickly and efficiently. Foster a corporate agility that enables swift adaptation to crises, new technological landscapes, regulatory changes, and evolving consumer expectations.

Why is adaptability important to companies?

It's a common misconception that being reactive to change is sufficient for a company's survival and growth. In my consulting experience,

Table 18.1 How to improve the resilience of your company.

Theme	Key Resilience Factors	Actionable Steps	Illustrative Company Stories
Strategic Agility	Anticipate and embrace change.	Regularly scan industry trends and be willing to pivot business models.	Netflix foresaw the shift to streaming, while Kodak failed to embrace digital photography.
	Innovate continuously.	Encourage new ideas and allocate resources for R&D.	Apple innovated with the iPhone and iPad, while Polaroid did not move beyond film photography.
	Adopt a strong digital strategy.	Develop a comprehensive digital strategy, including online presence and digital marketing.	Netflix embraced digital early, while Blockbuster was late to adopt a digital strategy.
	Leverage data and analytics for decision-making.	Invest in advanced data analytics tools and capabilities to make informed decisions.	Ant Group leverages big data and analytics to transform financial services.
	Foster partnerships and collaborations.	Engage in strategic partnerships and collaborations with other companies and institutions.	John Deere forms strategic partnerships with tech companies and research institutions.

(*continued*)

Table 18.1   (*continued*)

Theme	Key Resilience Factors	Actionable Steps	Illustrative Company Stories
Operational Excellence	Use a customer-centric approach.	Understand and adapt to changing consumer preferences.	Apple focused on user experience, while Tower Records missed the digital music shift.
	Ensure financial flexibility and risk management.	Maintain a strong balance sheet, manage debts prudently, and have contingency plans.	All companies need to balance investment and have financial contingencies.
	Cultivate a flexible and adaptive organizational structure.	Adopt a flexible organizational structure that can quickly adjust to changing market conditions.	Ant Group's adaptive organizational structure allows rapid response to regulatory changes.
	Develop robust contingency and risk management plans.	Identify potential risks and vulnerabilities and develop comprehensive contingency plans.	John Deere's robust risk management involves comprehensive contingency planning.
	Prioritize sustainability and social responsibility.	Integrate sustainability and social responsibility into the business model.	Ant Group incorporates sustainability into its business model with initiatives like Ant Forest, which encourages users to engage in eco-friendly activities.

Theme	Key Resilience Factors	Actionable Steps	Illustrative Company Stories
Cultural Strength	Build a resilient and adaptive organizational culture.	Cultivate a culture that values resilience, adaptability, learning, and innovation.	Microsoft pivoted under Nadella, focusing on cloud and AI, while Kodak resisted change.
	Foster visionary and agile leadership.	Develop leadership that is forward-thinking, adaptable, and capable of strategic decisions.	Leadership styles of Steve Jobs and Satya Nadella illustrate the importance of visionary yet adaptable leadership.
	Embrace continuous learning and development.	Foster a culture of lifelong learning and skill development within the organization.	John Deere continually evolves its product line by integrating advanced technologies.
	Promote psychological safety and employee well-being.	Create an environment where employees feel safe to express ideas and voice concerns.	John Deere invests in employee development and safety initiatives, fostering a culture that values well-being.

I've observed that this approach is not just inadequate; it's potentially detrimental. Here's why:

- **Speed of change:** In today's fast-paced world, especially with the rapid advancements in AI and technology, change happens quickly and often unexpectedly. Companies that are merely reactive are always a step behind, playing catch-up instead of leading the way.

- **Missed opportunities:** Being reactive means a company is focused on responding to external forces rather than proactively seeking opportunities. By the time a reactive company responds, the opportunity might have already been seized by a more proactive competitor.

- **Resource inefficiency:** Reactive companies tend to make decisions in crisis mode, often leading to rushed and less-than-optimal solutions that require more resources to fix later. This is both inefficient and costly.

- **Employee morale and culture:** A reactive stance can breed a culture of constant urgency and stress. It can demotivate employees, as they feel they're always in a state of firefighting rather than contributing to strategic, forward-thinking initiatives.

- **Customer perception:** Customers can sense when a company is always playing catch-up. It can lead to a perception of the company as outdated or behind the times, which can erode trust and loyalty.

For these reasons, it's crucial for companies to move beyond the misconception that being reactive to change is enough. In an era marked by rapid technological advancements and shifting market dynamics, the ability to embed change into the organizational fabric and navigate it with agility is not just a strategic advantage; it's a necessity for long-term success.

How can a company become adaptable?

Toyota provides a compelling example of a company that has consistently anticipated change and even purposely triggered change within itself to cultivate a culture of continuous improvement and adaptability. This approach is deeply rooted in the Toyota Production System (TPS), also known as "Lean manufacturing."

Continuous Improvement and Adaptation: Toyota Production System (TPS)
- **Kaizen (continuous improvement):** Toyota institutionalized the concept of continuous, incremental improvement (kaizen). The company constantly seeks ways to improve efficiency, reduce waste, and enhance product quality.

- **Jidoka (automation with a human touch):** Toyota implemented this principle to ensure that production defects are addressed immediately and prevent faulty products from moving down the line, effectively embracing change at the microlevel in their manufacturing processes.

Anticipating and Leading Market Change: Hybrid and Hydrogen Fuel Cell Vehicles

- **Hybrid Technology:** In the late 1990s, well before the global push for sustainability and emission reductions gained momentum, Toyota introduced the Prius, the world's first mass-produced hybrid vehicle. This was a significant risk at the time, because the market for such vehicles was unproven.

- **Hydrogen Fuel Cell Vehicles:** More recently, Toyota invested in hydrogen fuel cell technology, introducing the Mirai, despite the market for hydrogen fuel cells still being in its infancy. This move is part of Toyota's long-term vision for sustainable mobility, anticipating future market shifts toward alternative energy vehicles.

Internal Change to Foster Adaptability: Toyota New Global Architecture (TNGA)

- **Toyota New Global Architecture (TNGA):** In the 2010s, Toyota launched TNGA, a new strategy for vehicle platforms and powertrain components. This initiative was not just about reducing costs but also about making the organization more flexible and responsive to market changes. It involved a significant overhaul of their engineering and manufacturing processes to allow for more shared components and quicker response to market demands.

Toyota's approach exemplifies a company that doesn't rest on its laurels but instead actively seeks out change, uses it as an opportunity for growth, and embeds adaptability into its corporate culture. By doing so, Toyota trains itself to navigate and thrive amid change, maintaining its position as a global leader in the automotive industry.

What did Toyota do to achieve such a level of adaptability?

Toyota's philosophy of purposely triggering change within itself to better navigate and thrive amid change is deeply rooted in the Toyota Production System (TPS) and its overarching management philosophy. This approach is based on two core principles: continuous improvement (kaizen) and respect for people. Here's how these principles foster a culture of proactive change:

Continuous Improvement (Kaizen)

- Toyota instills a mindset that there is always room for improvement, no matter how successful a process or product may be. This mindset encourages employees at all levels to constantly look for ways to enhance efficiency, reduce waste, and improve quality.

- Problems are not viewed negatively but are seen as opportunities for learning and improvement. Employees are encouraged to identify issues and collaborate on solving them, ensuring that the organization continuously evolves and improves.

- Innovation is not just reserved for R&D departments; it's part of the daily work. Every employee is encouraged to come up with small, incremental changes that can lead to significant improvements over time.

Respect for People

- Employees are considered the most valuable asset. Toyota empowers its employees to take initiative and make decisions. This empowerment fosters a sense of ownership and a proactive attitude toward change.

- Toyota promotes a culture of teamwork where sharing knowledge and collaborative problem-solving are the norms. This approach helps in adapting to changes more effectively as it combines the strengths and perspectives of diverse team members.

- Continuous learning and development are integral. By investing in its people, Toyota ensures that the workforce is skilled, adaptable, and ready to embrace new challenges.

Structured yet Flexible Processes

- While Toyota has standardized processes to ensure quality and efficiency, it also maintains flexibility within these processes to adapt to changes quickly, whether they are changes in consumer demand, technology, or the market environment.

- Toyota plans for the future with a long-term vision but remains flexible enough to make short-term adjustments. This balance allows the company to stay focused on its goals while being agile enough to respond to immediate changes.

By integrating these principles into its culture, Toyota doesn't just react to change; it anticipates and drives change. The company understands that the business environment is dynamic and that staying ahead requires a proactive approach to change, continuous improvement, and a deep respect for people. This philosophy has made Toyota not only a leader in the automotive industry but also a model for operational excellence and adaptability across various sectors.

PART

VI

Implementing an Action Plan

Throughout this book, we've explored what it means to be IRRE-PLACEABLE in the age of AI. We've explored this concept from various perspectives to create a cohesive approach that consistently addresses all facets of your life—personal, professional, parental, and entrepreneurial. Now it's time to put all of this into action.

In this final part of the book, I'll provide you with an example of a concrete plan to implement the strategies we've discussed. Remember, this is just a template—ensure that you tailor it to your needs so you can effectively adhere to it.

CHAPTER

19

Your Action Plan

Based on the concepts and strategies presented throughout the book, this chapter presents 15 actions to implement for the coming months to become IRREPLACEABLE in an AI-driven world.

The First Week

Here are four actions you can take in the first week to become IRREPLACEABLE:

Action 1: Go through the IRREPLACEABLE Quotient (IRQ) at www.irreplaceable.ai and identify your areas for improvement across the three competencies of the future:

- AI-Ready
- Human-Ready
- Change-Ready

Set specific, measurable goals for competency development. For example, within the next three months, identify and implement AI tools that can save you at least five hours per week.

Action 2: In your daily life and interactions with others, push yourself to change your mindset. Begin building an AI mindset by focusing on prioritizing efficiency over effort, value over volume, collaboration over control, balance over burnout, and reflection over rush. Refer to Chapter 8.

Action 3: Assess activities to be automated with AI or eliminated by leveraging the 20% rule presented in Chapter 8 of the book. The purpose is that you make time for the activities you will need to implement over the coming weeks to become IRREPLACEABLE.

Action 4: Take control of your digital life by monitoring and limiting AI-generated distractions. Implement the strategies suggested in the book, such as controlling notifications on your devices and establishing specific times for checking emails and social media—refer to Chapter 12. The purpose here is also to build free time that you will be able to leverage in the coming days to implement new IRREPLACEABLE actions.

The First Month

After the first week, there are several more steps you can take to round out that first month of becoming IRREPLACEABLE.

Action 5: Start building up your Humics. As you have been able to free up some of your time thanks to automation—Action 3—you can now dedicate 30 minutes daily to developing them. Choose one of the three Humics to focus on each week, such as genuine creativity, social authenticity, or critical thinking. Engage in activities or exercises that challenge and develop this skill, such as brainstorming sessions, active listening practice, or problem-solving scenarios. Follow the detailed approach suggested in Part 2 of the book. Read the suggested additional material.

Action 6: Build the habit of regularly maintaining your AI literacy. Leverage the time you have made available during the first week to dedicate 15% of your time daily to AI literacy. Achieve that by reading articles and books, watching interviews, listening to podcasts, or taking online courses to constantly strengthen and update your understanding of AI, its applications, and potential impacts on your industry and society.

Action 7: Identify activities that could be elevated by AI—use the 20% rule presented in Chapter 8. Identify AI tools that could be relevant to your work and start exploring how to use them. Follow the task elevation approach presented in the book.

Action 8: Learn about the data privacy settings of your most-used platforms and applications. Review and customize them. Apply the approach suggested in Chapter 14 to take control of your private data.

Action 9: Start taking the habit of strengthening your resilience. Dedicate a few minutes each day to practice mindfulness, breathing, and physical exercise as described in Chapter 9.

The First Three Months

Continue performing the actions that you started during the last month. In addition, perform the following over the next several months:

Action 10: Nurture your children's autonomy, competence, and human bonds in AI use. Follow the approach suggested in Chapter 11 to ensure they grow alongside AI.

Action 11: Advocate for responsible AI by promoting initiatives that benefit humanity. Actively advocate for AI that propels human progress such as applications in healthcare, environmental conservation, and education; vote with your actions by purchasing products and services from companies that use AI transparently and ethically, and by boycotting those that don't. Speak up against AI used for destructive or unethical purposes as described in Chapter 14.

Action 12: Practice resilience and adaptability: Embrace adaptability by focusing on potential gains and celebrating adversity as presented in Chapter 9. Also, actively seek out and initiate changes in your life.

Action 13: Share your knowledge and involve others. Initiate conversations with colleagues or team members about the impact of AI and the importance of skill development. Engage in active learning techniques, such as explaining AI concepts you've learned in your own words to a friend or colleague. Organize lunch-and-learn sessions or a book club discussion on topics related to AI, innovation, or personal growth.

Moving Forward

After three months of becoming IRREPLACEABLE, follow these steps:

Action 14: Take the IRREPLACEABLE Quotient (IRQ) again to assess the progress you made over the last three months. If needed, read the book again, or at least the parts you need to consolidate, so that it really anchors in your mind.

Action 15: Share and celebrate. Update your professional profiles and résumé to highlight your IRREPLACEABLE skills and experiences. Celebrate your progress and share your learnings with others to inspire and motivate them on their own IRREPLACEABLE journey, through blog posts, social media updates, or presentations. Use the hashtag #irreplaceable.

Moving forward, persist with the practices you've adopted over the past three months and embed them as lifelong habits; they are the pillars of your IRREPLACEABLE future success.

Make this action plan yours and evolve it as you go. Recognize that this is not a destination but an ongoing journey in a landscape that is ever-changing—you, the environment, and the ever-evolving AI. Hence, embrace the cycle of perpetual learning, unlearning, and relearning.

Summary of the Key Actions You've Learned in the Book

Table 19.1 recaps the three competencies of the future to become IRREPLACEABLE.

Table 19.1 Three competencies and approaches to achieve them.

Compe-tency	Description	Sample approaches taught in the book	Refer-ence
AI-Ready	"AI-Ready" involves not only leveraging AI for augmented performance but also safeguarding against its negative impacts, such as ethical issues or addictions.		
Augmen-tation	Augment yourself with AI by creating an AI mindset, strategically leveraging AI, and maintaining AI literacy.	• Adopt an AI mindset by prioritizing efficiency over effort, value over volume, collaboration over control, balance over burnout, and reflection over rush. • Identify activities that can be automated, elevated, or eliminated using AI. • Select, integrate, and educate yourself on appropriate AI tools. • Dedicate 15% of work hours to learning and updating AI literacy. Knowing 30% about a topic is enough for fluency. • Regularly reassess and adjust your AI strategies.	*Chapter 8*
Protec-tion	Protect yourself and your children from the negative impacts of AI, such as distractions, addictions, or data privacy issues.	• Identify and challenge undesirable emotions and distorted thoughts to prevent AI addiction. • Be aware of and protect against misinformation, such as deepfakes and manipulated content. • Customize privacy settings, share only necessary data, and use trusted services to protect personal information. • Regularly review and clean your digital footprint. • Control notifications, schedule social media check-ins and email checks to minimize distractions.	*Chapters 12 and 13*

(continued)

Table 19.1   (*continued*)

Compe- tency	Description	Sample approaches taught in the book	Refer- ence
Responsi- bility	Use and build AI responsibly: mindful, ethical, respectful, and sustainable.	• Nurture children's autonomy, human bonds, and competence in AI use. • Identify and engage in non-AI activities following the "Joy and Growth Principle." • Advocate for AI initiatives that benefit humanity and speak out against unethical AI uses. • Make conscious consumer choices to support companies that use AI transparently and ethically. • Teach AI ethics and love by interacting respectfully and sharing your human values with it.	*Chapters* 11 *and* 14
Human- Ready	"Human-Ready" emphasizes nurturing the "Humics," abilities that are distinctly human and that AI can't authentically replicate. This focus ensures the highest level of synergy with AI, because these abilities are deeply embedded in aspects of humanity—our unique life experiences, emotions, personal stories, and personalities. Love is unique to humans and is expressed through the Humics. Outcomes derived from the Humics are valued more when they originate from a human, rather than from AI. For example, humans value a human coach more than they value an AI coach.		

Compe- tency	Description	Sample approaches taught in the book	Refer- ence
Genuine Creativity	Generate original ideas and solutions, artistic expressions, and novel approaches to problems. Think outside the box, drawing on inspiration, intuition, and subjective experiences.	• Engage in creative thinking during and after exercising. • Put yourself in a "hypnagogic state" to boost creativity. • Achieve a "flow" state to heighten focus on internal thoughts and creativity. • Practice generating original ideas, artistic expressions, and novel problem-solving approaches. • Draw on inspiration, intuition, and subjective experiences to think outside the box.	*Chapters* 3, 5, 6 *and* 7
Critical Thinking	Analyze and evaluate information by applying independent judgment and ethical reason-ing. Critique the validity of information, use intuition to make decisions, and engage in self-reflection to understand your biases, purpose, and underlying motivations. Ask better questions to get better answers. Build trust.	• Educate yourself about the 188 human cognitive biases and reflect on your decision-making process. • Build and trust your intuition by learning from past decisions. • Develop the habit of critically analyzing the information you consume. • Spend time understanding your motivations, values, and biases through self-reflection. • Regularly reflect on your actions, decisions, and their outcomes.	*Chapters* 3, 5, 6 *and* 7

(continued)

Table 19.1   (*continued*)

Competency	Description	Sample approaches taught in the book	Reference
Social Authenticity	Forge deep, meaningful relationships, understand complex social cues, and express empathy in ways that are profoundly connected to our consciousness and sense of self. This includes genuine emotional connections and the capacity for moral judgment. It also involves leadership to guide and positively influence other people.	• Practice active listening and seeing situations from others' perspectives to develop empathy. • Improve communication skills through storytelling, articulation, and nonverbal cues. • Learn conflict resolution strategies, such as maintaining neutrality and finding common ground. • Cultivate social awareness by paying attention to social cues and respecting cultural differences. • Strengthen team collaboration by identifying and appreciating diverse skills and perspectives.	*Chapters 3, 5, 6 and 7*

Compe-tency	Description	Sample approaches taught in the book	Refer-ence
Change-Ready	"Change-Ready" emphasizes developing resilience and adaptability to thrive amidst the rapid changes and heightened challenges brought about by the advancement of AI.		
Resil-ience	Build a dynamic process of maintaining or regaining your mental well-being in the face of obstacles, changes, or pressures.	• Practice breathing exercises regularly to build resilience. • Connect with nature to maintain mental well-being. • Engage in mindfulness practices to develop resilience. • Celebrate adversity as an opportunity for growth and learning.	*Chapter 9*
Adapt-ability	Quickly and efficiently adjust to new situations, environments, or changes.	• Actively seek out and initiate changes in your life. • Focus on the potential gains from changes rather than the losses. • Collaborate with others to increase collective adaptability. • Cultivate a flexible mindset and be open to new experiences.	*Chapter 9*
Relearn-ing how to learn	Engage in unlearning to discard outdated knowledge, and pave the way for relearning—acquiring new competencies in a fresh context.	• Create emotional connections with learning material to improve memory retention. • Employ interleaved practice by mixing different types of problems or subjects in a study session. • Actively engage with material by explaining it in your own words to strengthen neural pathways.	*Chapter 11*

CHAPTER

20

Final Words

As you embark on this exhilarating journey into an AI-driven future, it's clear that the path ahead is one of tremendous opportunity and transformation. By embracing the IRREPLACEABLE framework and cultivating the competencies of being AI-Ready, Human-Ready, and Change-Ready, you position yourself not just to survive, but to thrive in this new era.

For ourselves and our children, becoming IRREPLACEABLE is a profound journey of self-discovery and reinvention. It challenges us to look within, identify our unique strengths and passions, and develop the skills and mindset needed to create value in an AI-augmented world. It invites us to redefine our relationship with technology, seeing AI not as a threat, but as a powerful ally in our quest for personal and professional growth.

For our businesses, becoming IRREPLACEABLE is a strategic imperative. It requires bold leadership, a culture of continuous learning and innovation, and a willingness to fundamentally rethink traditional business models and processes. It demands a new kind of partnership between humans and machines, one that leverages the unique strengths of each to drive breakthrough performance, value creation, and differentiation.

As we've explored throughout this book, the rise of AI presents both challenges and opportunities. It disrupts industries, transforms

261

the nature of work, and raises profound ethical and societal questions. AI destroys the present, but enables us to build a better future. Yet amid this disruption, there is also immense potential for you, your kids, and your company.

This is not a journey we can undertake alone. Becoming truly IRREPLACEABLE requires collaboration, partnership, and a shared commitment to shaping a future that benefits all. It calls for open dialogue, diverse perspectives, and a willingness to tackle tough challenges head on.

As I've engaged with readers, clients, and colleagues around the world, I've been inspired by the stories of individuals and organizations who are already embracing this IRREPLACEABLE mindset. From the teacher who is using AI to personalize learning and unlock student potential to the startup that is harnessing machine learning to solve global health challenges, these pioneers are charting the course for a brighter, more resilient future.

Their stories remind us that becoming IRREPLACEABLE is not a destination but a journey—one that requires courage, curiosity, and a steadfast commitment to growth. It's a journey that will undoubtedly be marked by setbacks and challenges, but also by incredible breakthroughs and triumphs.

But the path to be IRREPLACEABLE isn't just about achievement; it's about evolution. It invites us to imagine a world where AI's automation frees us from mundane, repetitive, and boring occupations to more exciting and value-adding activities.

AI is taking the front seat. We are transitioning from being the creators and providers of answers to becoming the ones who ask the questions and curate information. We are moving from being the engine of progress to being the compass of progress. AI is the new engine.

It also means reimagining the nature of work itself, recognizing that the societal value of a job doesn't always translate to a paycheck. With AI as our ally, we can create a world where people are free to pursue their passions, care for their loved ones, and contribute to their communities in meaningful ways.

We can redefine success, not in terms of productivity, GDP, or stock prices, but in terms of human flourishing and planetary health. With that, we have an unprecedented opportunity to rediscover and reinvent what it means to be human.

This is the essence of Abraham Maslow's hierarchy of needs: a progression from the basic demands of existence to the pinnacle of self-actualization. Yes, the IRREPLACEABLE framework is our lift to the top of the Maslow pyramid! AI is the catalyst that propels us upward, freeing us to explore the uncharted territories of our potential.

AI isn't merely a catalyst for economic productivity but a means to elevate the human spirit, envisaging a future where technology amplifies our most human qualities. AI grants us the space, time, and mental freedom to explore the most critical questions of our existence, such as our purpose in life.

The journey to be IRREPLACEABLE extends to the very fabric of our society. As parents and leaders in the age of AI, we have a sacred duty to create a world that works for everyone. This means harnessing the power of AI to solve global challenges, from eradicating poverty and disease to reversing climate change and creating opportunities for all.

This is the world we must fight for—a world where AI serves the interests of humanity, not the other way around. A world where being IRREPLACEABLE isn't just a personal aspiration, but a collective imperative. A world where every person has the chance to live a life of purpose, joy, and connection.

The journey begins now. It starts with a simple choice: to be a passive spectator of change, or to be an active agent of transformation. To cling to the familiar, or to boldly embrace the unknown. To settle for what is, or to strive for what can be.

This book is just the trigger. The true transformation continues online with the Academy at www.irreplaceable.ai, where you'll find a vibrant community of fellow IRREPLACEABLEs, ready to support you, challenge you, and inspire you to reach new heights.

Take the IRREPLACEABLE Quotient (IRQ) test and discover your strengths and growth areas at www.irreplaceable.ai.

Dive into the wealth of resources, expert discussions, and cutting-edge insights available on my LinkedIn page (www.linkedin.com/in/pascalbornet), X account (@pascal_bornet), and YouTube channel (@pascal_bornet).

Share your own stories and breakthroughs with the hashtag #irreplaceable, and become a beacon of light for others on this path.

Notes

Preface

1. Roser, Max, et al., "Life Expectancy," Our World in Data, 2020, https://ourworldindata.org/life-expectancy
2. Roser, Max, and Esteban Ortiz-Ospina, "Literacy," Our World in Data, 2019, https://ourworldindata.org/literacy
3. Roser, Max, and Esteban Ortiz-Ospina, "Global Extreme Poverty," Our World in Data, 2013, https://ourworldindata.org/poverty
4. UN Inter-Agency Group for Child Mortality Estimation, 2020, https://childmortality.org/about
5. Ritchie, Hannah, and Max, Roser, "CO_2 and Greenhouse Gas Emissions," Our World in Data, 2020, https://ourworldindata.org/co2-and-greenhouse-gas-emissions

Chapter 1: Don't Believe All You Hear About AI!

1. Siggelkow, Nicolaj, and Christian Terwiesch, "The Age of Continuous Connection," *Harvard Business Review*, May–June 2019, https://hbr.org/2019/05/the-age-of-continuous-connection

Chapter 2: The Essence of Being IRREPLACEABLE

1. Fæste, Lars, Martin Reeves, and Kevin Whitaker, "The Science of Organizational Change," BCG Henderson Institute, May 2, 2019, https://www.bcg.com/featured-insights/winning-the-20s/science-of-change
2. "Why Do Most Transformations Fail? A Conversation with Harry Robinson," July 10, 2019, https://www.mckinsey.com/business-functions/transformation/our-insights/why-do-most-transformations-fail-a-conversation-with-harry-robinson

Chapter 7: Bringing Your Humics to a Whole New Level

1. LinkedIn Talent Solutions, "Most Promising Jobs: A Reevaluation," LinkedIn Talent Solutions Blog, 2022, https://business.linkedin.com/talent-solutions/blog/trends-and-research/2022/most-promising-jobs-reevaluation
2. World Economic Forum, "The Future of Jobs Report 2022," World Economic Forum, October 2022, https://www3.weforum.org/docs/WEF_Future_of_Jobs_2022.pdf
3. Adobe, "Creative Salary Survey," The Blog, accessed May 24, 2024, https://theblog.adobe.com/creative-salary-survey/
4. McKinsey & Company, "Need Some Creative Inspiration? The Most Innovative Companies of 2022," McKinsey Design, 2022, https://www.mckinsey.com/business-functions/mckinsey-design/our-insights/need-some-creative-inspiration-the-most-innovative-companies-of-2022

Chapter 8: Augmenting Yourself with AI at Work

1. Fabrizio Dell'Acqua et al., "Navigating the Jagged Technological Frontier: Field Experimental Evidence of the Effects of AI on Knowledge Worker Productivity and Quality," 2023, https://www.hbs.edu/ris/Publication%20Files/24-013_d9b45b68-9e74-42d6-a1c6-c72fb70c7282.pdf
2. Yu, Eileen, "Workers with AI Skills Can Expect Higher Salaries—Depending on Their Role," March 7, 2024, https://www.zdnet.com/article/workers-with-ai-skills-can-expect-higher-salaries-depending-on-their-role/

3. Sidoti, Olivia, and Emily A. Vogels, "What Americans Know About AI, Cybersecurity and Big Tech," August 17, 2023, https://www.pewresearch.org/internet/2023/08/17/what-americans-know-about-ai-cybersecurity-and-big-tech/

4. D. Crystal, *English as a Global Language*, 2nd ed. (Cambridge University Press, 2003); Neeley, Tsedal, "Global Business Speaks English: Why You Need a Language Strategy Now," *Harvard Business Review*, May 2012, https://www.hbs.edu/faculty/Pages/item.aspx?num=42451

5. Hart Research Associates, July 2023, https://fm.cnbc.com/applications/cnbc.com/resources/editorialfiles/2023/07/21/econsurveypart2.pdf

Chapter 9: Fostering Resilience and Adaptability in a Rapidly Evolving World

1. Kurzweil, Ray, "The Law of Accelerating Returns," Kurzweil Accelerating Intelligence, March 2001.

2. "Gallup Poll Social Series: Mood of the Nation," January 3–16, 2022, https://news.gallup.com/file/poll/389318/220202IssueSatisfaction.pdf

3. "Stress: The Health Epidemic of the 21st Century," *SciTech Connect*, 2016, https://scitechconnect.elsevier.com/stress-health-epidemic-21st-century

4. Liu, Qingqing et al., "Changes in the global burden of depression from 1990 to 2017: Findings from the Global Burden of Disease study," August 10, 2019, https://www.sciencedirect.com/science/article/pii/S0022395619307381

5. United Nations, "News in Brief," October 6, 2022, https://news.un.org/en/tags/suicide-prevention

Chapter 10: The Future of Work Is...No Work?

1. Gettysburg College, "One third of your life is spent at work," https://www.gettysburg.edu/news/stories?id=79db7b34-630c-4f49-ad32-4ab9ea48e72b&pageTitle=1%2F3+of+your+life+is+spent+at+work

2. Clifton, Jim, "The World's Broken Workplace," Gallup, June 13, 2017. https://news.gallup.com/opinion/chairman/212045/world-broken-workplace.aspx?g_source=position1&g_medium=related&g_campaign=tiles

3. International Labour Organization, "Safety and Health at the Heart of the Future of Work," 2019, https://www.ilo.org/wcmsp5/groups/public/---dgreports/---dcomm/documents/publication/wcms:686645.pdf

4. World Health Organization, "WHO Mortality Database," https://www
.who.int/healthinfo/mortality_data/en/

5. Uppsala Conflict Data Program (UCDP), Department of Peace and
Conflict Research, Uppsala University, https://ucdp.uu.se/downloads/
charts/

6. New China TV, "Jack Ma and Elon Musk hold debate in Shanghai,"
2019, https://youtu.be/f3lUEnMaiAU

7. WORLDCRUNCH, "The Four-Day School Week: Passing Fad or the
Future of Education," April 26, 2024, https://worldcrunch.com/culture-
society/countries-4-day-school-week

8. McCurry, Justin, "Japan urges overworked employees to take Monday
mornings off," *Guardian*, August 3, 2018, https://www.theguardian.com/
world/2018/aug/03/japan-overworked-employees-monday-mornings-off

9. Reuters, "Do more with less: New Zealand firm's four-day week,"
November 5, 2019, https://www.reuters.com/article/us-worklifebalance-
newzealand/do-more-with-less-new-zealand-firms-four-day-week-
idUSKBN1XF1TM

Chapter 11: Educating Future-Proof Minds in the Age of AI

1. David J. Hill, "Finland's Latest Educational Move Will Produce a
Generation of Entrepreneurs," SingularityHub, April 4, 2015, https://
singularityhub.com/2015/04/04/finlands-latest-educational-move-will-
produce-a-generation-of-entrepreneurs/

2. "Empathy? In Denmark they're learning it in school," Morning Future,
April 26, 2019, https://www.morningfuture.com/en/2019/04/26/empathy-
happiness-school-denmark/

3. Claudia Goldin and Lawrence F. Katz. *The Race between Education and
Technology*. Belknap Press, 2008.

4. Stephane, "Skill, re-skill and re-skill again. How to keep up with the
future of work," July 31, 2017, https://www.weforum.org/agenda/2017/07/
skill-reskill-prepare-for-future-of-work/

5. Zak, P. J., "Why Your Brain Loves Good Storytelling," *Harvard Business
Review*, October 28, 2014, https://hbr.org/2014/10/why-your-brain-loves-
good-storytelling

6. American Psychological Association, "Playing Video Games Linked
to Aggressive Behavior in Some, but Not All, Teenagers," November 25, 2013,
https://www.apa.org/news/press/releases/2013/11/video-games#:~:
text=While%20one%20widely%20held%20view,studies%20reviewed
%20in%20the%20article

Chapter 12: Navigating AI Distractions

1. Bianchi, Tiago, "Google: annual advertising revenue 2001–2023," February 1, 2024, https://www.statista.com/statistics/266249/advertising-revenue-of-google/
2. National Highway Traffic Safety Administration, "U Drive. U Text. U Pay," Traffic Safety Marketing, accessed May 24, 2024, https://www.trafficsafetymarketing.gov/get-materials/distracted-driving/u-drive-u-text-u-pay

Chapter 13: Overcoming AI-Generated Addictions

1. Khubchandani, Jagdish, Sushil Sharma, James H. Price, "COVID-19 Pandemic and the Burden of Internet Addiction in the United States," *Psychiatry International* 2(4) November 4, 2021, https://doi.org/10.3390/psychiatryint2040031
2. Petrosyan, Ani, "Dangers of the metaverse according to internet users worldwide in 2021," July 7, 2022, Statista, https://www.statista.com/statistics/1288822/metaverse-dangers/
3. "Popular AI friendship apps may have negative effects on wellbeing and cause addictive behaviour, finds study," October 19, 2023, https://www.surrey.ac.uk/news/popular-ai-friendship-apps-may-have-negative-effects-wellbeing-and-cause-addictive-behaviour-finds

Chapter 14: Managing Your Data Effectively and Using AI Ethically

1. "A Day in the Life of Your Data," April 2021, https://www.apple.com/privacy/docs/A_Day_in_the_Life_of_Your_Data.pdf
2. "Mobile App Download Statistics & Usage Statistics," Buildfire, 2024, https://buildfire.com/app-statistics/
3. "How Much Is Your Data Worth: The Complete Breakdown for 2024," Invisibly, July 13, 2021, https://www.invisibly.com/learn-blog/how-much-is-data-worth
4. Statista, "Social media companies ranked by average revenue per user (ARPU) in 2022," https://www.statista.com/statistics/1371738/social-media-apps-arpu-global/

5. Privacy Affairs, "Dark Web Price Index 2022," https://www.privacyaffairs .com/dark-web-price-index-2023
6. List of cognitive biases, https://en.wikipedia.org/wiki/List_of_cognitive_ biases

Chapter 16: Making Your Company AI-Ready

1. Boston Consulting Group, "From Potential to Profit with GenAI," last modified 2024, https://www.bcg.com/publications/2024/from-potential-to-profit-with-genai
2. Microsoft, "AI at Work: Here Now, Comes the Hard Part," Microsoft Work Trend Index, 2024, https://www.microsoft.com/en-us/worklab/ work-trend-index/ai-at-work-is-here-now-comes-the-hard-part
3. Julia Angwin, Jeff Larson, Suray Mattu, and Lauren Kirchner, "Machine Bias," ProPublica, May 23, 2016, https://www.propublica.org/article/ machine-bias-risk-assessments-in-criminal-sentencing

Chapter 17: Shifting to a Human-Ready Business

1. Beverland, Michael B., Francis J. Farrelly, and Charles R.C. Lim, "Crafting Authenticity: The Validation of Identity in the Creative Professions," *Journal of Management Studies* 53, no. 5 (July 2016): 726–53.

Chapter 18: Making Your Business Change-Ready

1. UN News, "2023 Recorded as Fifth Hottest Year Ever, Other Extreme Weather Events: WMO," United Nations, December 31, 2023, https:// news.un.org/en/story/2023/12/1144372
2. Hayes, Adam, "What Caused Black Monday: The Stock Market Crash of 1987?" Investopedia, updated March 13, 2023, https://www.investopedia. com/ask/answers/042115/what-caused-black-monday-stock-market-crash-1987.asp
3. World Bank Group, "Global Economic Prospects, January 2019: Darkening Skies," World Bank, 2019, https://pubdocs.worldbank.org/ en/869591574200501599/Recession-Chapter-1.pdf

Acknowledgments

Writing this book has been an incredible journey, one that I could not have embarked on without the support, guidance, and patience of a remarkable group of people.

First and foremost, my agent, Leah Spiro, whose invaluable coaching and unwavering patience have been the guiding lights through this process. Kim Wimpsett and Andrew Eck, my developmental editors, your keen insights have been instrumental in refining the core messages of my work.

I extend heartfelt thanks to Thomas Jestin and Ernie Hayden, whose detailed reviews and timely advice enriched the quality of this manuscript. Fred Eck, Emilie Viasnoff, Jorge Storm, Arnaud Morvan, Jochen Wirtz, Pooja Sund, Andy Holley, Ema Roloff, Gloria Zvaravanhu, Nandan Mullakara, Breaden Kurchina, Erin Kurchina, Lasse Rindom, and Bernard Goldstein, you have each brought unique perspectives that have greatly contributed to this book's depth. Your willingness to spend time offering feedback has made a significant difference.

To my dear friends Ian Barkin, Seb Bonhomme, Manoj Yadav, and Martin Weis, your encouragement kept me buoyant even when the challenges of writing seemed insurmountable. Your belief in my ideas and the gentle prodding to keep going did not go unnoticed.

To my life partner, Pascaline, your support at all levels has been my foundation. Your strength and understanding allowed me to pursue this dream. Mayleen and Kylian, my kids, your patience and acceptance while I was engrossed in writing this book mean the world to me. I promise more adventures and less distraction in the future. To Pierre, who left us too early and to my family in France, who is the foundation of all this!

To Angelica, whose dinnertime questions sparked the inspiration for this book and kept the wheels in my head turning—your skepticism and curiosity with AI have left an indelible mark on these pages.

Each of you has played a crucial role in this project, and I am eternally grateful for your contributions, large and small. Thank you for being part of my journey.

About the Author

Pascal Bornet is an award-winning expert, author, and keynote speaker on artificial intelligence (AI) and automation. He has received multiple awards and is regularly ranked as one of the top 10 global AI and automation experts. He is also an influencer with more than a million followers on social media.

Bornet developed his expertise over more than 20 years as a senior executive at McKinsey and EY, where he created and led their intelligent automation practices and implemented AI and automation initiatives for hundreds of organizations around the world.

For the past decades, Bornet's research has focused on the intersection of AI and humans, where he believes the greatest value lies. He is a fervent advocate for human-centric AI, and he believes that with the right approach, AI can make our world more human.

He has authored two best-selling books, *Intelligent Automation* and *Irreplaceable*, and his insights have been featured in prestigious publications such as *Forbes*, Bloomberg, *McKinsey Quarterly*, and the *London Times*. He is also a lecturer at several universities, a member of the Forbes Technology Council, and a senior advisor for several startups and charities.

Index